FP 1/14	WY 7/14	RE 7/15	HO 2/16

right state

[redacted]

[redacted]

WRITTEN BY **MAT JOHNSON** ART BY **ANDREA MUTTI** LETTERS BY PAT BROSSEAU

[redacted]

[redacted]

VERTIGO

[redacted]

Jonathan Vankin and Will Dennis Editors   Gregory Lockard Assistant Editor   Robbin Brosterman Design Director – Books

Karen Berger Senior VP – Executive Editor, Vertigo   Bob Harras VP – Editor-In-Chief

Diane Nelson President   Dan DiDio and Jim Lee Co-Publishers   Geoff Johns Chief Creative Officer
John Rood Executive VP – Sales, Marketing and Business Development   Amy Genkins Senior VP – Business and Legal Affairs
Nairi Gardiner Senior VP – Finance   Jeff Boison VP – Publishing Operations   Mark Chiarello VP – Art Direction and Design
John Cunningham VP – Marketing   Terri Cunningham VP – Talent Relations and Services   Alison Gill Senior VP – Manufacturing and Operations
Hank Kanalz Senior VP – Digital   Jay Kogan VP – Business and Legal Affairs, Publishing   Jack Mahan VP – Business Affairs, Talent
Nick Napolitano VP – Manufacturing Administration   Sue Pohja VP – Book Sales
Courtney Simmons Senior VP – Publicity   Bob Wayne Senior VP – Sales

Cover Design by IAAH / iamalwayshungry. Nessim Higson + Lizzy Margiotta
Cover Photography by Daymon Gardner

Andrea Mutti would like to thank Dimitri Fogolin

SUSTAINABLE FORESTRY INITIATIVE

Certified Chain of Custody
At Least 25% Certified Forest Content
www.sfiprogram.org
SFI-01042
APPLIES TO TEXT STOCK ONLY

Library of Congress Cataloging-in-Publication Data

Johnson, Mat.
Right state / Mat Johnson, Andrea Mutti.
p. cm.
ISBN 978-1-4012-2943-6 (alk. paper)
1. Militia movements--Comic books, strips, etc. 2.
Presidents--Assassination attempts--Comic books, strips, etc. 3. Graphic
novels. 4. Political fiction. I. Mutti, Andrea, 1973- II. Title.
PN6727.J573R54 2012
741.5'973--dc23
2012019780

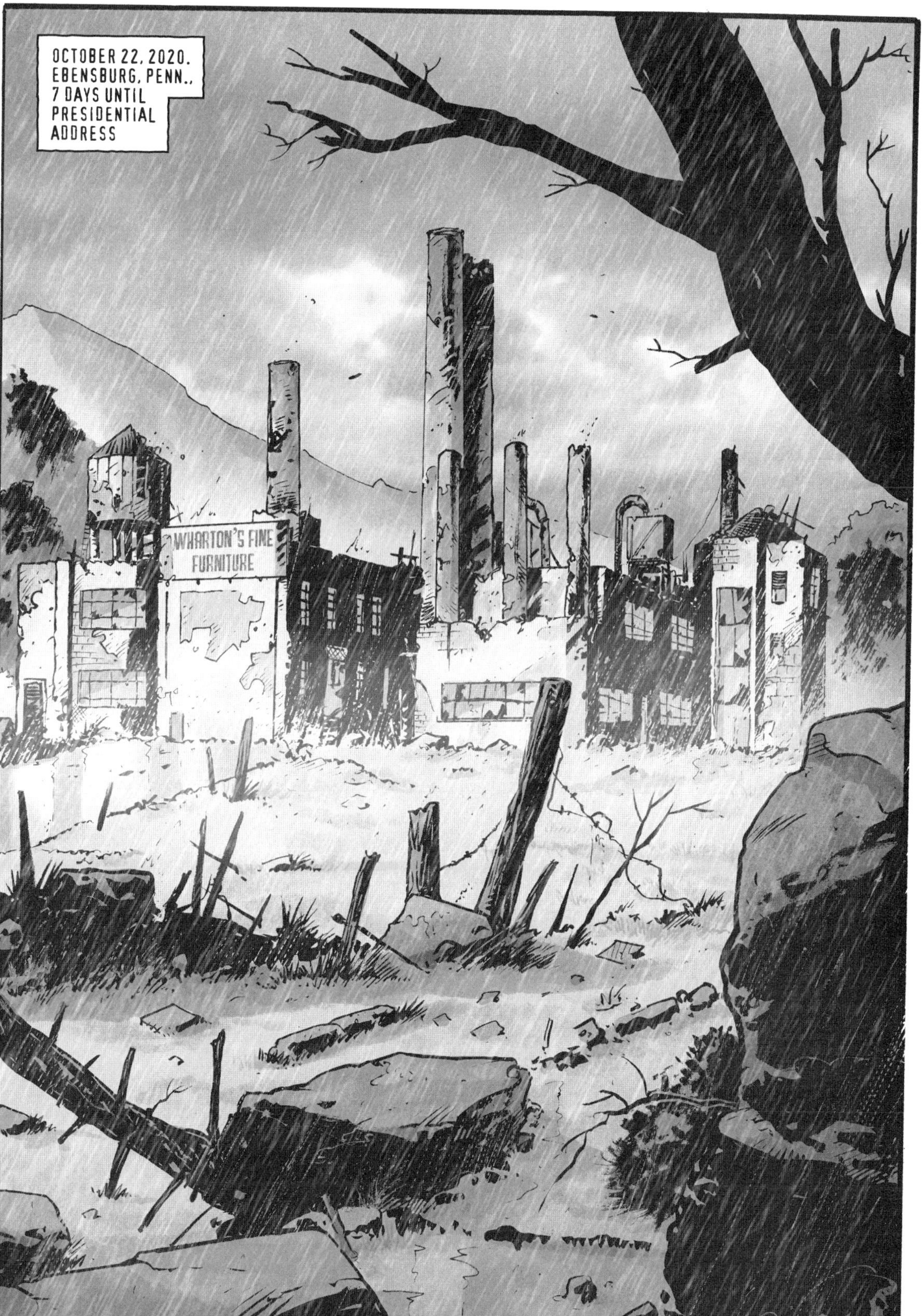
OCTOBER 22, 2020. EBENSBURG, PENN., 7 DAYS UNTIL PRESIDENTIAL ADDRESS
WHARTON'S FINE FURNITURE

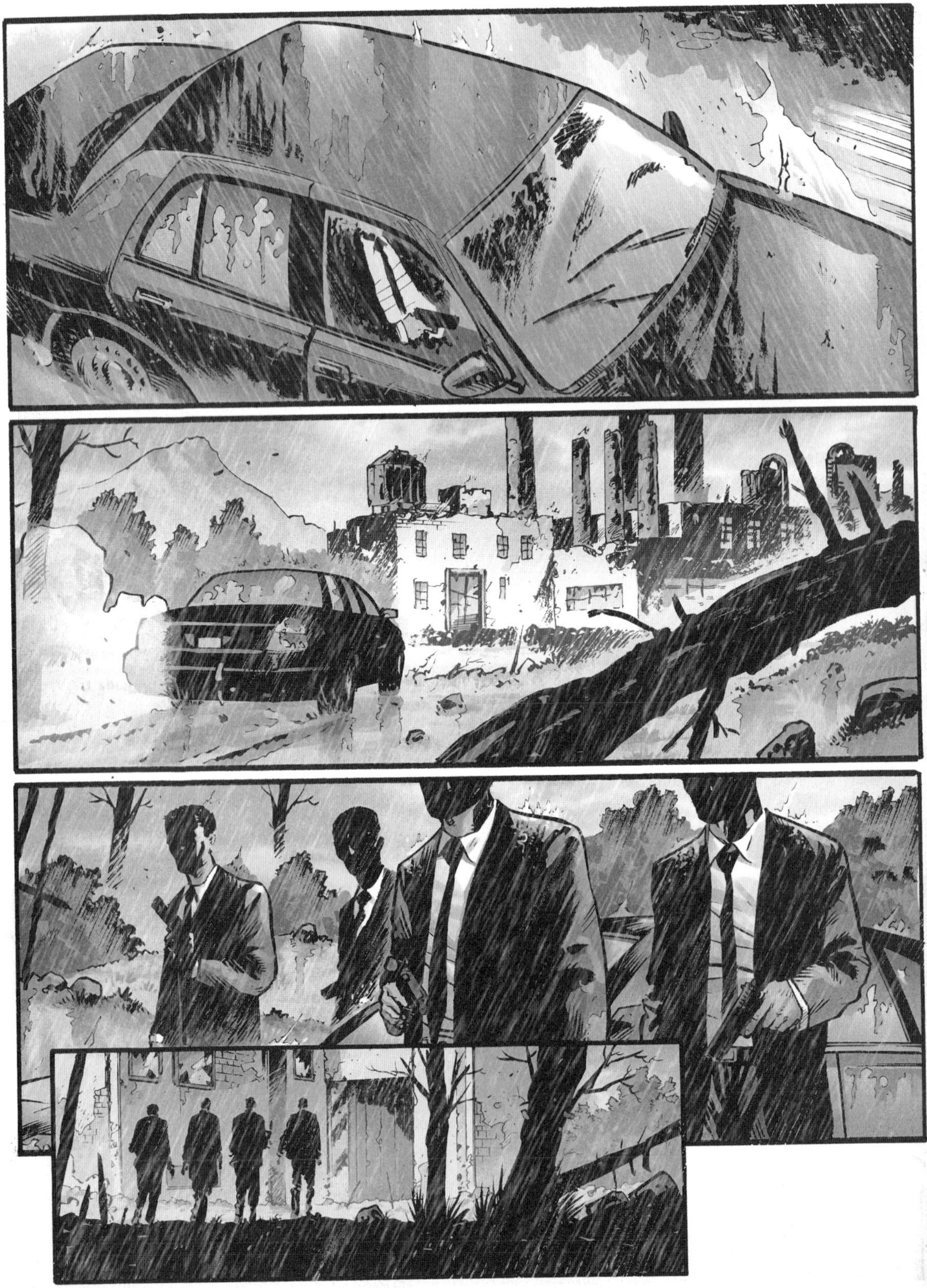

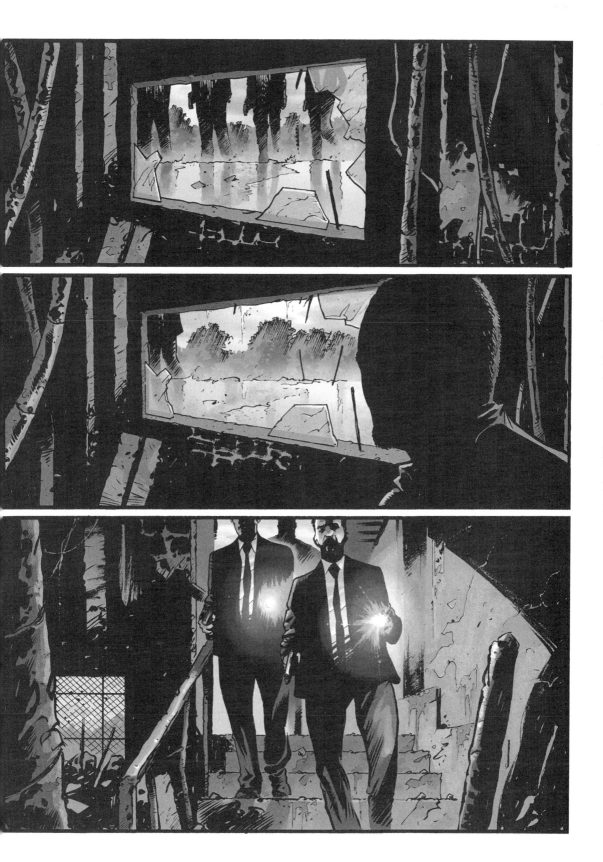

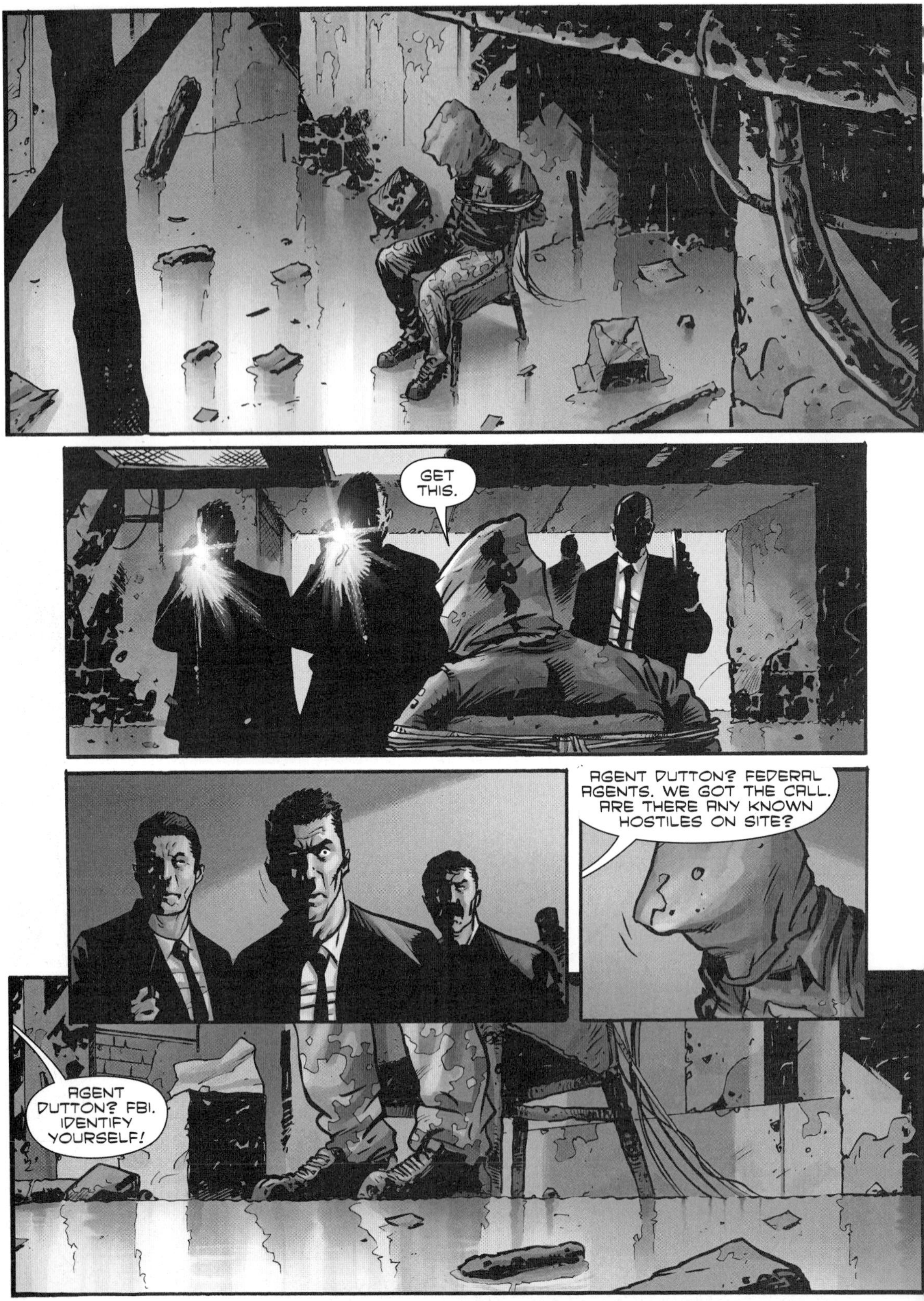
GET THIS.
AGENT DUTTON? FEDERAL AGENTS. WE GOT THE CALL. ARE THERE ANY KNOWN HOSTILES ON SITE?
AGENT DUTTON? FBI. IDENTIFY YOURSELF!

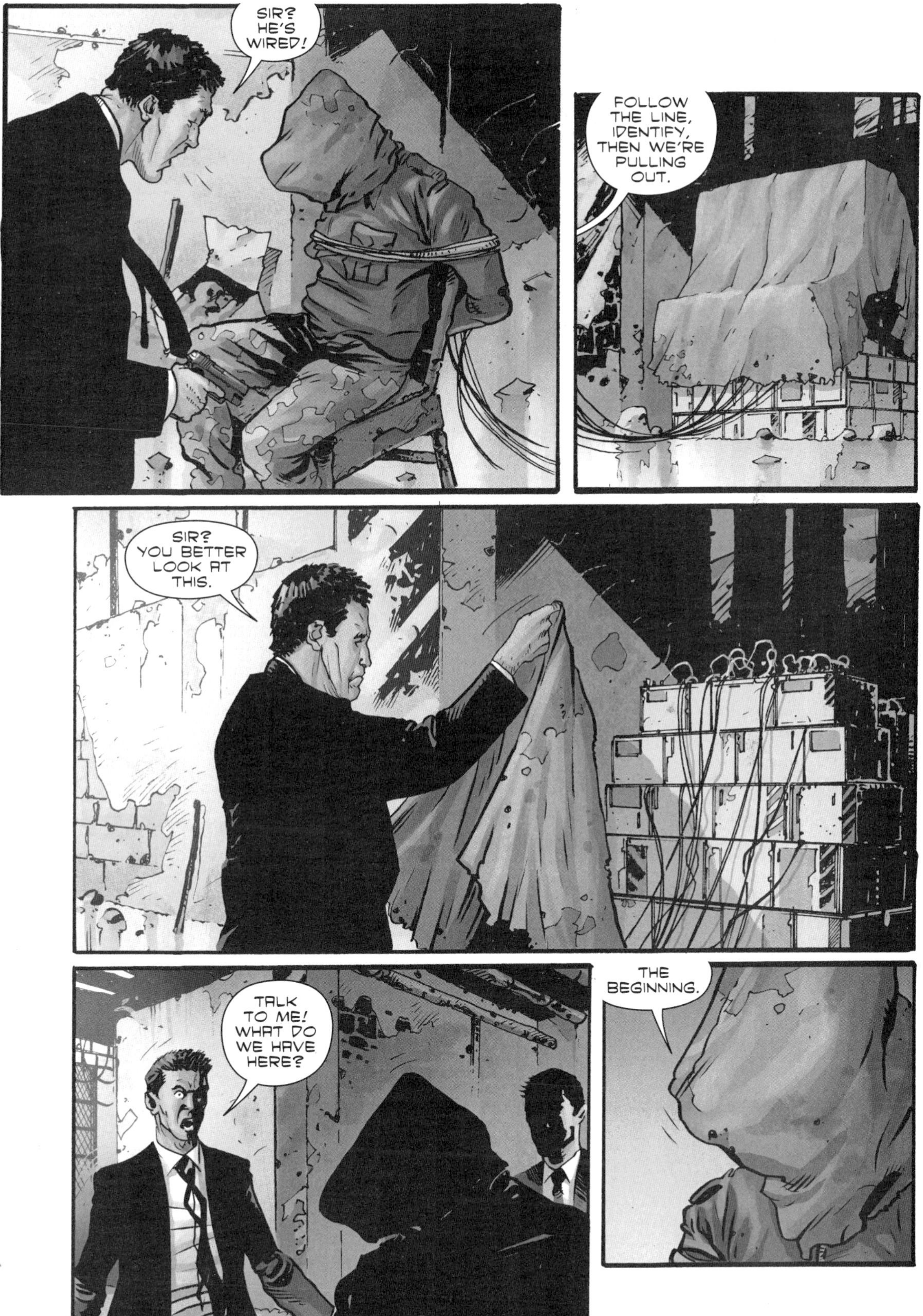
SIR? HE'S WIRED!
FOLLOW THE LINE, IDENTIFY, THEN WE'RE PULLING OUT.
SIR? YOU BETTER LOOK AT THIS.
TALK TO ME! WHAT DO WE HAVE HERE?
THE BEGINNING.

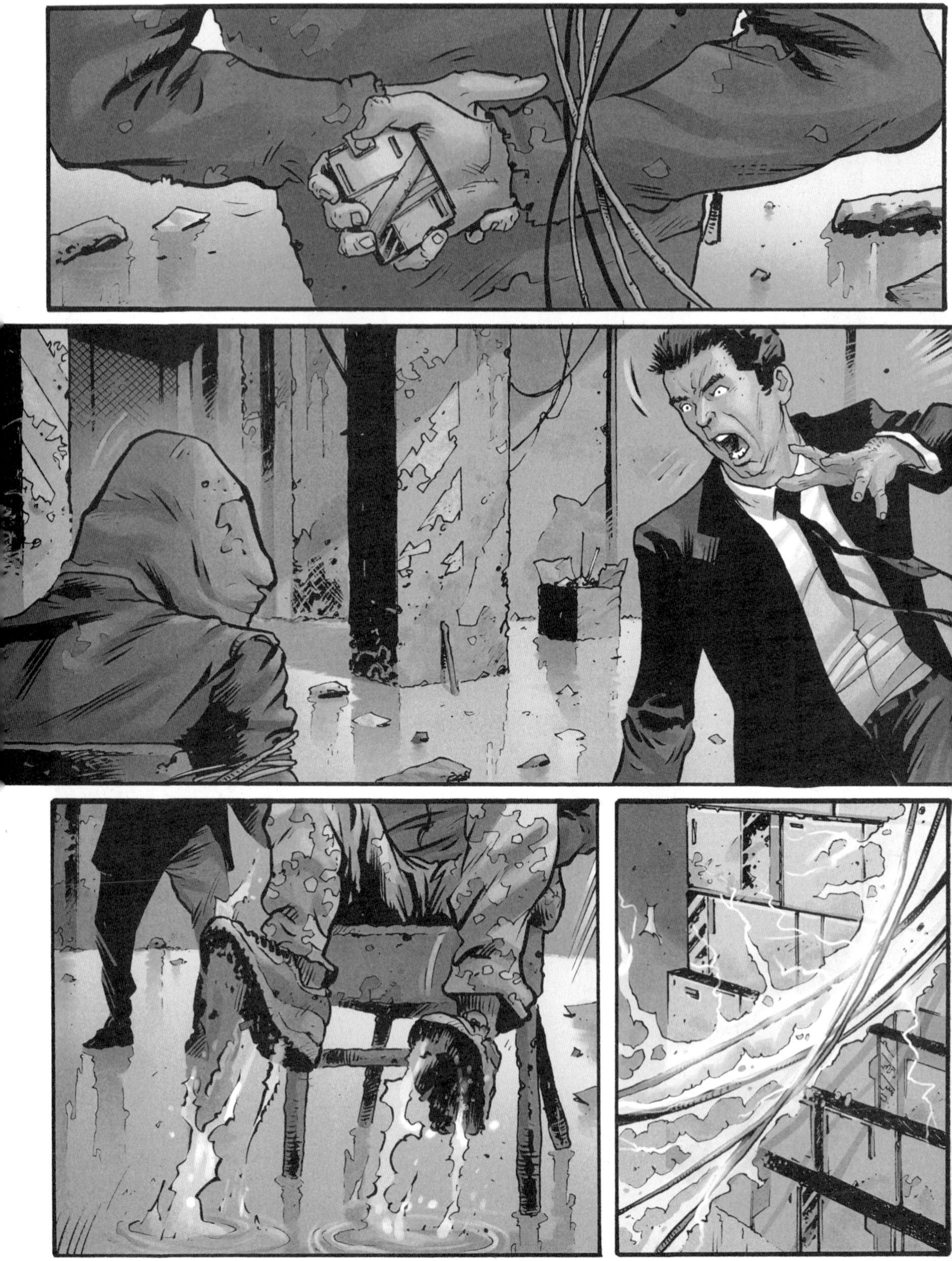

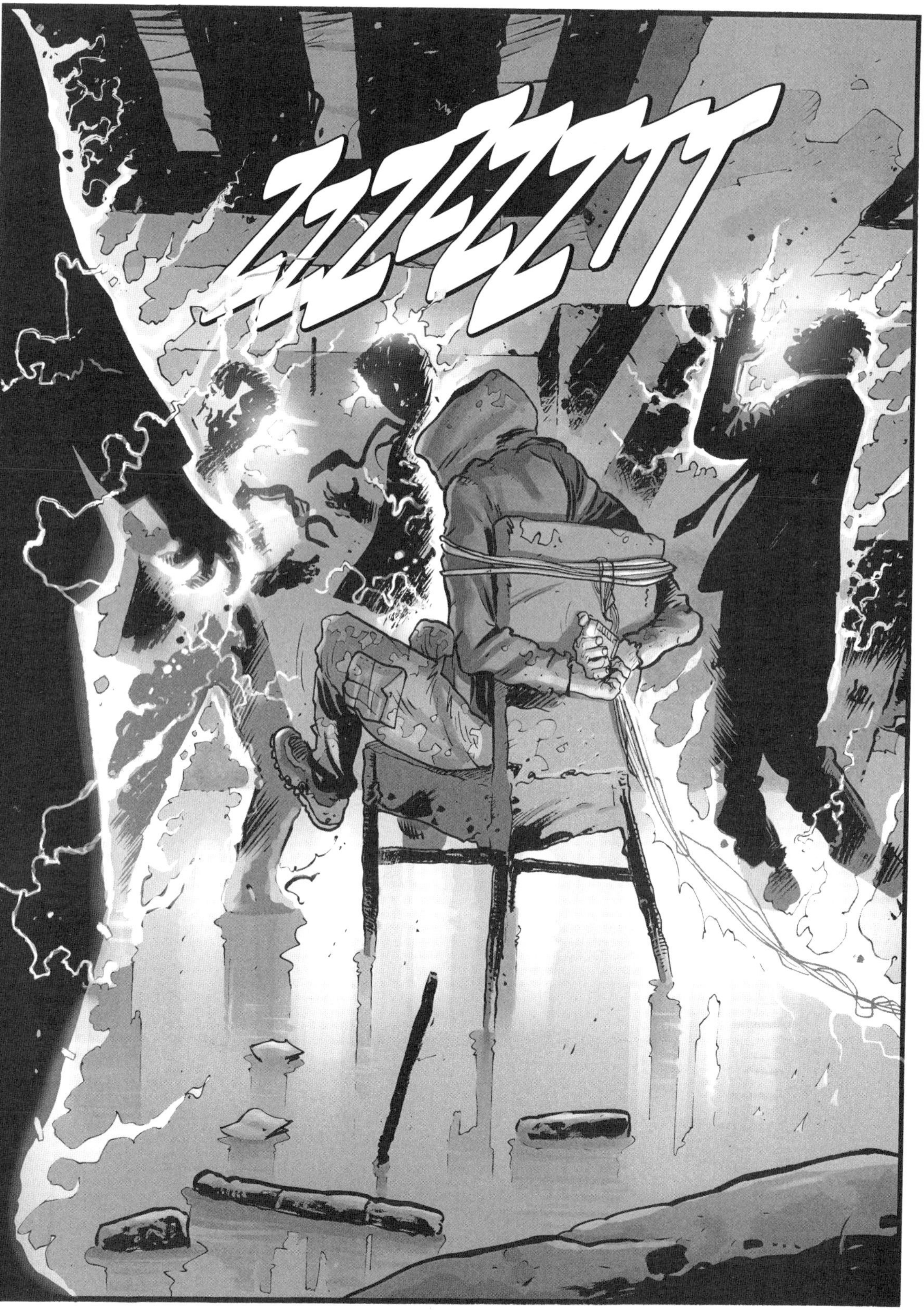
ZZZZZZTT

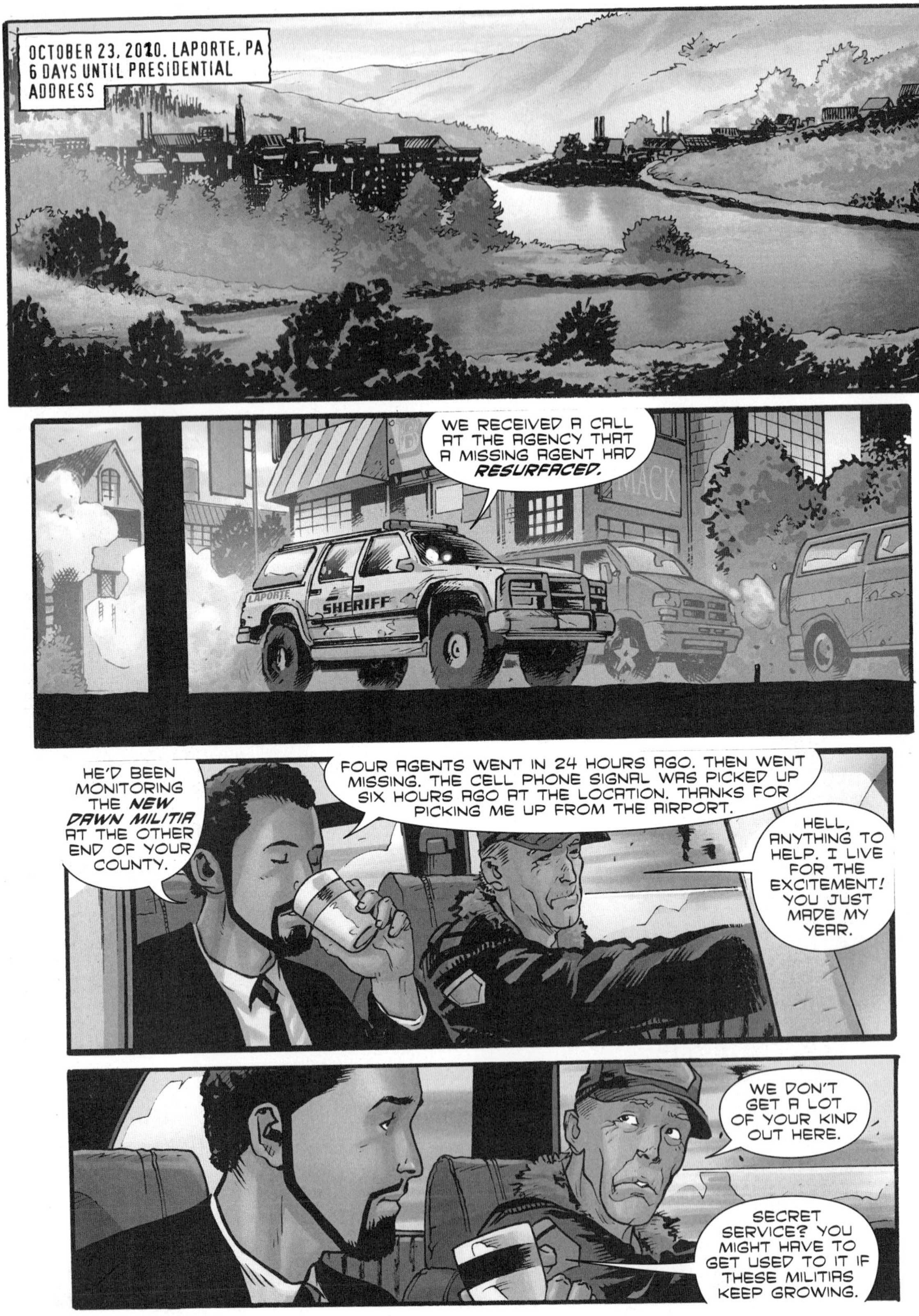
OCTOBER 23, 2010. LAPORTE, PA 6 DAYS UNTIL PRESIDENTIAL ADDRESS
WE RECEIVED A CALL AT THE AGENCY THAT A MISSING AGENT HAD RESURFACED.
LAPORTE SHERIFF
MACK
HE'D BEEN MONITORING THE NEW DAWN MILITIA AT THE OTHER END OF YOUR COUNTY.
FOUR AGENTS WENT IN 24 HOURS AGO. THEN WENT MISSING. THE CELL PHONE SIGNAL WAS PICKED UP SIX HOURS AGO AT THE LOCATION. THANKS FOR PICKING ME UP FROM THE AIRPORT.
HELL, ANYTHING TO HELP. I LIVE FOR THE EXCITEMENT! YOU JUST MADE MY YEAR.
WE DON'T GET A LOT OF YOUR KIND OUT HERE.
SECRET SERVICE? YOU MIGHT HAVE TO GET USED TO IT IF THESE MILITIAS KEEP GROWING.

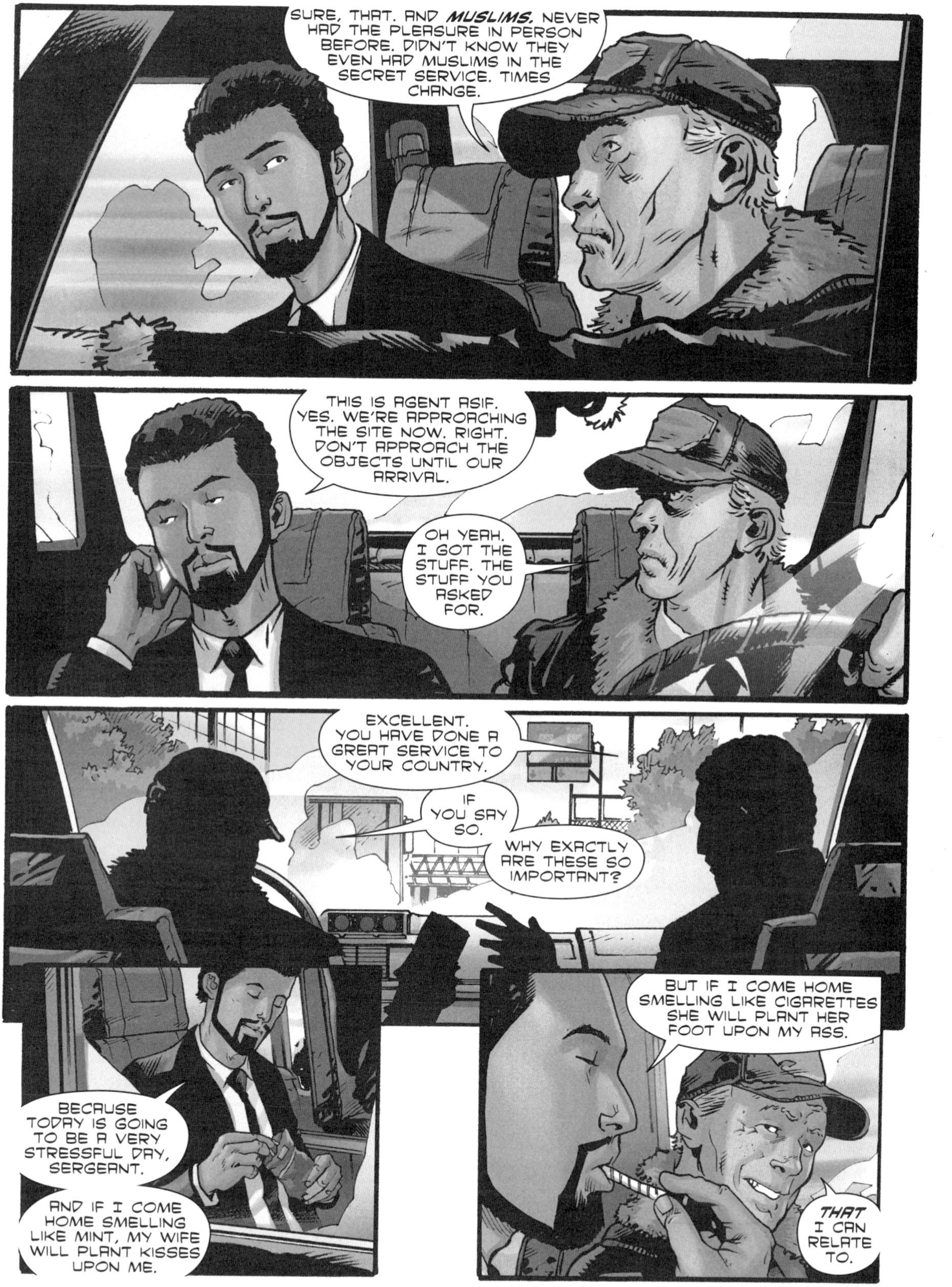

SURE, THAT. AND *MUSLIMS.* NEVER HAD THE PLEASURE IN PERSON BEFORE. DIDN'T KNOW THEY EVEN HAD MUSLIMS IN THE SECRET SERVICE. TIMES CHANGE.
THIS IS AGENT ASIF. YES. WE'RE APPROACHING THE SITE NOW. RIGHT. DON'T APPROACH THE OBJECTS UNTIL OUR ARRIVAL.
OH YEAH. I GOT THE STUFF. THE STUFF YOU ASKED FOR.
EXCELLENT. YOU HAVE DONE A GREAT SERVICE TO YOUR COUNTRY.
IF YOU SAY SO.
WHY EXACTLY ARE THESE SO IMPORTANT?
BECAUSE TODAY IS GOING TO BE A VERY STRESSFUL DAY, SERGEANT.
AND IF I COME HOME SMELLING LIKE MINT, MY WIFE WILL PLANT KISSES UPON ME.
BUT IF I COME HOME SMELLING LIKE CIGARETTES SHE WILL PLANT HER FOOT UPON MY ASS.
THAT I CAN RELATE TO.

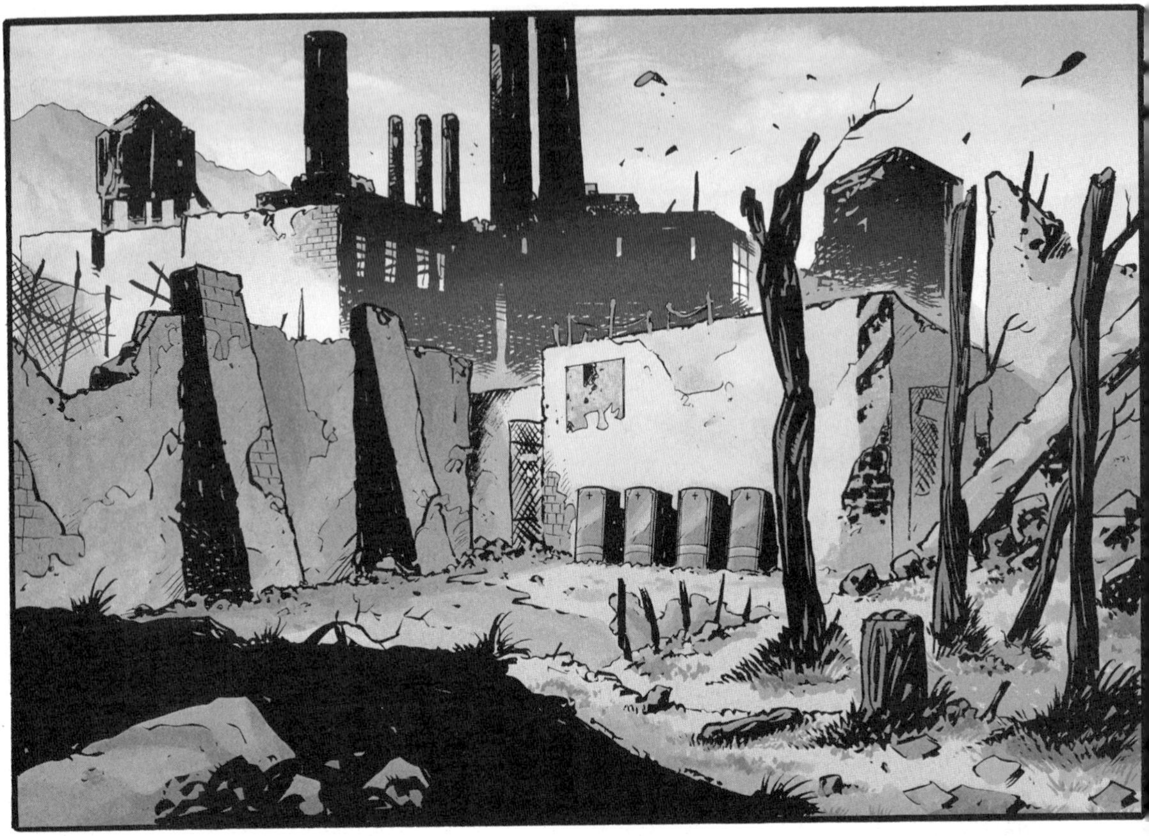

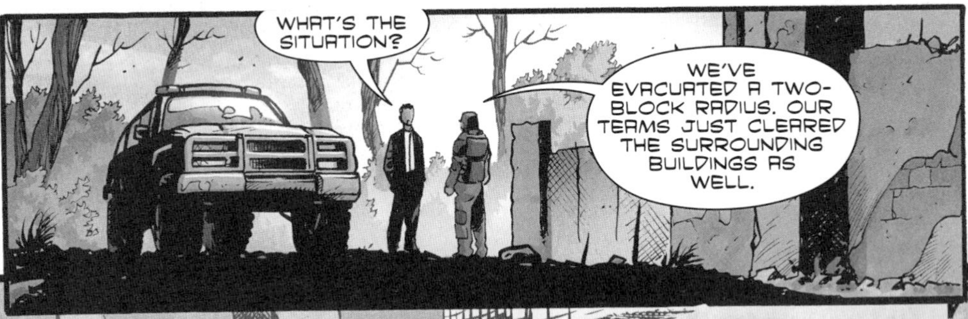
WHAT'S THE SITUATION?
WE'VE EVACUATED A TWO-BLOCK RADIUS. OUR TEAMS JUST CLEARED THE SURROUNDING BUILDINGS AS WELL.

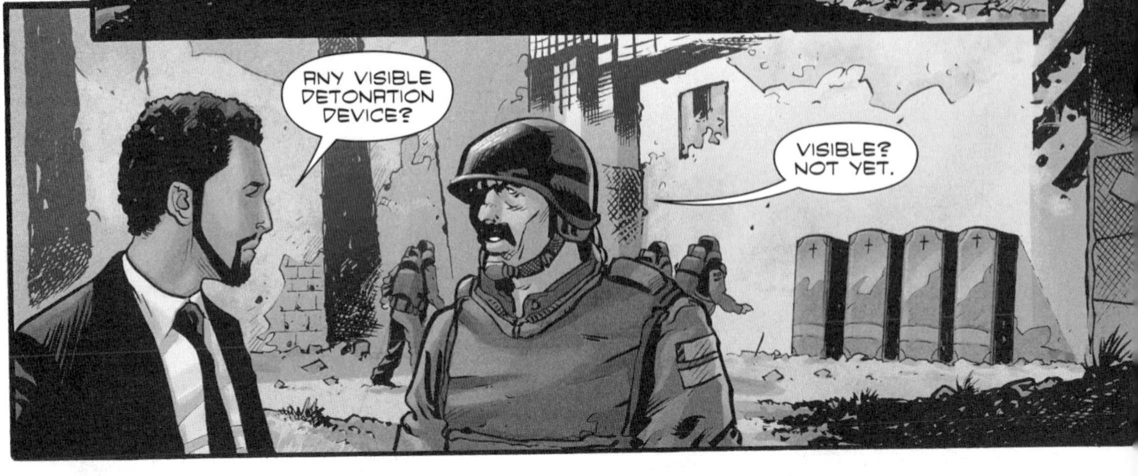
ANY VISIBLE DETONATION DEVICE?
VISIBLE? NOT YET.

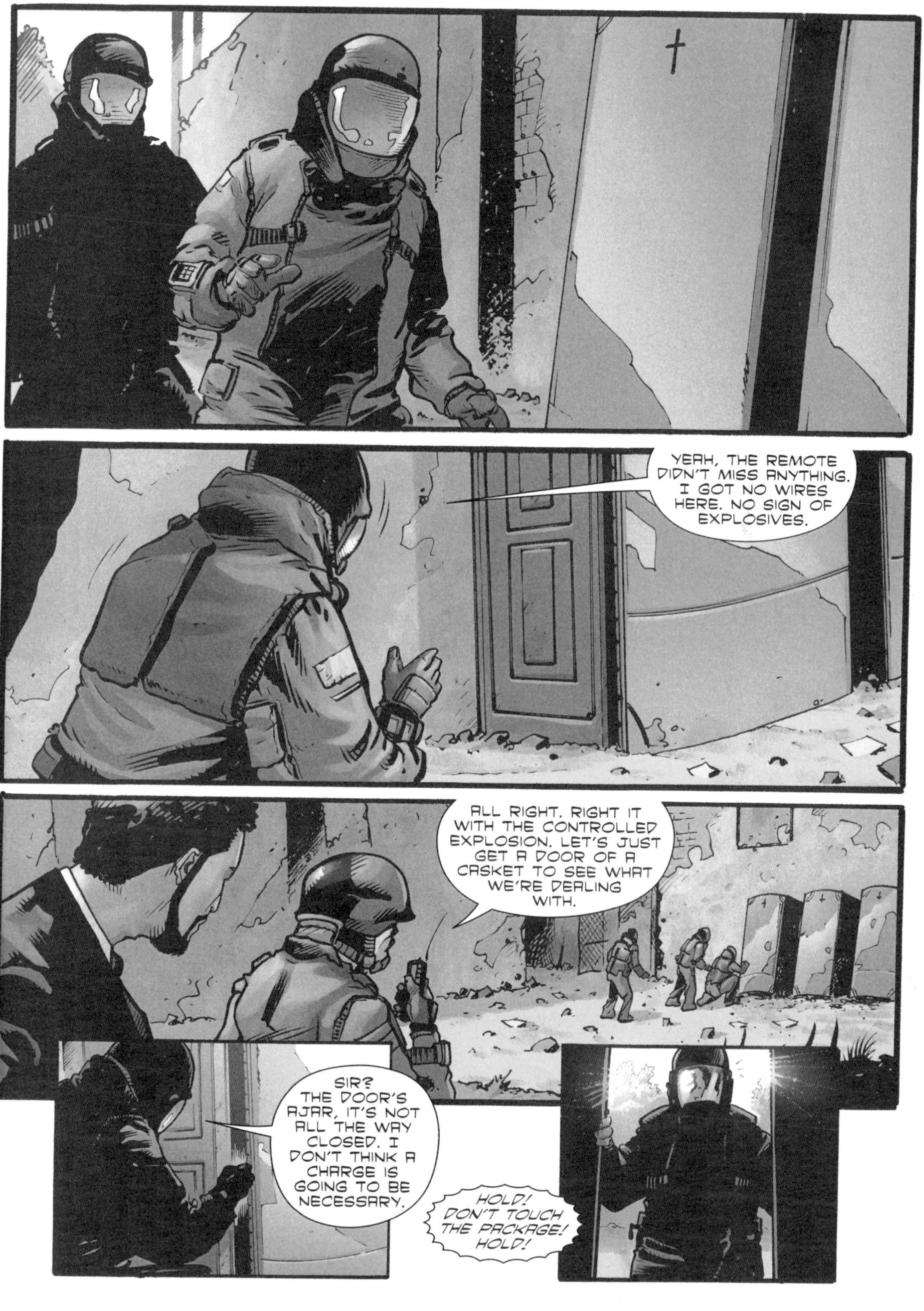
YEAH, THE REMOTE DIDN'T MISS ANYTHING. I GOT NO WIRES HERE. NO SIGN OF EXPLOSIVES.
ALL RIGHT. RIGHT IT WITH THE CONTROLLED EXPLOSION. LET'S JUST GET A DOOR OF A CASKET TO SEE WHAT WE'RE DEALING WITH.
SIR? THE DOOR'S AJAR, IT'S NOT ALL THE WAY CLOSED. I DON'T THINK A CHARGE IS GOING TO BE NECESSARY.
HOLD! DON'T TOUCH THE PACKAGE! HOLD!

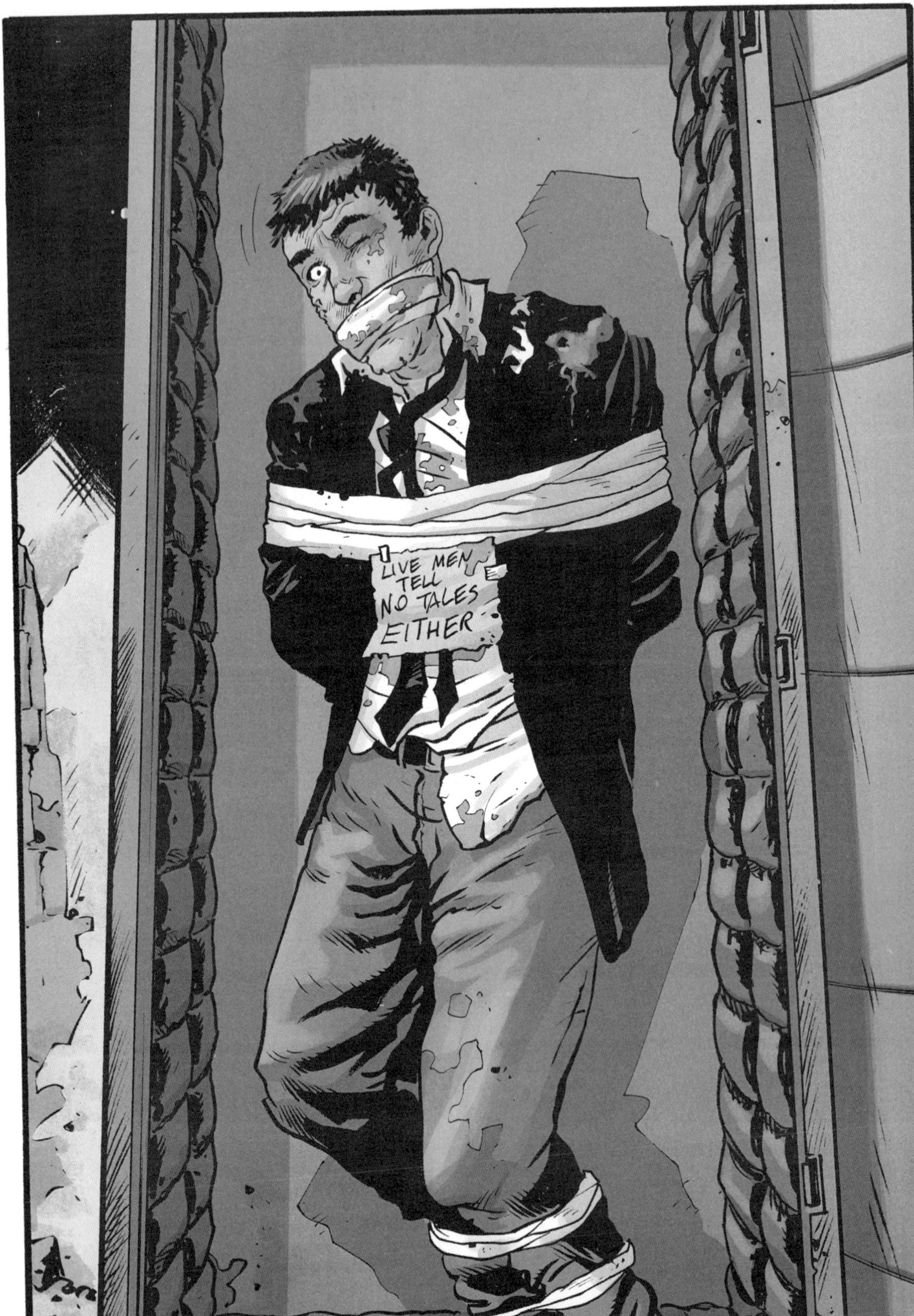
LIVE MEN TELL NO TALES EITHER

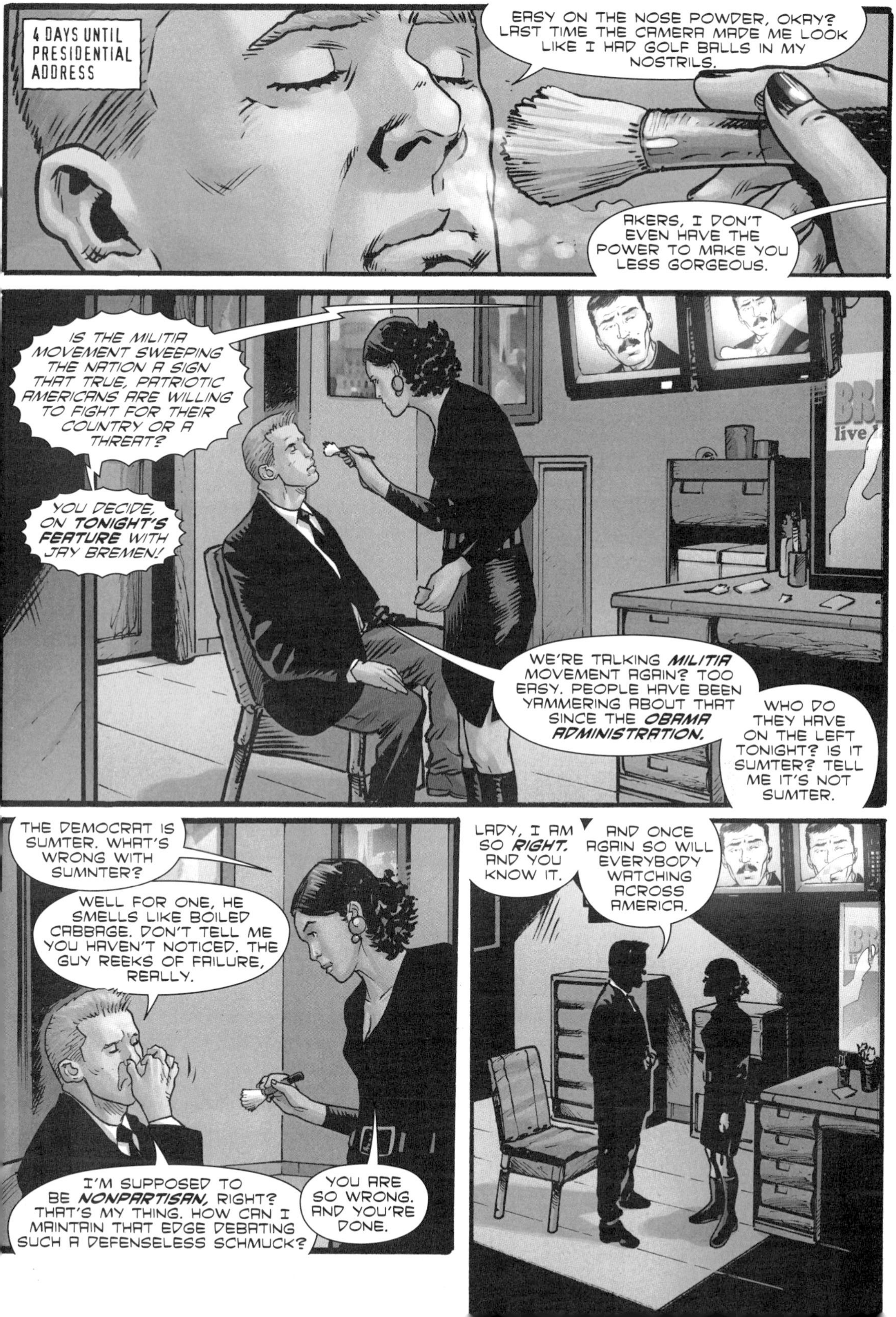
4 DAYS UNTIL PRESIDENTIAL ADDRESS
EASY ON THE NOSE POWDER, OKAY? LAST TIME THE CAMERA MADE ME LOOK LIKE I HAD GOLF BALLS IN MY NOSTRILS.
AKERS, I DON'T EVEN HAVE THE POWER TO MAKE YOU LESS GORGEOUS.
IS THE MILITIA MOVEMENT SWEEPING THE NATION A SIGN THAT TRUE, PATRIOTIC AMERICANS ARE WILLING TO FIGHT FOR THEIR COUNTRY OR A THREAT?
YOU DECIDE, ON TONIGHT'S FEATURE WITH JAY BREMEN!
WE'RE TALKING MILITIA MOVEMENT AGAIN? TOO EASY. PEOPLE HAVE BEEN YAMMERING ABOUT THAT SINCE THE OBAMA ADMINISTRATION.
WHO DO THEY HAVE ON THE LEFT TONIGHT? IS IT SUMTER? TELL ME IT'S NOT SUMTER.
THE DEMOCRAT IS SUMTER. WHAT'S WRONG WITH SUMNTER?
WELL FOR ONE, HE SMELLS LIKE BOILED CABBAGE. DON'T TELL ME YOU HAVEN'T NOTICED. THE GUY REEKS OF FAILURE, REALLY.
I'M SUPPOSED TO BE NONPARTISAN, RIGHT? THAT'S MY THING. HOW CAN I MAINTAIN THAT EDGE DEBATING SUCH A DEFENSELESS SCHMUCK?
YOU ARE SO WRONG. AND YOU'RE DONE.
LADY, I AM SO RIGHT. AND YOU KNOW IT.
AND ONCE AGAIN SO WILL EVERYBODY WATCHING ACROSS AMERICA.

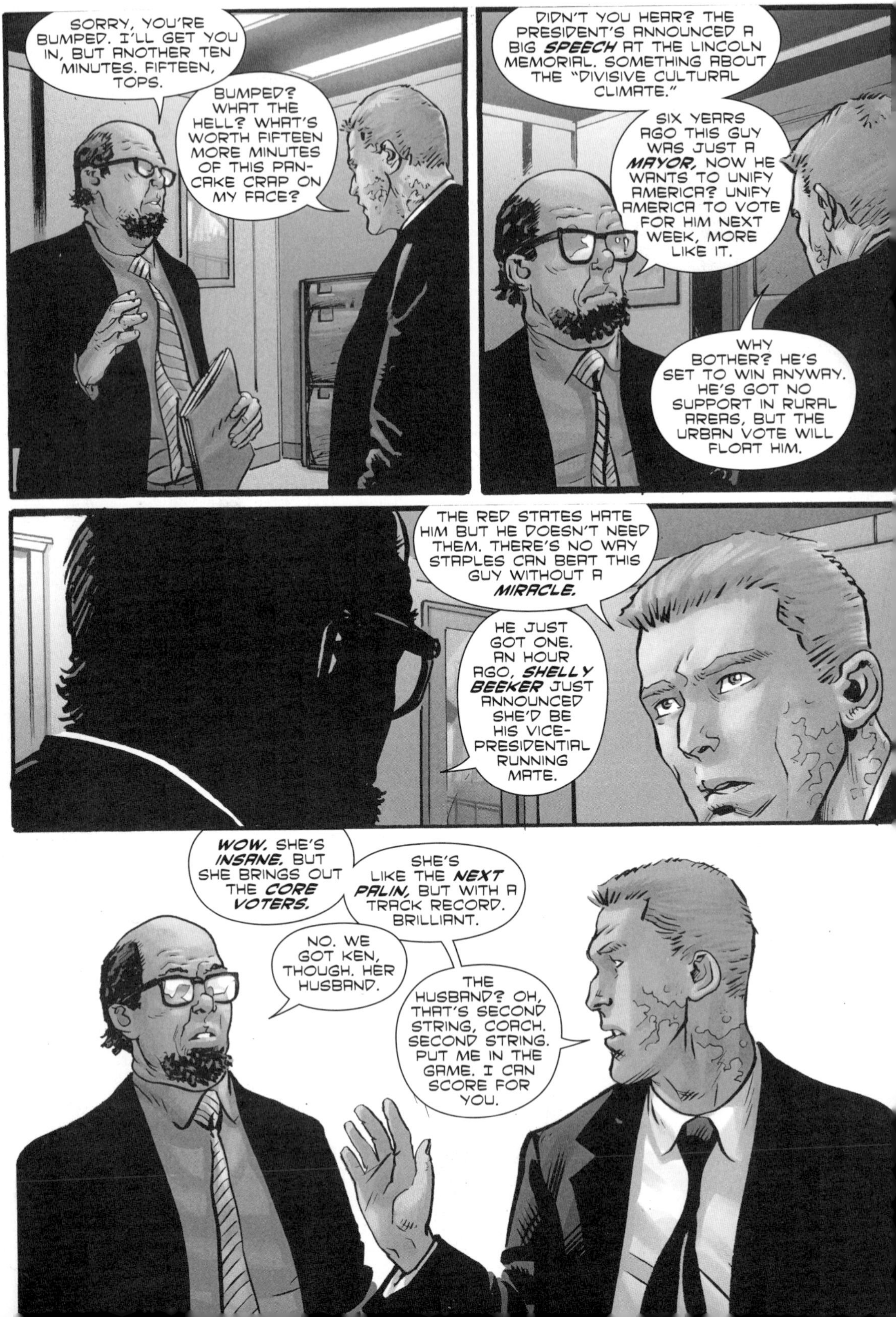
SORRY, YOU'RE BUMPED. I'LL GET YOU IN, BUT ANOTHER TEN MINUTES. FIFTEEN, TOPS.
BUMPED? WHAT THE HELL? WHAT'S WORTH FIFTEEN MORE MINUTES OF THIS PAN-CAKE CRAP ON MY FACE?
DIDN'T YOU HEAR? THE PRESIDENT'S ANNOUNCED A BIG SPEECH AT THE LINCOLN MEMORIAL. SOMETHING ABOUT THE "DIVISIVE CULTURAL CLIMATE."
SIX YEARS AGO THIS GUY WAS JUST A MAYOR, NOW HE WANTS TO UNIFY AMERICA? UNIFY AMERICA TO VOTE FOR HIM NEXT WEEK, MORE LIKE IT.
WHY BOTHER? HE'S SET TO WIN ANYWAY. HE'S GOT NO SUPPORT IN RURAL AREAS, BUT THE URBAN VOTE WILL FLOAT HIM.
THE RED STATES HATE HIM BUT HE DOESN'T NEED THEM. THERE'S NO WAY STAPLES CAN BEAT THIS GUY WITHOUT A MIRACLE.
HE JUST GOT ONE. AN HOUR AGO, SHELLY BEEKER JUST ANNOUNCED SHE'D BE HIS VICE-PRESIDENTIAL RUNNING MATE.
WOW. SHE'S INSANE. BUT SHE BRINGS OUT THE CORE VOTERS.
SHE'S LIKE THE NEXT PALIN, BUT WITH A TRACK RECORD. BRILLIANT.
NO. WE GOT KEN, THOUGH. HER HUSBAND.
THE HUSBAND? OH, THAT'S SECOND STRING, COACH. SECOND STRING. PUT ME IN THE GAME. I CAN SCORE FOR YOU.

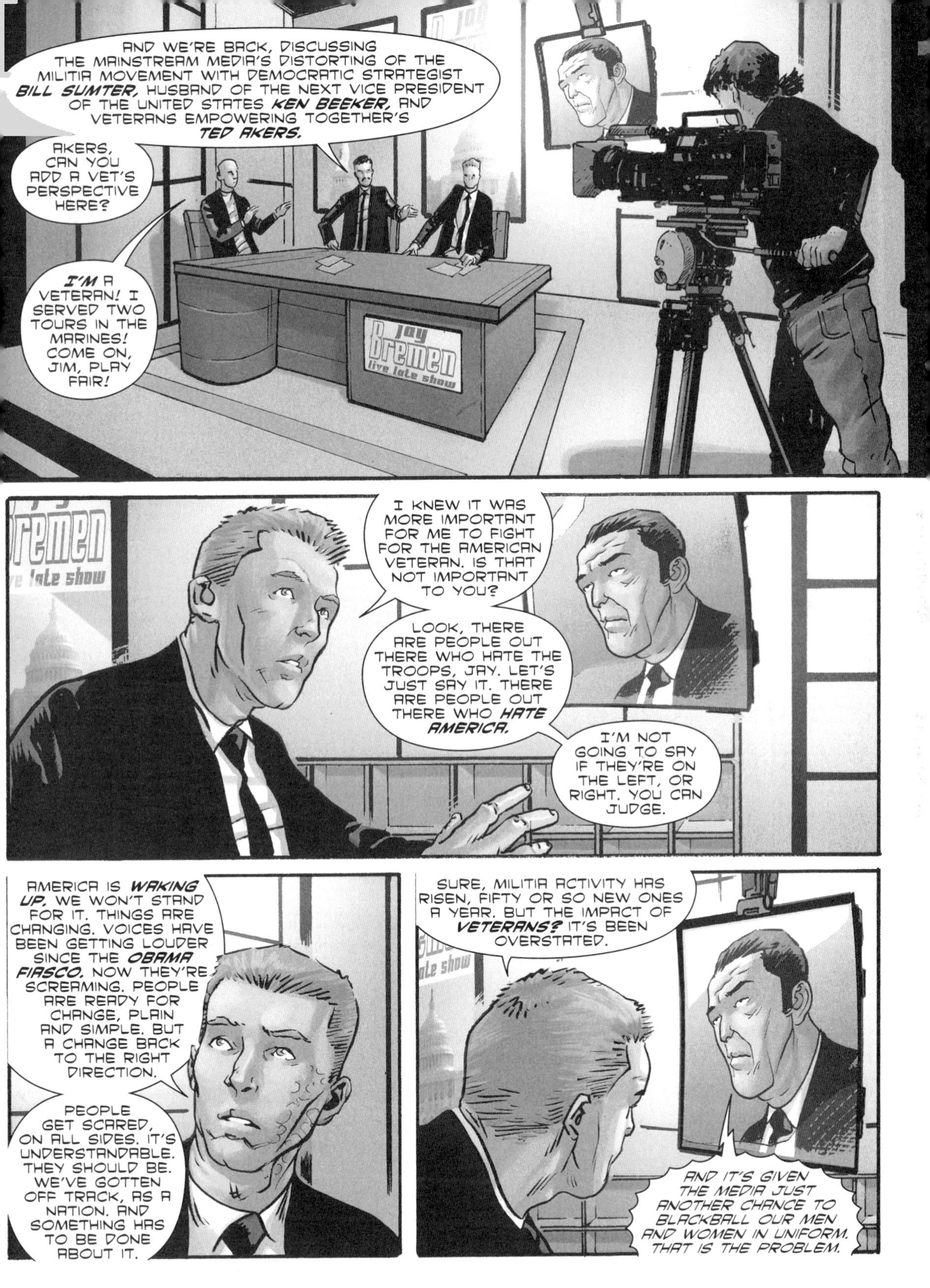

AND WE'RE BACK, DISCUSSING THE MAINSTREAM MEDIA'S DISTORTING OF THE MILITIA MOVEMENT WITH DEMOCRATIC STRATEGIST BILL SUMTER, HUSBAND OF THE NEXT VICE PRESIDENT OF THE UNITED STATES KEN BEEKER, AND VETERANS EMPOWERING TOGETHER'S TED AKERS.
AKERS, CAN YOU ADD A VET'S PERSPECTIVE HERE?
I'M A VETERAN! I SERVED TWO TOURS IN THE MARINES! COME ON, JIM, PLAY FAIR!
jay Bremen live late show
I KNEW IT WAS MORE IMPORTANT FOR ME TO FIGHT FOR THE AMERICAN VETERAN. IS THAT NOT IMPORTANT TO YOU?
LOOK, THERE ARE PEOPLE OUT THERE WHO HATE THE TROOPS, JAY. LET'S JUST SAY IT. THERE ARE PEOPLE OUT THERE WHO HATE AMERICA.
I'M NOT GOING TO SAY IF THEY'RE ON THE LEFT, OR RIGHT. YOU CAN JUDGE.
AMERICA IS WAKING UP. WE WON'T STAND FOR IT. THINGS ARE CHANGING. VOICES HAVE BEEN GETTING LOUDER SINCE THE OBAMA FIASCO. NOW THEY'RE SCREAMING. PEOPLE ARE READY FOR CHANGE, PLAIN AND SIMPLE. BUT A CHANGE BACK TO THE RIGHT DIRECTION.
PEOPLE GET SCARED, ON ALL SIDES. IT'S UNDERSTANDABLE. THEY SHOULD BE. WE'VE GOTTEN OFF TRACK, AS A NATION. AND SOMETHING HAS TO BE DONE ABOUT IT.
SURE, MILITIA ACTIVITY HAS RISEN, FIFTY OR SO NEW ONES A YEAR. BUT THE IMPACT OF VETERANS? IT'S BEEN OVERSTATED.
AND IT'S GIVEN THE MEDIA JUST ANOTHER CHANCE TO BLACKBALL OUR MEN AND WOMEN IN UNIFORM. THAT IS THE PROBLEM.

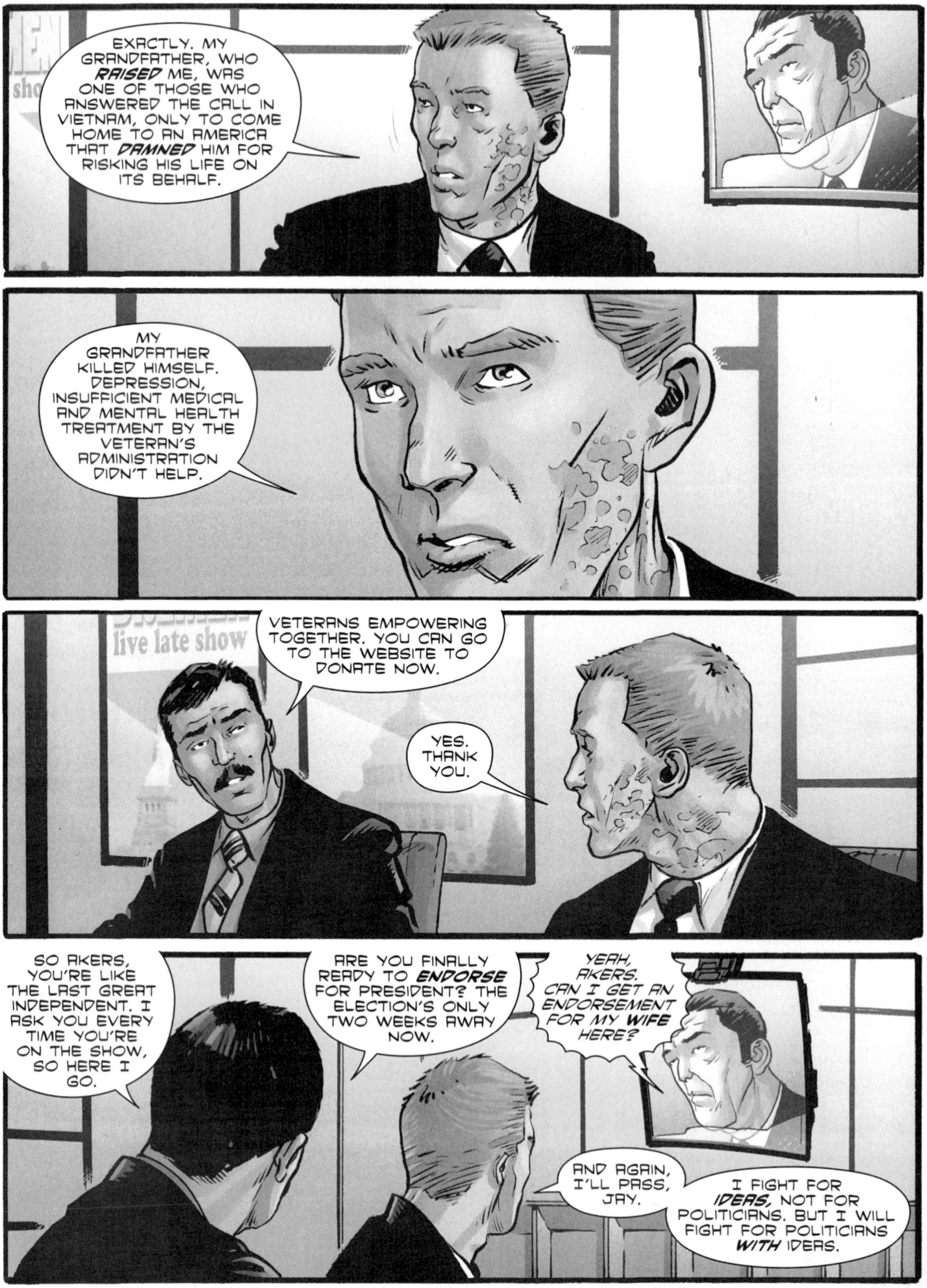
EXACTLY. MY GRANDFATHER, WHO RAISED ME, WAS ONE OF THOSE WHO ANSWERED THE CALL IN VIETNAM, ONLY TO COME HOME TO AN AMERICA THAT DAMNED HIM FOR RISKING HIS LIFE ON ITS BEHALF.
MY GRANDFATHER KILLED HIMSELF. DEPRESSION, INSUFFICIENT MEDICAL AND MENTAL HEALTH TREATMENT BY THE VETERAN'S ADMINISTRATION DIDN'T HELP.
live late show
VETERANS EMPOWERING TOGETHER. YOU CAN GO TO THE WEBSITE TO DONATE NOW.
YES. THANK YOU.
SO AKERS, YOU'RE LIKE THE LAST GREAT INDEPENDENT. I ASK YOU EVERY TIME YOU'RE ON THE SHOW, SO HERE I GO.
ARE YOU FINALLY READY TO ENDORSE FOR PRESIDENT? THE ELECTION'S ONLY TWO WEEKS AWAY NOW.
YEAH, AKERS. CAN I GET AN ENDORSEMENT FOR MY WIFE HERE?
AND AGAIN, I'LL PASS, JAY.
I FIGHT FOR IDEAS, NOT FOR POLITICIANS. BUT I WILL FIGHT FOR POLITICIANS WITH IDEAS.

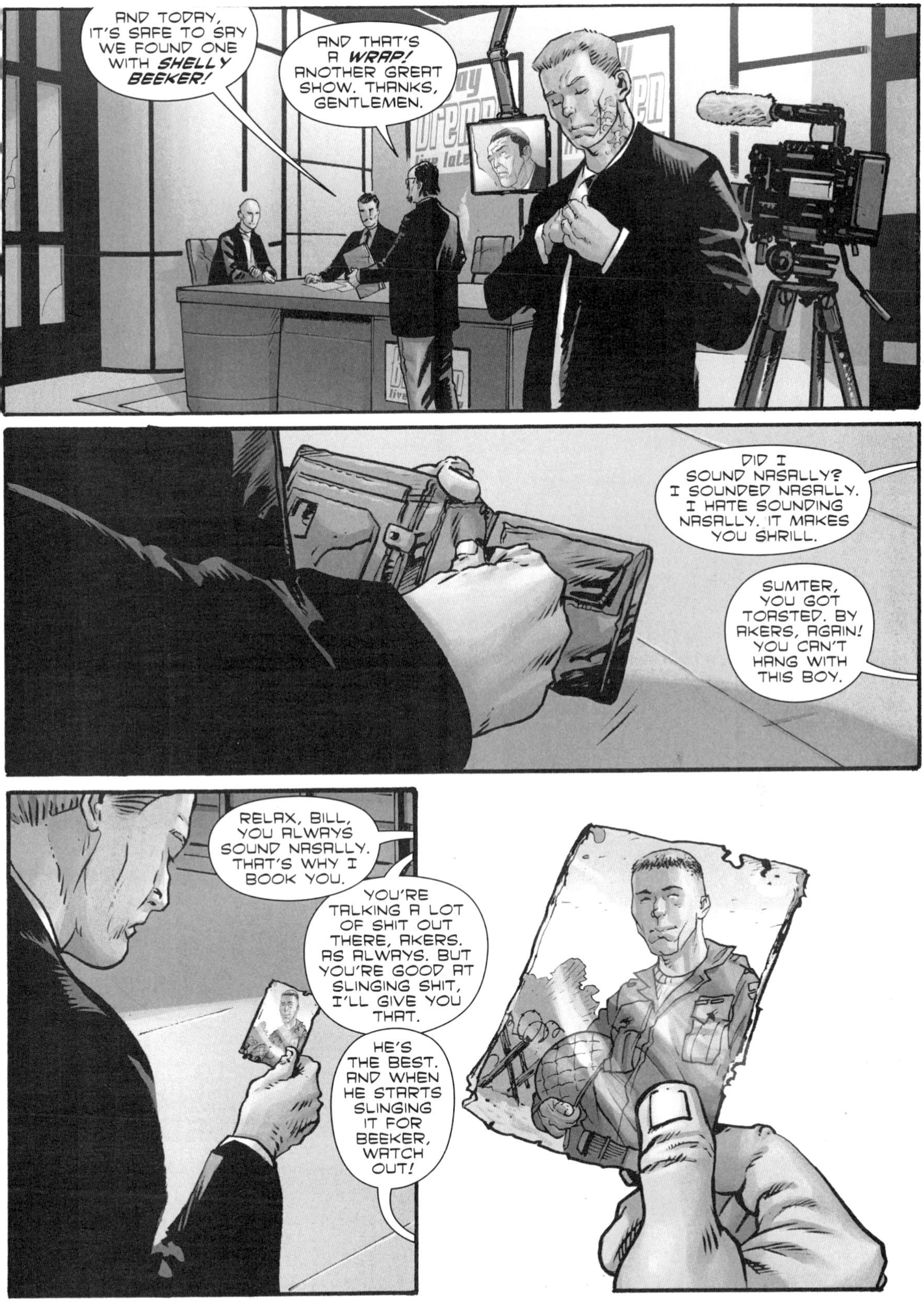
AND TODAY, IT'S SAFE TO SAY WE FOUND ONE WITH SHELLY BEEKER!
AND THAT'S A WRAP! ANOTHER GREAT SHOW. THANKS, GENTLEMEN.
DID I SOUND NASALLY? I SOUNDED NASALLY. I HATE SOUNDING NASALLY. IT MAKES YOU SHRILL.
SUMTER, YOU GOT TOASTED. BY AKERS, AGAIN! YOU CAN'T HANG WITH THIS BOY.
RELAX, BILL, YOU ALWAYS SOUND NASALLY. THAT'S WHY I BOOK YOU.
YOU'RE TALKING A LOT OF SHIT OUT THERE, AKERS. AS ALWAYS. BUT YOU'RE GOOD AT SLINGING SHIT, I'LL GIVE YOU THAT.
HE'S THE BEST. AND WHEN HE STARTS SLINGING IT FOR BEEKER, WATCH OUT!

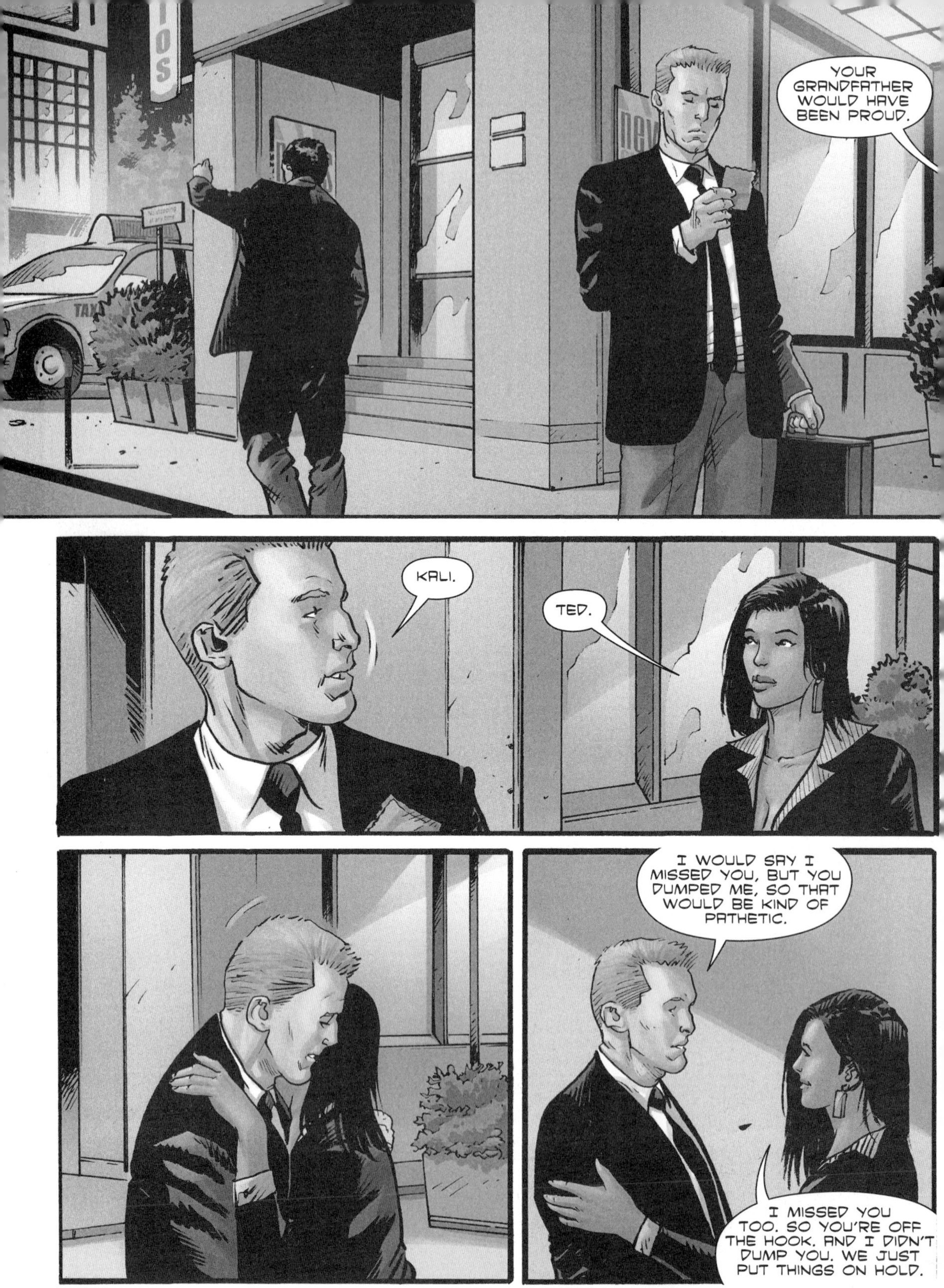
YOUR GRANDFATHER WOULD HAVE BEEN PROUD.
KALI.
TED.
I WOULD SAY I MISSED YOU, BUT YOU DUMPED ME, SO THAT WOULD BE KIND OF PATHETIC.
I MISSED YOU TOO. SO YOU'RE OFF THE HOOK. AND I DIDN'T DUMP YOU. WE JUST PUT THINGS ON HOLD.

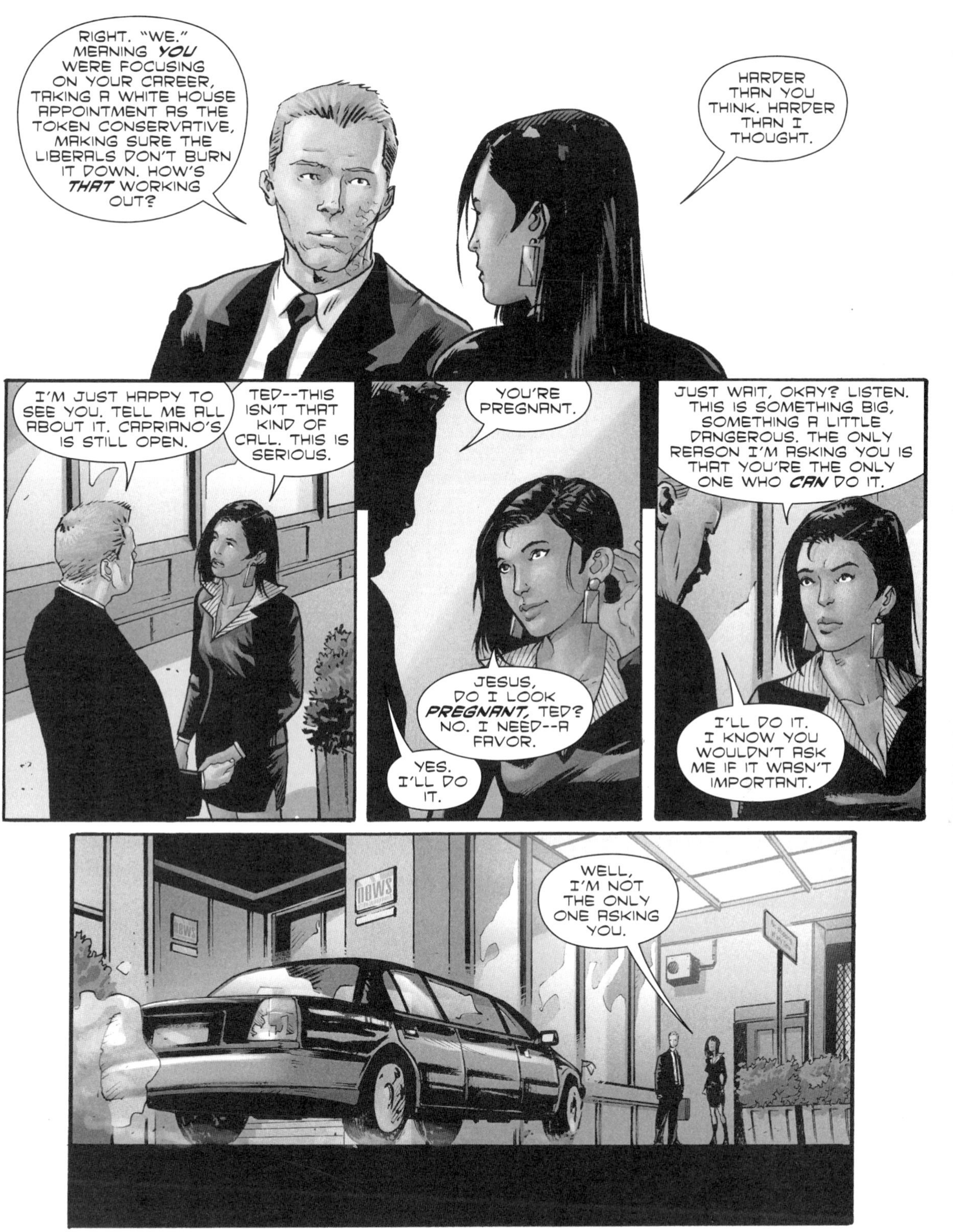

RIGHT. "WE." MEANING *YOU* WERE FOCUSING ON YOUR CAREER, TAKING A WHITE HOUSE APPOINTMENT AS THE TOKEN CONSERVATIVE, MAKING SURE THE LIBERALS DON'T BURN IT DOWN. HOW'S *THAT* WORKING OUT?
HARDER THAN YOU THINK. HARDER THAN I THOUGHT.
I'M JUST HAPPY TO SEE YOU. TELL ME ALL ABOUT IT. CAPRIANO'S IS STILL OPEN.
TED--THIS ISN'T THAT KIND OF CALL. THIS IS SERIOUS.
YOU'RE PREGNANT.
JESUS, DO I LOOK *PREGNANT,* TED? NO. I NEED--A FAVOR.
YES. I'LL DO IT.
JUST WAIT, OKAY? LISTEN. THIS IS SOMETHING BIG, SOMETHING A LITTLE DANGEROUS. THE ONLY REASON I'M ASKING YOU IS THAT YOU'RE THE ONLY ONE WHO *CAN* DO IT.
I'LL DO IT. I KNOW YOU WOULDN'T ASK ME IF IT WASN'T IMPORTANT.
NEWS
WELL, I'M NOT THE ONLY ONE ASKING YOU.

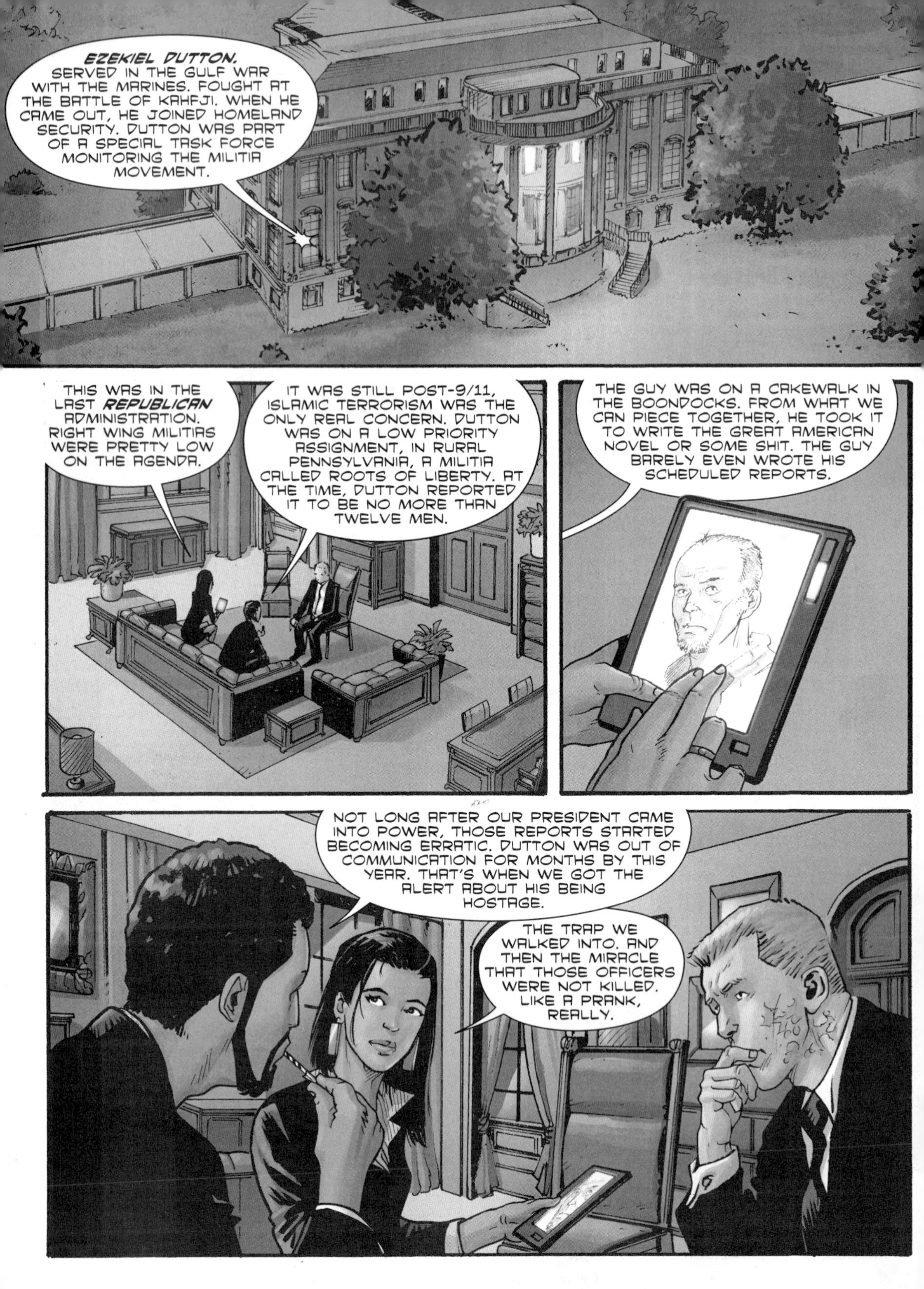
EZEKIEL DUTTON. SERVED IN THE GULF WAR WITH THE MARINES. FOUGHT AT THE BATTLE OF KAHFJI. WHEN HE CAME OUT, HE JOINED HOMELAND SECURITY. DUTTON WAS PART OF A SPECIAL TASK FORCE MONITORING THE MILITIA MOVEMENT.
THIS WAS IN THE LAST REPUBLICAN ADMINISTRATION. RIGHT WING MILITIAS WERE PRETTY LOW ON THE AGENDA.
IT WAS STILL POST-9/11, ISLAMIC TERRORISM WAS THE ONLY REAL CONCERN. DUTTON WAS ON A LOW PRIORITY ASSIGNMENT, IN RURAL PENNSYLVANIA, A MILITIA CALLED ROOTS OF LIBERTY. AT THE TIME, DUTTON REPORTED IT TO BE NO MORE THAN TWELVE MEN.
THE GUY WAS ON A CAKEWALK IN THE BOONDOCKS. FROM WHAT WE CAN PIECE TOGETHER, HE TOOK IT TO WRITE THE GREAT AMERICAN NOVEL OR SOME SHIT. THE GUY BARELY EVEN WROTE HIS SCHEDULED REPORTS.
NOT LONG AFTER OUR PRESIDENT CAME INTO POWER, THOSE REPORTS STARTED BECOMING ERRATIC. DUTTON WAS OUT OF COMMUNICATION FOR MONTHS BY THIS YEAR. THAT'S WHEN WE GOT THE ALERT ABOUT HIS BEING HOSTAGE.
THE TRAP WE WALKED INTO. AND THEN THE MIRACLE THAT THOSE OFFICERS WERE NOT KILLED. LIKE A PRANK, REALLY.

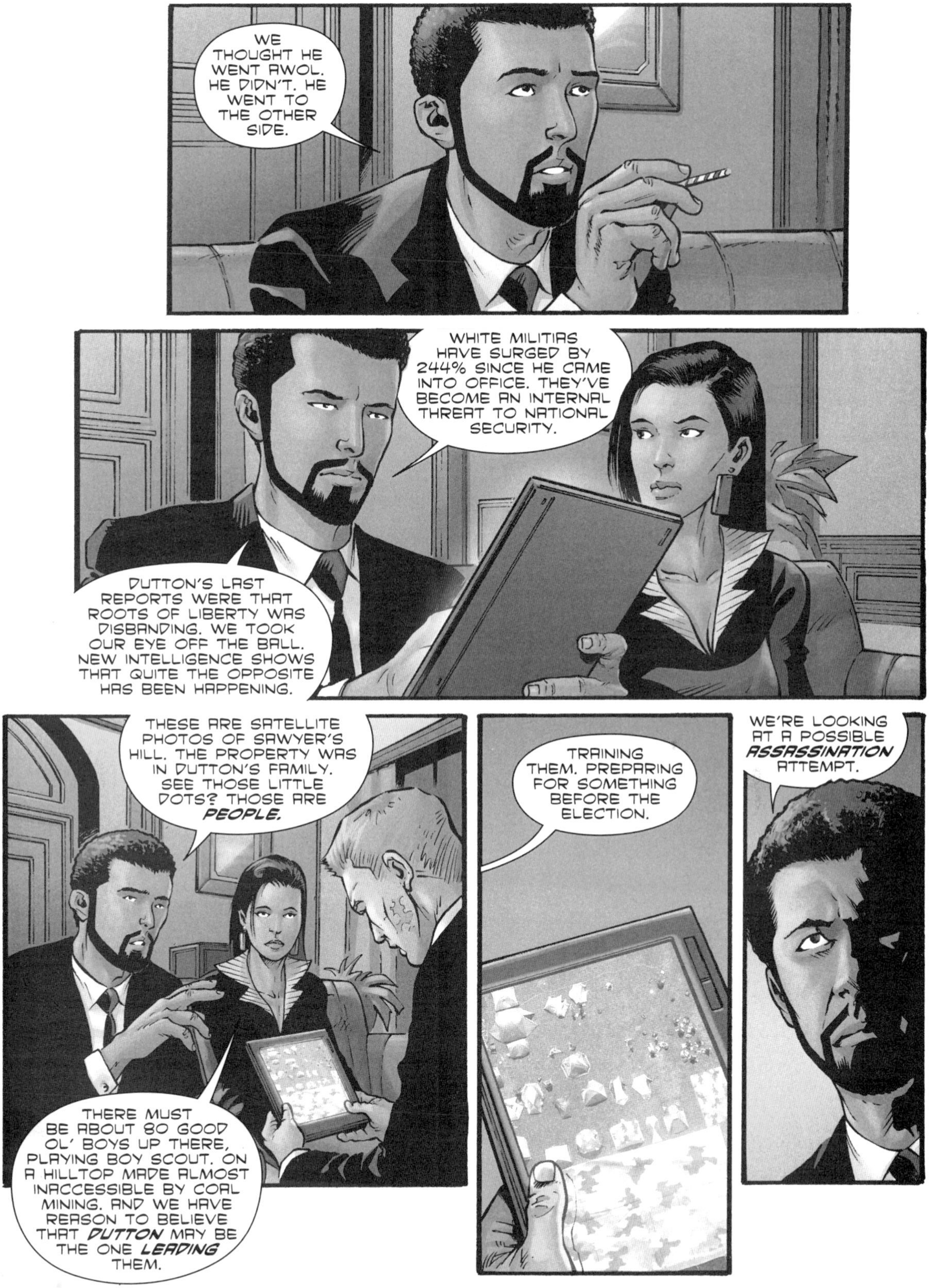
WE THOUGHT HE WENT AWOL. HE DIDN'T. HE WENT TO THE OTHER SIDE.
WHITE MILITIAS HAVE SURGED BY 244% SINCE HE CAME INTO OFFICE. THEY'VE BECOME AN INTERNAL THREAT TO NATIONAL SECURITY.
DUTTON'S LAST REPORTS WERE THAT ROOTS OF LIBERTY WAS DISBANDING. WE TOOK OUR EYE OFF THE BALL. NEW INTELLIGENCE SHOWS THAT QUITE THE OPPOSITE HAS BEEN HAPPENING.
THESE ARE SATELLITE PHOTOS OF SAWYER'S HILL. THE PROPERTY WAS IN DUTTON'S FAMILY. SEE THOSE LITTLE DOTS? THOSE ARE *PEOPLE.*
THERE MUST BE ABOUT 80 GOOD OL' BOYS UP THERE, PLAYING BOY SCOUT. ON A HILLTOP MADE ALMOST INACCESSIBLE BY COAL MINING. AND WE HAVE REASON TO BELIEVE THAT *DUTTON* MAY BE THE ONE *LEADING* THEM.
TRAINING THEM. PREPARING FOR SOMETHING BEFORE THE ELECTION.
WE'RE LOOKING AT A POSSIBLE *ASSASSINATION* ATTEMPT.

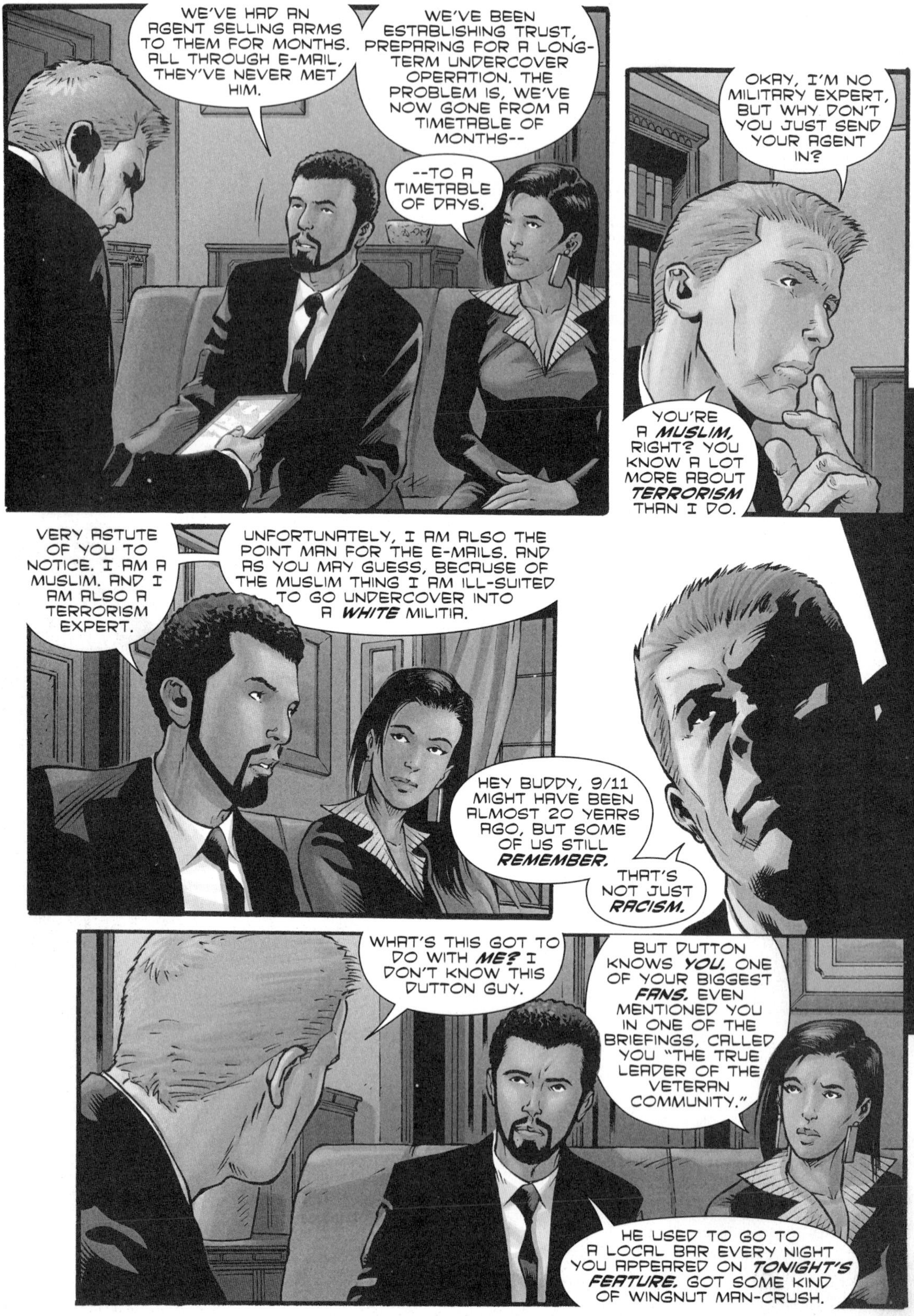
WE'VE HAD AN AGENT SELLING ARMS TO THEM FOR MONTHS. ALL THROUGH E-MAIL, THEY'VE NEVER MET HIM.
WE'VE BEEN ESTABLISHING TRUST, PREPARING FOR A LONG-TERM UNDERCOVER OPERATION. THE PROBLEM IS, WE'VE NOW GONE FROM A TIMETABLE OF MONTHS--
--TO A TIMETABLE OF DAYS.
OKAY, I'M NO MILITARY EXPERT, BUT WHY DON'T YOU JUST SEND YOUR AGENT IN?
YOU'RE A MUSLIM, RIGHT? YOU KNOW A LOT MORE ABOUT TERRORISM THAN I DO.
VERY ASTUTE OF YOU TO NOTICE. I AM A MUSLIM. AND I AM ALSO A TERRORISM EXPERT.
UNFORTUNATELY, I AM ALSO THE POINT MAN FOR THE E-MAILS. AND AS YOU MAY GUESS, BECAUSE OF THE MUSLIM THING I AM ILL-SUITED TO GO UNDERCOVER INTO A WHITE MILITIA.
HEY BUDDY, 9/11 MIGHT HAVE BEEN ALMOST 20 YEARS AGO, BUT SOME OF US STILL REMEMBER.
THAT'S NOT JUST RACISM.
WHAT'S THIS GOT TO DO WITH ME? I DON'T KNOW THIS DUTTON GUY.
BUT DUTTON KNOWS YOU. ONE OF YOUR BIGGEST FANS. EVEN MENTIONED YOU IN ONE OF THE BRIEFINGS, CALLED YOU "THE TRUE LEADER OF THE VETERAN COMMUNITY."
HE USED TO GO TO A LOCAL BAR EVERY NIGHT YOU APPEARED ON TONIGHT'S FEATURE. GOT SOME KIND OF WINGNUT MAN-CRUSH.

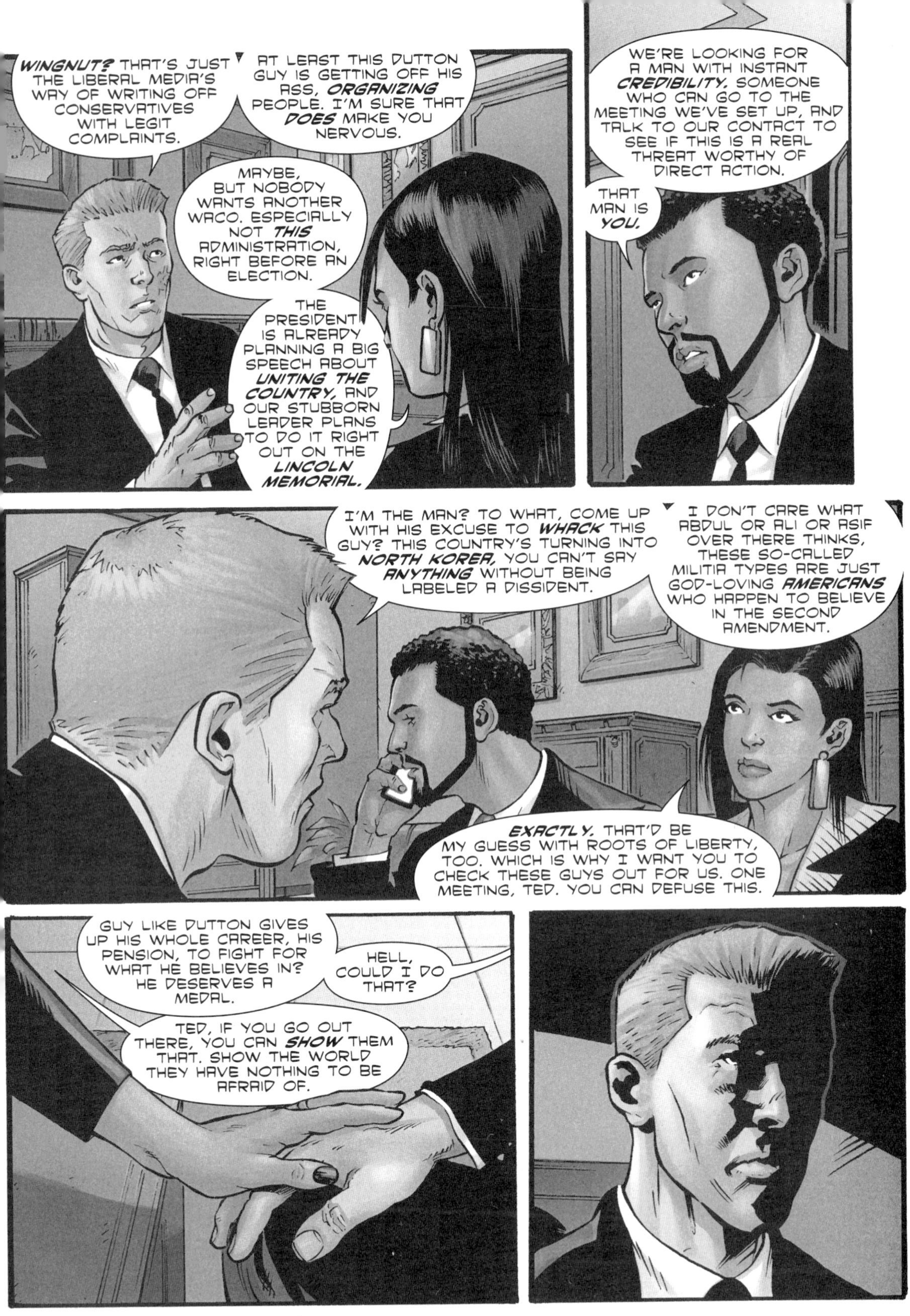
WINGNUT? THAT'S JUST THE LIBERAL MEDIA'S WAY OF WRITING OFF CONSERVATIVES WITH LEGIT COMPLAINTS.
AT LEAST THIS DUTTON GUY IS GETTING OFF HIS ASS, ORGANIZING PEOPLE. I'M SURE THAT DOES MAKE YOU NERVOUS.
MAYBE, BUT NOBODY WANTS ANOTHER WACO. ESPECIALLY NOT THIS ADMINISTRATION, RIGHT BEFORE AN ELECTION.
THE PRESIDENT IS ALREADY PLANNING A BIG SPEECH ABOUT UNITING THE COUNTRY, AND OUR STUBBORN LEADER PLANS TO DO IT RIGHT OUT ON THE LINCOLN MEMORIAL.
WE'RE LOOKING FOR A MAN WITH INSTANT CREDIBILITY. SOMEONE WHO CAN GO TO THE MEETING WE'VE SET UP, AND TALK TO OUR CONTACT TO SEE IF THIS IS A REAL THREAT WORTHY OF DIRECT ACTION.
THAT MAN IS YOU.
I'M THE MAN? TO WHAT, COME UP WITH HIS EXCUSE TO WHACK THIS GUY? THIS COUNTRY'S TURNING INTO NORTH KOREA, YOU CAN'T SAY ANYTHING WITHOUT BEING LABELED A DISSIDENT.
I DON'T CARE WHAT ABDUL OR ALI OR ASIF OVER THERE THINKS, THESE SO-CALLED MILITIA TYPES ARE JUST GOD-LOVING AMERICANS WHO HAPPEN TO BELIEVE IN THE SECOND AMENDMENT.
EXACTLY. THAT'D BE MY GUESS WITH ROOTS OF LIBERTY, TOO. WHICH IS WHY I WANT YOU TO CHECK THESE GUYS OUT FOR US. ONE MEETING, TED. YOU CAN DEFUSE THIS.
GUY LIKE DUTTON GIVES UP HIS WHOLE CAREER, HIS PENSION, TO FIGHT FOR WHAT HE BELIEVES IN? HE DESERVES A MEDAL.
HELL, COULD I DO THAT?
TED, IF YOU GO OUT THERE, YOU CAN SHOW THEM THAT. SHOW THE WORLD THEY HAVE NOTHING TO BE AFRAID OF.

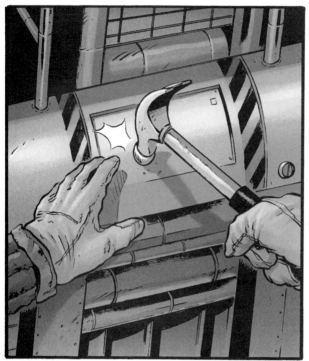

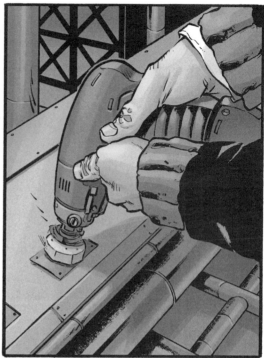

SECURITY SECTION

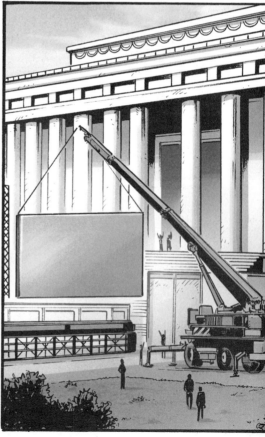

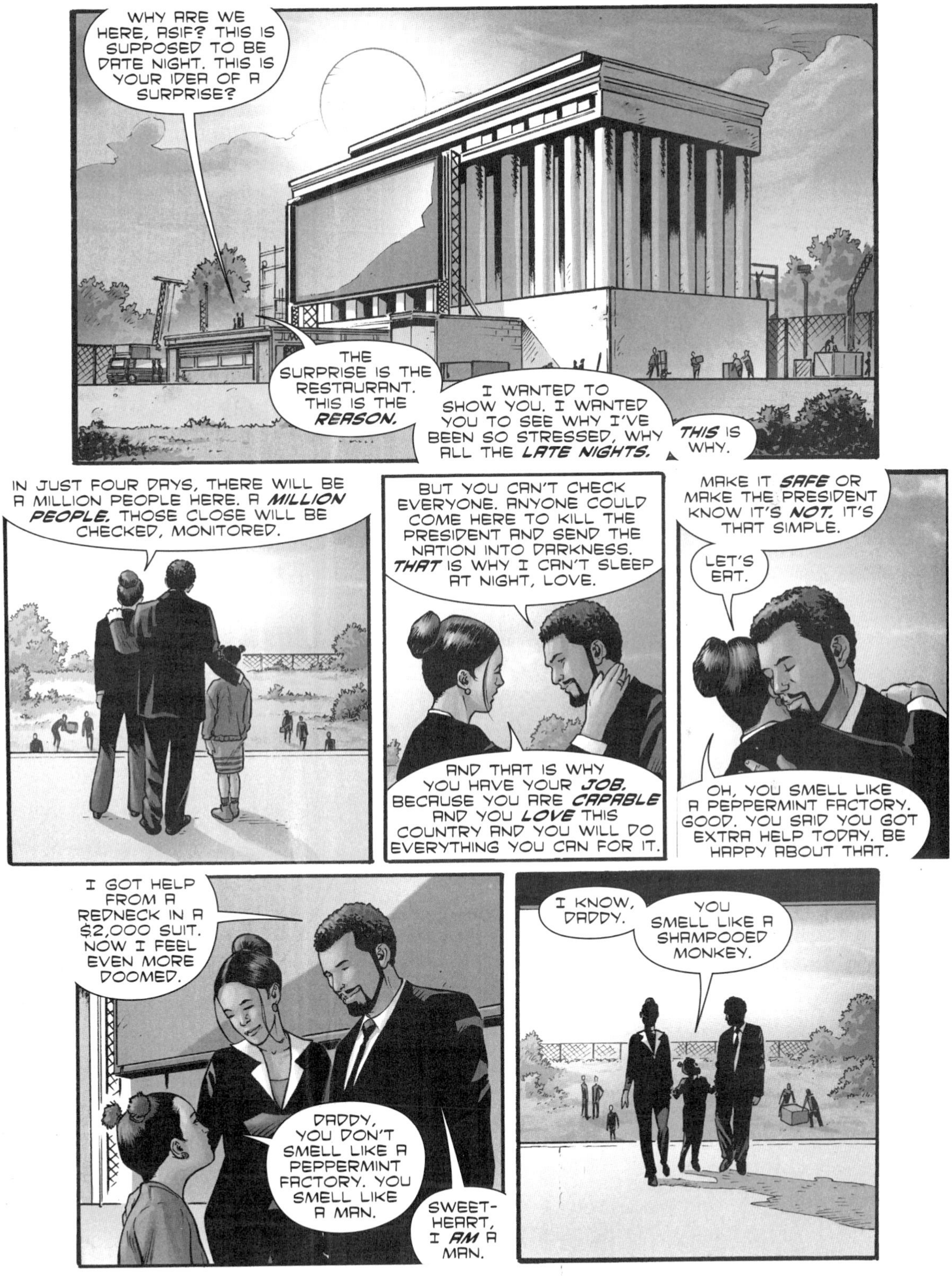

WHY ARE WE HERE, ASIF? THIS IS SUPPOSED TO BE DATE NIGHT. THIS IS YOUR IDEA OF A SURPRISE?
THE SURPRISE IS THE RESTAURANT. THIS IS THE REASON.
I WANTED TO SHOW YOU. I WANTED YOU TO SEE WHY I'VE BEEN SO STRESSED, WHY ALL THE LATE NIGHTS.
THIS IS WHY.
IN JUST FOUR DAYS, THERE WILL BE A MILLION PEOPLE HERE. A MILLION PEOPLE. THOSE CLOSE WILL BE CHECKED, MONITORED.
BUT YOU CAN'T CHECK EVERYONE. ANYONE COULD COME HERE TO KILL THE PRESIDENT AND SEND THE NATION INTO DARKNESS. THAT IS WHY I CAN'T SLEEP AT NIGHT, LOVE.
AND THAT IS WHY YOU HAVE YOUR JOB. BECAUSE YOU ARE CAPABLE AND YOU LOVE THIS COUNTRY AND YOU WILL DO EVERYTHING YOU CAN FOR IT.
MAKE IT SAFE OR MAKE THE PRESIDENT KNOW IT'S NOT. IT'S THAT SIMPLE.
LET'S EAT.
OH, YOU SMELL LIKE A PEPPERMINT FACTORY. GOOD. YOU SAID YOU GOT EXTRA HELP TODAY. BE HAPPY ABOUT THAT.
I GOT HELP FROM A REDNECK IN A $2,000 SUIT. NOW I FEEL EVEN MORE DOOMED.
DADDY, YOU DON'T SMELL LIKE A PEPPERMINT FACTORY. YOU SMELL LIKE A MAN.
SWEET-HEART, I AM A MAN.
I KNOW, DADDY.
YOU SMELL LIKE A SHAMPOOED MONKEY.

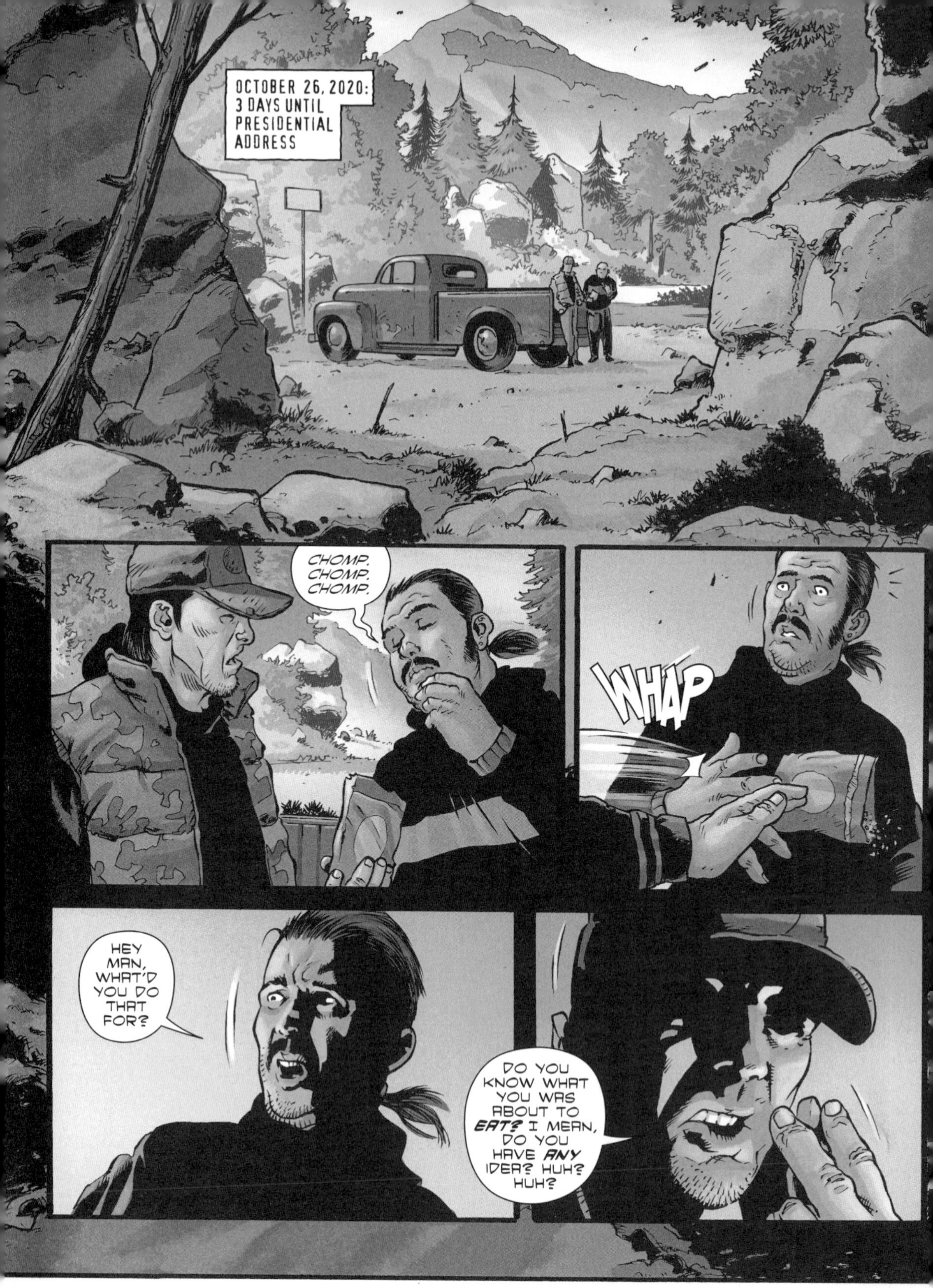
OCTOBER 26, 2020: 3 DAYS UNTIL PRESIDENTIAL ADDRESS
CHOMP. CHOMP. CHOMP.
WHAP
HEY MAN, WHAT'D YOU DO THAT FOR?
DO YOU KNOW WHAT YOU WAS ABOUT TO EAT? I MEAN, DO YOU HAVE ANY IDEA? HUH? HUH?

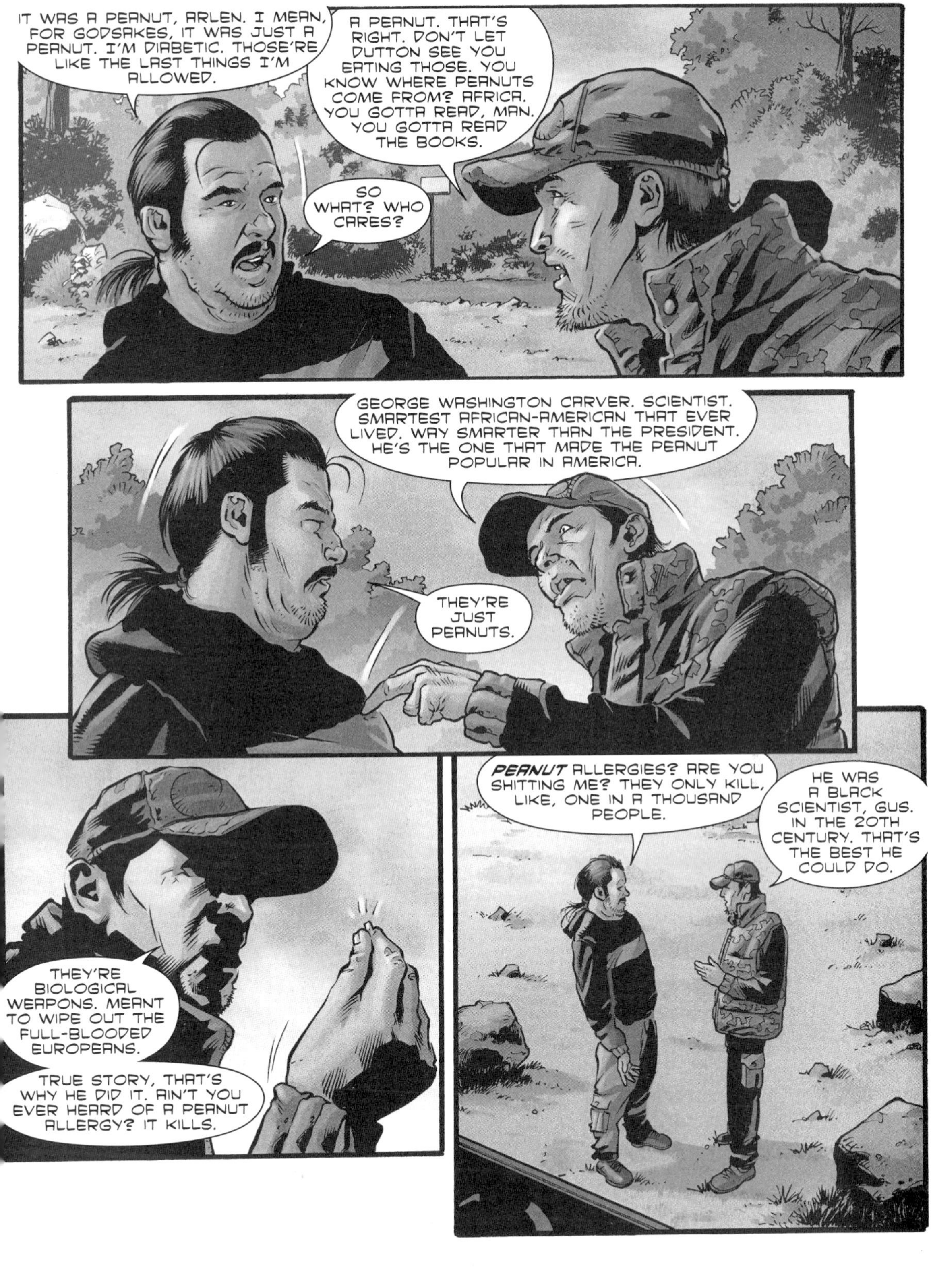
IT WAS A PEANUT, ARLEN. I MEAN, FOR GODSAKES, IT WAS JUST A PEANUT. I'M DIABETIC. THOSE'RE LIKE THE LAST THINGS I'M ALLOWED.
A PEANUT. THAT'S RIGHT. DON'T LET DUTTON SEE YOU EATING THOSE. YOU KNOW WHERE PEANUTS COME FROM? AFRICA. YOU GOTTA READ, MAN. YOU GOTTA READ THE BOOKS.
SO WHAT? WHO CARES?
GEORGE WASHINGTON CARVER. SCIENTIST. SMARTEST AFRICAN-AMERICAN THAT EVER LIVED. WAY SMARTER THAN THE PRESIDENT. HE'S THE ONE THAT MADE THE PEANUT POPULAR IN AMERICA.
THEY'RE JUST PEANUTS.
THEY'RE BIOLOGICAL WEAPONS. MEANT TO WIPE OUT THE FULL-BLOODED EUROPEANS.
TRUE STORY, THAT'S WHY HE DID IT. AIN'T YOU EVER HEARD OF A PEANUT ALLERGY? IT KILLS.
PEANUT ALLERGIES? ARE YOU SHITTING ME? THEY ONLY KILL, LIKE, ONE IN A THOUSAND PEOPLE.
HE WAS A BLACK SCIENTIST, GUS. IN THE 20TH CENTURY. THAT'S THE BEST HE COULD DO.

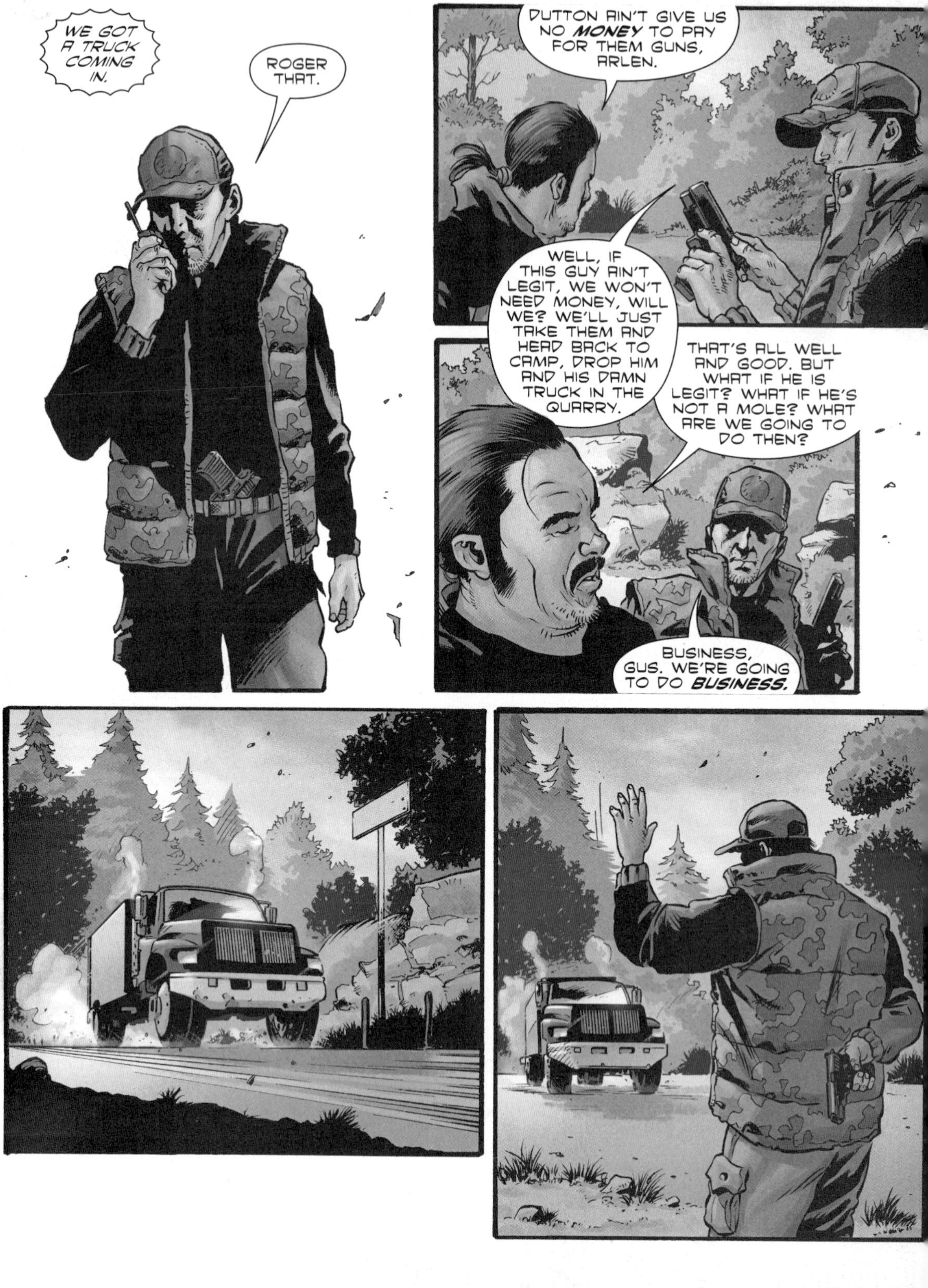
WE GOT A TRUCK COMING IN.
ROGER THAT.
DUTTON AIN'T GIVE US NO MONEY TO PAY FOR THEM GUNS, ARLEN.
WELL, IF THIS GUY AIN'T LEGIT, WE WON'T NEED MONEY, WILL WE? WE'LL JUST TAKE THEM AND HEAD BACK TO CAMP, DROP HIM AND HIS DAMN TRUCK IN THE QUARRY.
THAT'S ALL WELL AND GOOD. BUT WHAT IF HE IS LEGIT? WHAT IF HE'S NOT A MOLE? WHAT ARE WE GOING TO DO THEN?
BUSINESS, GUS. WE'RE GOING TO DO BUSINESS.

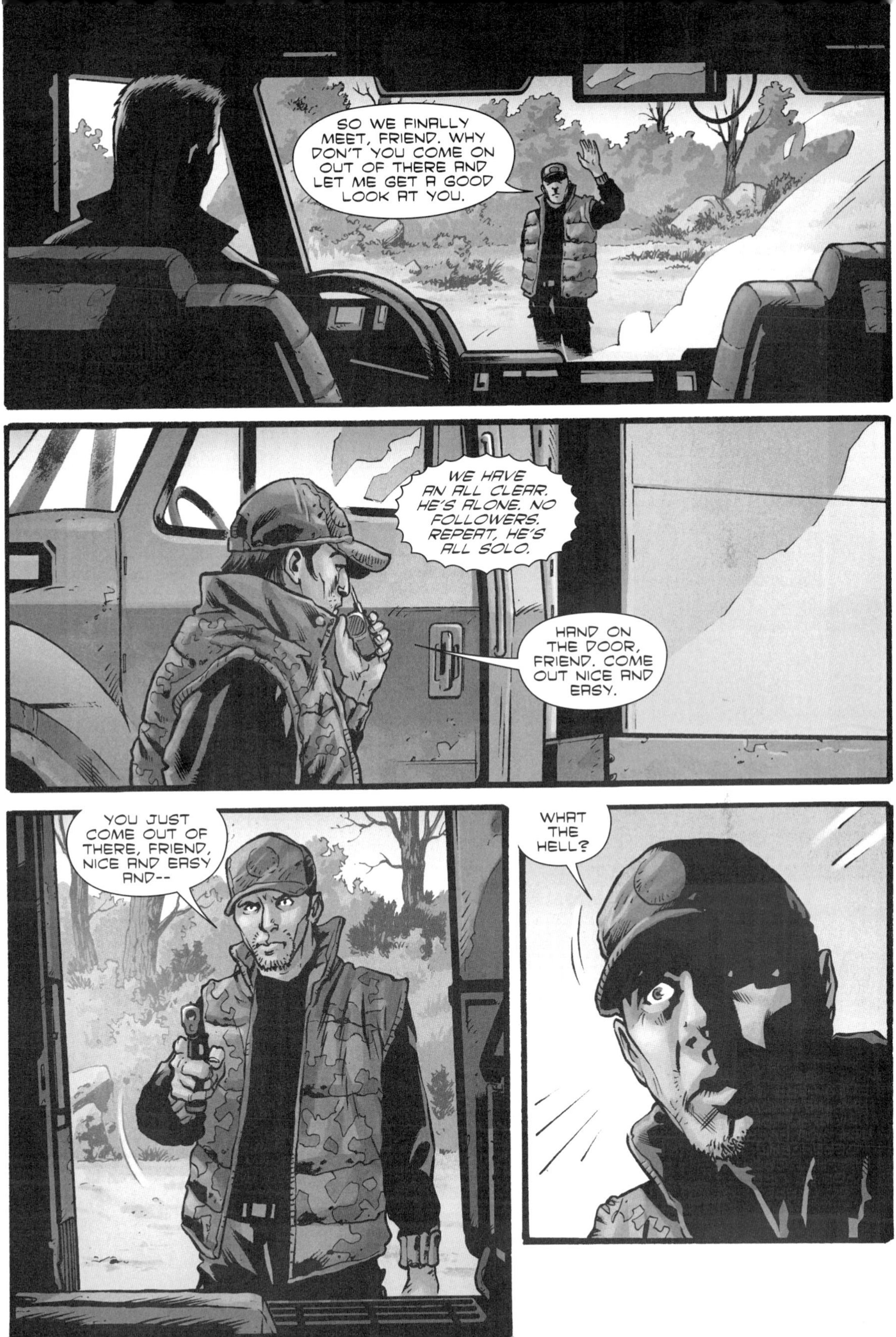
SO WE FINALLY MEET, FRIEND. WHY DON'T YOU COME ON OUT OF THERE AND LET ME GET A GOOD LOOK AT YOU.
WE HAVE AN ALL CLEAR. HE'S ALONE. NO FOLLOWERS. REPEAT, HE'S ALL SOLO.
HAND ON THE DOOR, FRIEND. COME OUT NICE AND EASY.
YOU JUST COME OUT OF THERE, FRIEND, NICE AND EASY AND--
WHAT THE HELL?

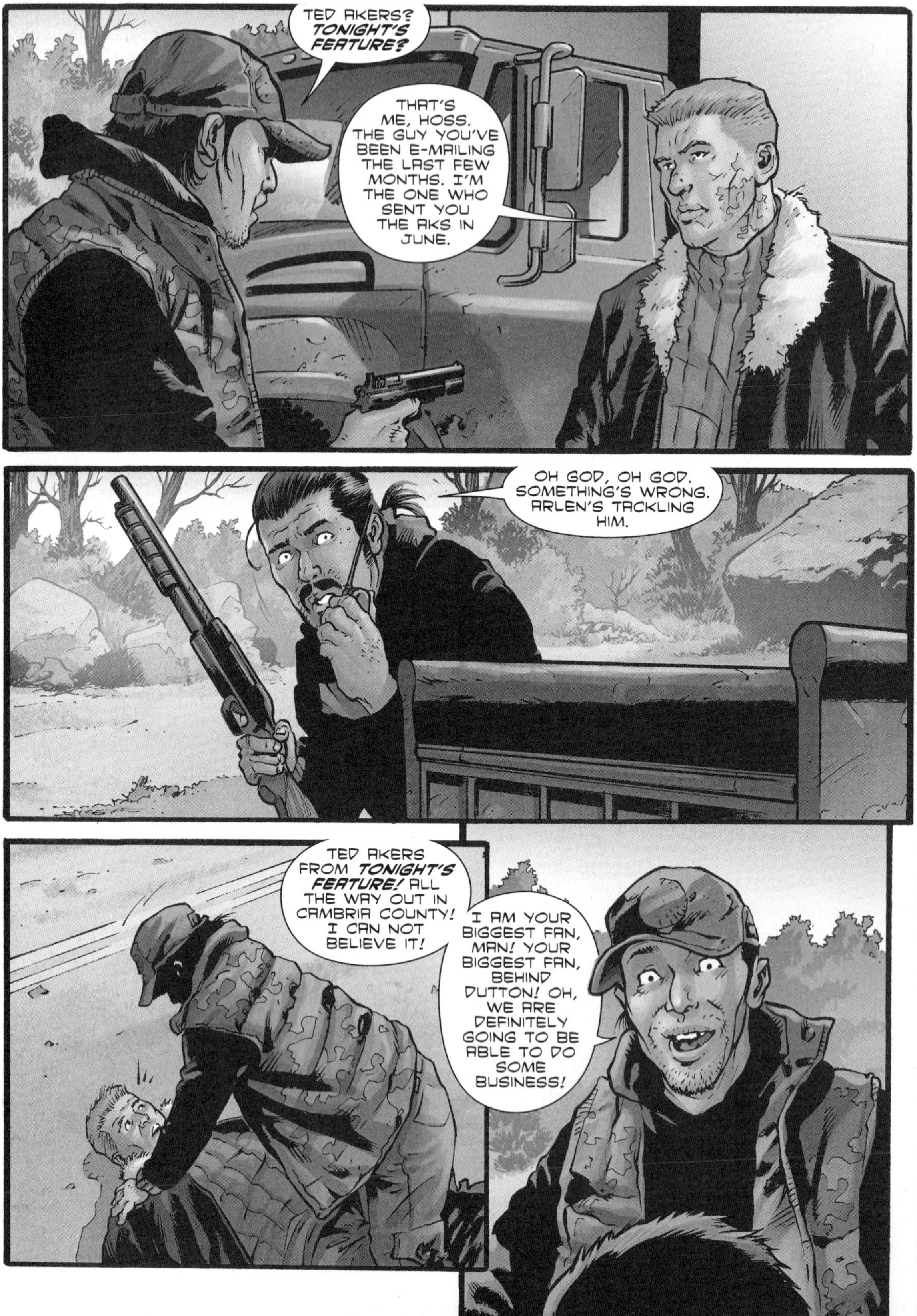
TED AKERS? *TONIGHT'S FEATURE?*
THAT'S ME, HOSS. THE GUY YOU'VE BEEN E-MAILING THE LAST FEW MONTHS. I'M THE ONE WHO SENT YOU THE AKS IN JUNE.
OH GOD, OH GOD. SOMETHING'S WRONG. ARLEN'S TACKLING HIM.
TED AKERS FROM *TONIGHT'S FEATURE!* ALL THE WAY OUT IN CAMBRIA COUNTY! I CAN NOT BELIEVE IT!
I AM YOUR BIGGEST FAN, MAN! YOUR BIGGEST FAN, BEHIND DUTTON! OH, WE ARE DEFINITELY GOING TO BE ABLE TO DO SOME BUSINESS!

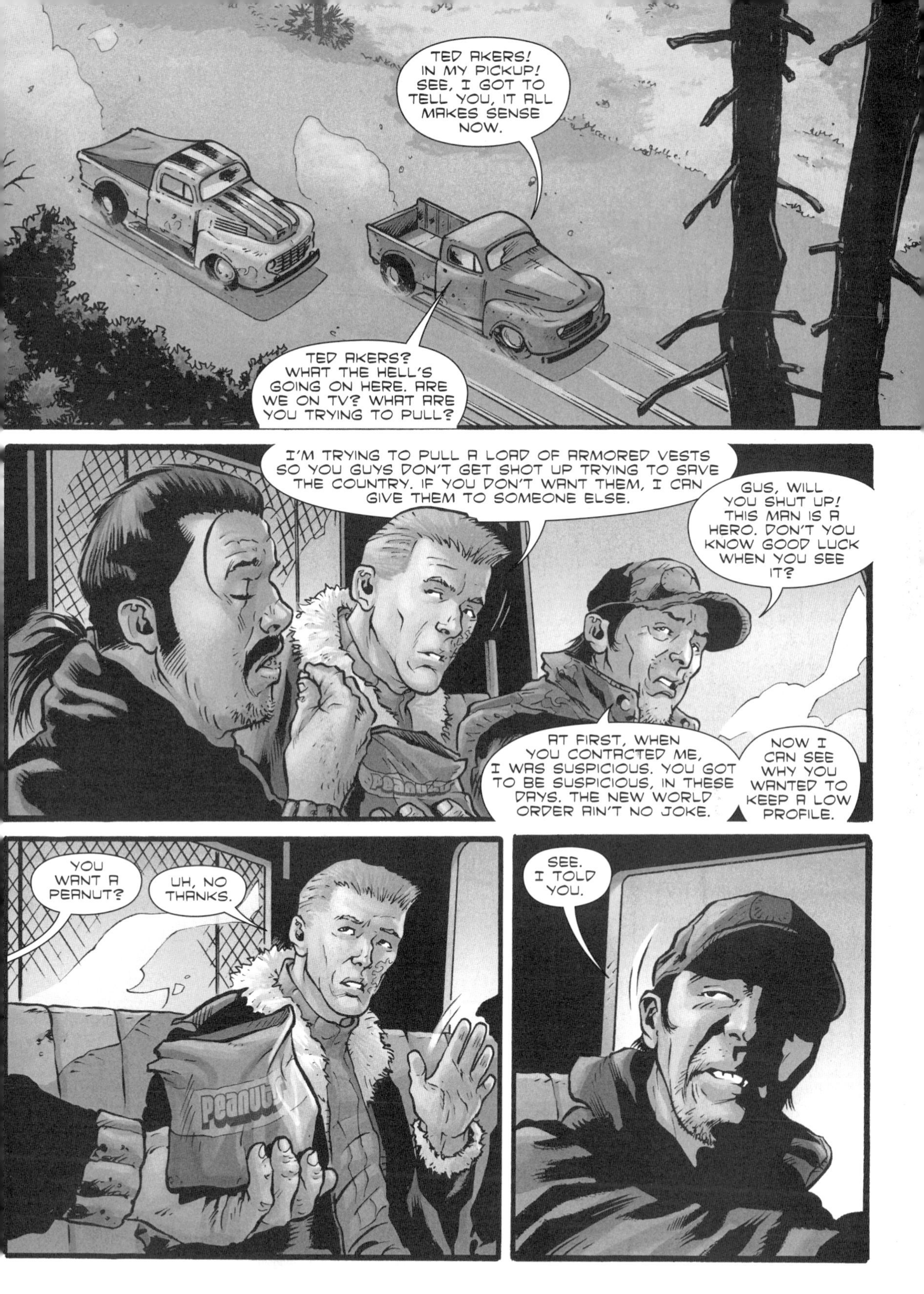
TED AKERS! IN MY PICKUP! SEE, I GOT TO TELL YOU, IT ALL MAKES SENSE NOW.
TED AKERS? WHAT THE HELL'S GOING ON HERE. ARE WE ON TV? WHAT ARE YOU TRYING TO PULL?
I'M TRYING TO PULL A LOAD OF ARMORED VESTS SO YOU GUYS DON'T GET SHOT UP TRYING TO SAVE THE COUNTRY. IF YOU DON'T WANT THEM, I CAN GIVE THEM TO SOMEONE ELSE.
GUS, WILL YOU SHUT UP! THIS MAN IS A HERO. DON'T YOU KNOW GOOD LUCK WHEN YOU SEE IT?
AT FIRST, WHEN YOU CONTACTED ME, I WAS SUSPICIOUS. YOU GOT TO BE SUSPICIOUS, IN THESE DAYS. THE NEW WORLD ORDER AIN'T NO JOKE.
NOW I CAN SEE WHY YOU WANTED TO KEEP A LOW PROFILE.
YOU WANT A PEANUT?
UH, NO THANKS.
SEE. I TOLD YOU.

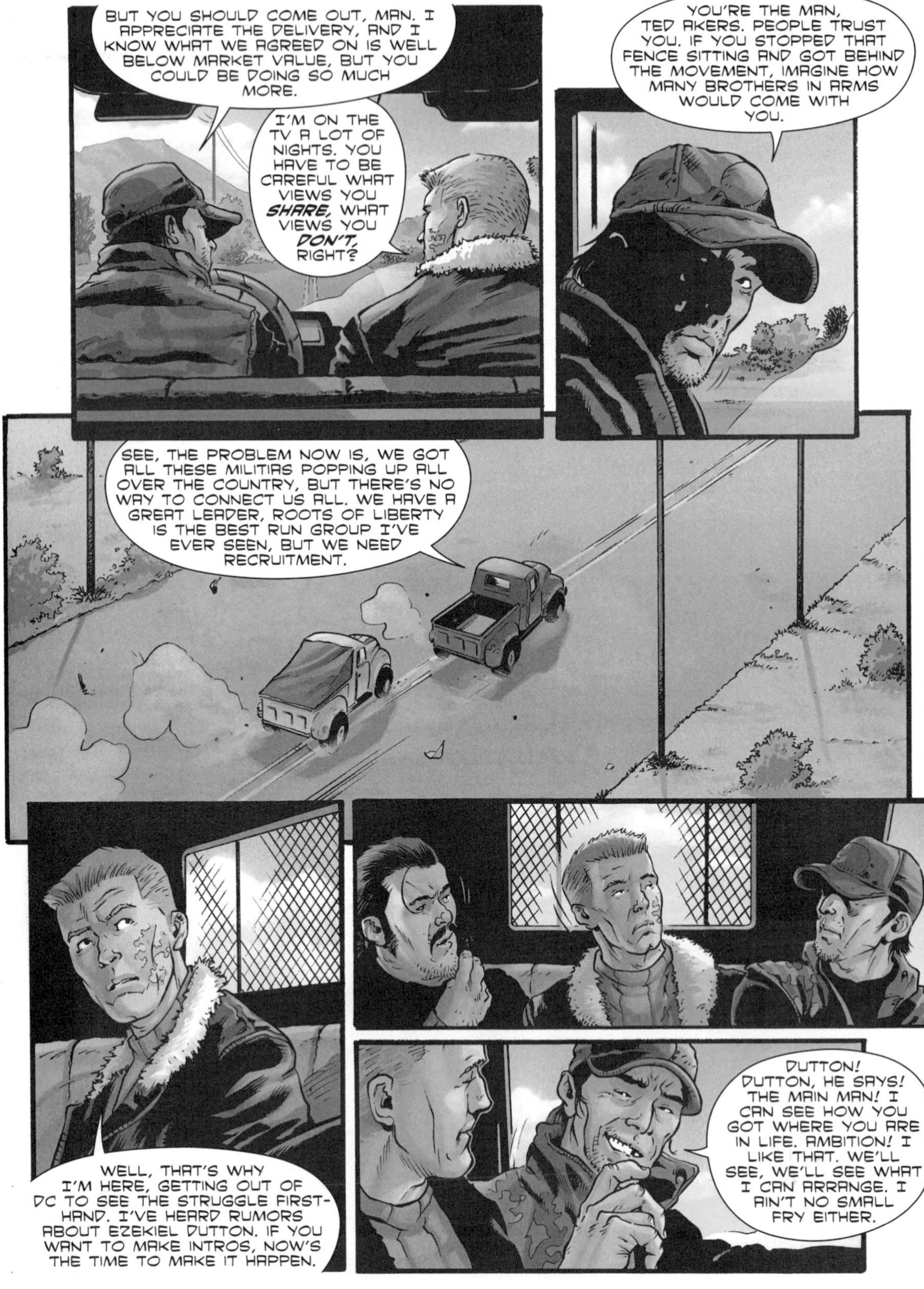
BUT YOU SHOULD COME OUT, MAN. I APPRECIATE THE DELIVERY, AND I KNOW WHAT WE AGREED ON IS WELL BELOW MARKET VALUE, BUT YOU COULD BE DOING SO MUCH MORE.
I'M ON THE TV A LOT OF NIGHTS. YOU HAVE TO BE CAREFUL WHAT VIEWS YOU SHARE, WHAT VIEWS YOU DON'T, RIGHT?
YOU'RE THE MAN, TED AKERS. PEOPLE TRUST YOU. IF YOU STOPPED THAT FENCE SITTING AND GOT BEHIND THE MOVEMENT, IMAGINE HOW MANY BROTHERS IN ARMS WOULD COME WITH YOU.
SEE, THE PROBLEM NOW IS, WE GOT ALL THESE MILITIAS POPPING UP ALL OVER THE COUNTRY, BUT THERE'S NO WAY TO CONNECT US ALL. WE HAVE A GREAT LEADER, ROOTS OF LIBERTY IS THE BEST RUN GROUP I'VE EVER SEEN, BUT WE NEED RECRUITMENT.
WELL, THAT'S WHY I'M HERE, GETTING OUT OF DC TO SEE THE STRUGGLE FIRST-HAND. I'VE HEARD RUMORS ABOUT EZEKIEL DUTTON. IF YOU WANT TO MAKE INTROS, NOW'S THE TIME TO MAKE IT HAPPEN.
DUTTON! DUTTON, HE SAYS! THE MAIN MAN! I CAN SEE HOW YOU GOT WHERE YOU ARE IN LIFE. AMBITION! I LIKE THAT. WE'LL SEE, WE'LL SEE WHAT I CAN ARRANGE. I AIN'T NO SMALL FRY EITHER.

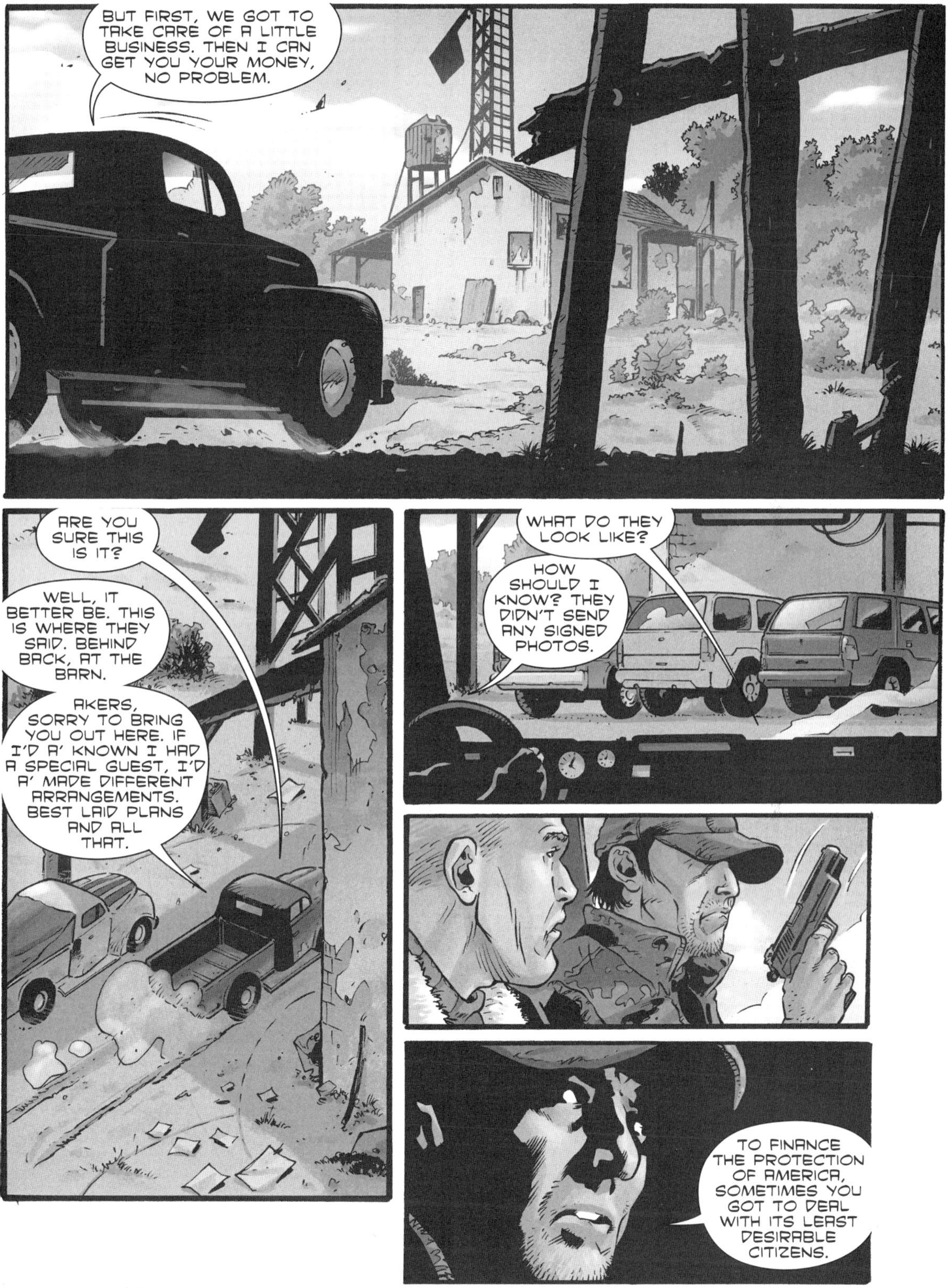
BUT FIRST, WE GOT TO TAKE CARE OF A LITTLE BUSINESS. THEN I CAN GET YOU YOUR MONEY, NO PROBLEM.
ARE YOU SURE THIS IS IT?
WELL, IT BETTER BE. THIS IS WHERE THEY SAID. BEHIND BACK, AT THE BARN.
AKERS, SORRY TO BRING YOU OUT HERE. IF I'D A' KNOWN I HAD A SPECIAL GUEST, I'D A' MADE DIFFERENT ARRANGEMENTS. BEST LAID PLANS AND ALL THAT.
WHAT DO THEY LOOK LIKE?
HOW SHOULD I KNOW? THEY DIDN'T SEND ANY SIGNED PHOTOS.
TO FINANCE THE PROTECTION OF AMERICA, SOMETIMES YOU GOT TO DEAL WITH ITS LEAST DESIRABLE CITIZENS.

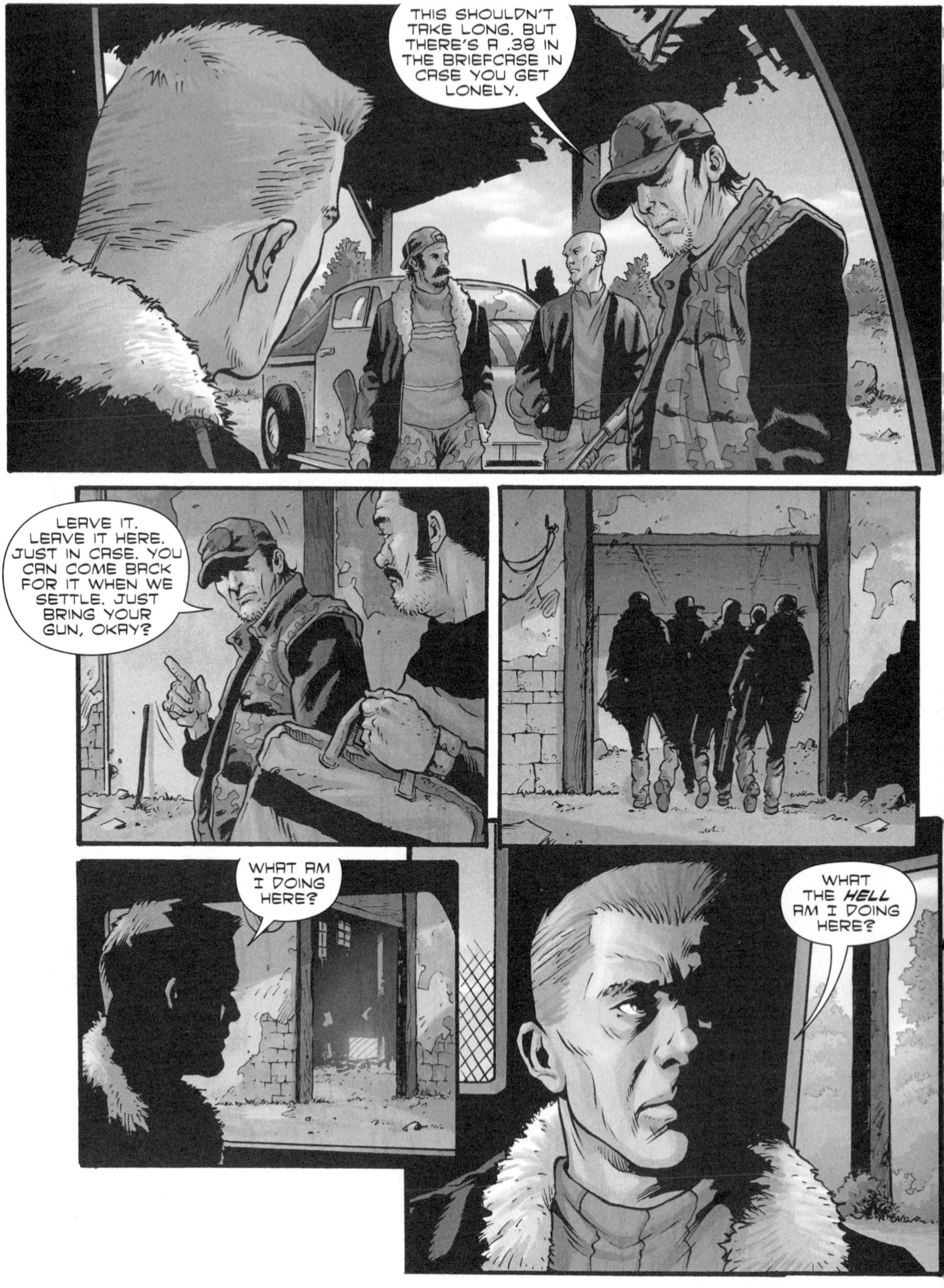
THIS SHOULDN'T TAKE LONG. BUT THERE'S A .38 IN THE BRIEFCASE IN CASE YOU GET LONELY.
LEAVE IT. LEAVE IT HERE. JUST IN CASE. YOU CAN COME BACK FOR IT WHEN WE SETTLE. JUST BRING YOUR GUN, OKAY?
WHAT AM I DOING HERE?
WHAT THE *HELL* AM I DOING HERE?

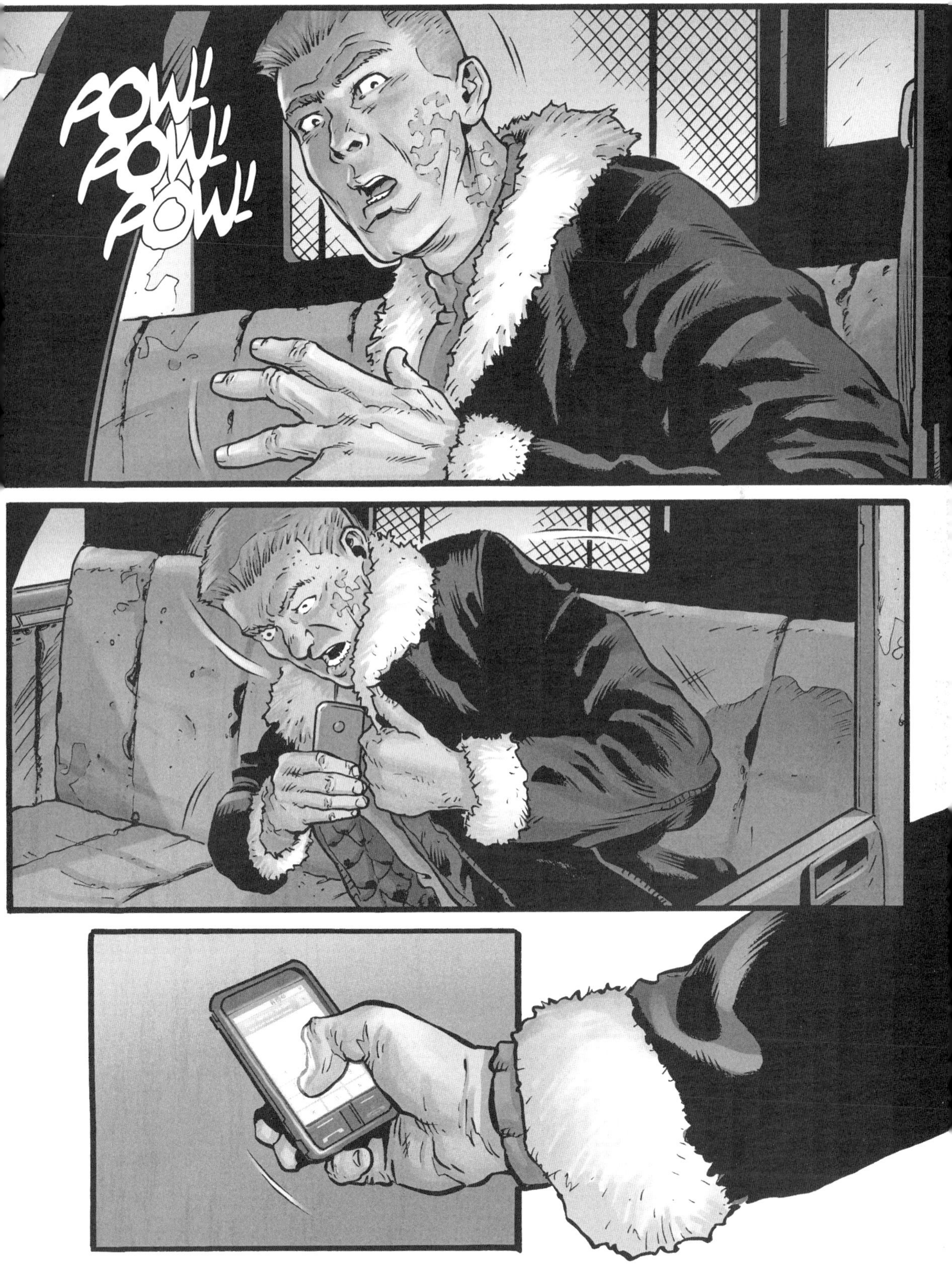
POW! POW! POW!

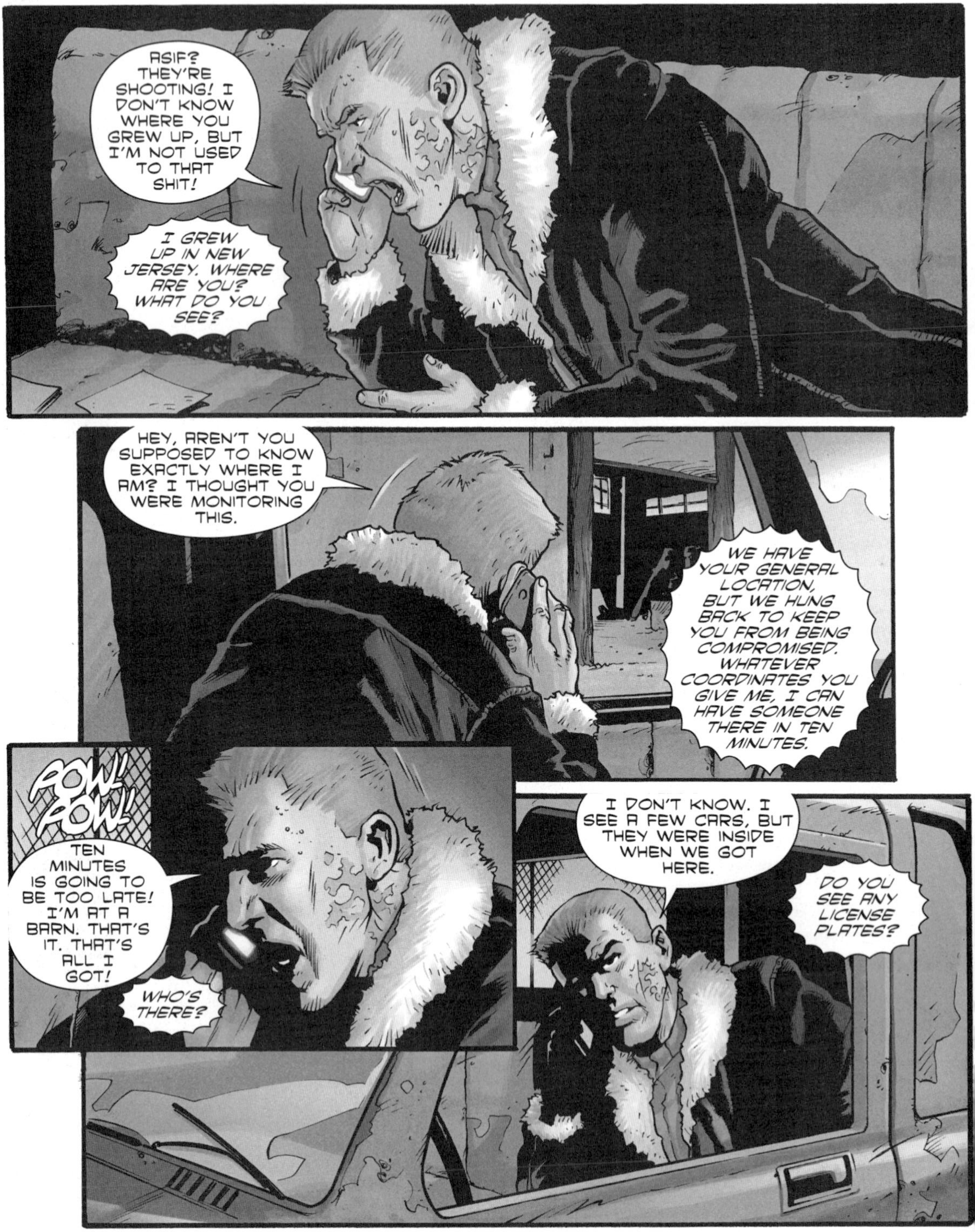
ASIF? THEY'RE SHOOTING! I DON'T KNOW WHERE YOU GREW UP, BUT I'M NOT USED TO THAT SHIT!
I GREW UP IN NEW JERSEY. WHERE ARE YOU? WHAT DO YOU SEE?
HEY, AREN'T YOU SUPPOSED TO KNOW EXACTLY WHERE I AM? I THOUGHT YOU WERE MONITORING THIS.
WE HAVE YOUR GENERAL LOCATION, BUT WE HUNG BACK TO KEEP YOU FROM BEING COMPROMISED. WHATEVER COORDINATES YOU GIVE ME, I CAN HAVE SOMEONE THERE IN TEN MINUTES.
POW! POW!
TEN MINUTES IS GOING TO BE TOO LATE! I'M AT A BARN. THAT'S IT. THAT'S ALL I GOT!
WHO'S THERE?
I DON'T KNOW. I SEE A FEW CARS, BUT THEY WERE INSIDE WHEN WE GOT HERE.
DO YOU SEE ANY LICENSE PLATES?

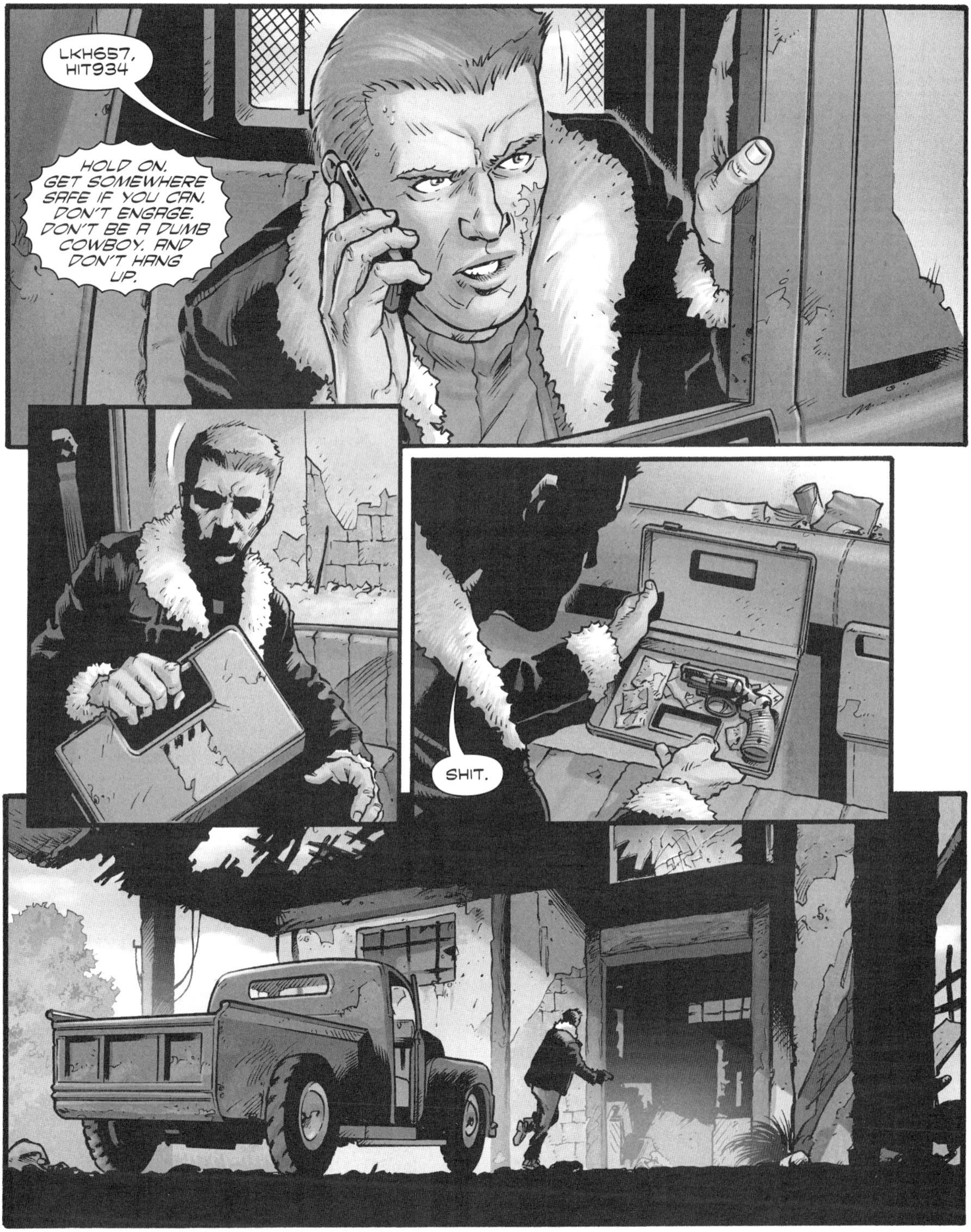
LKH657, HIT934
HOLD ON. GET SOMEWHERE SAFE IF YOU CAN. DON'T ENGAGE. DON'T BE A DUMB COWBOY. AND DON'T HANG UP.
SHIT.

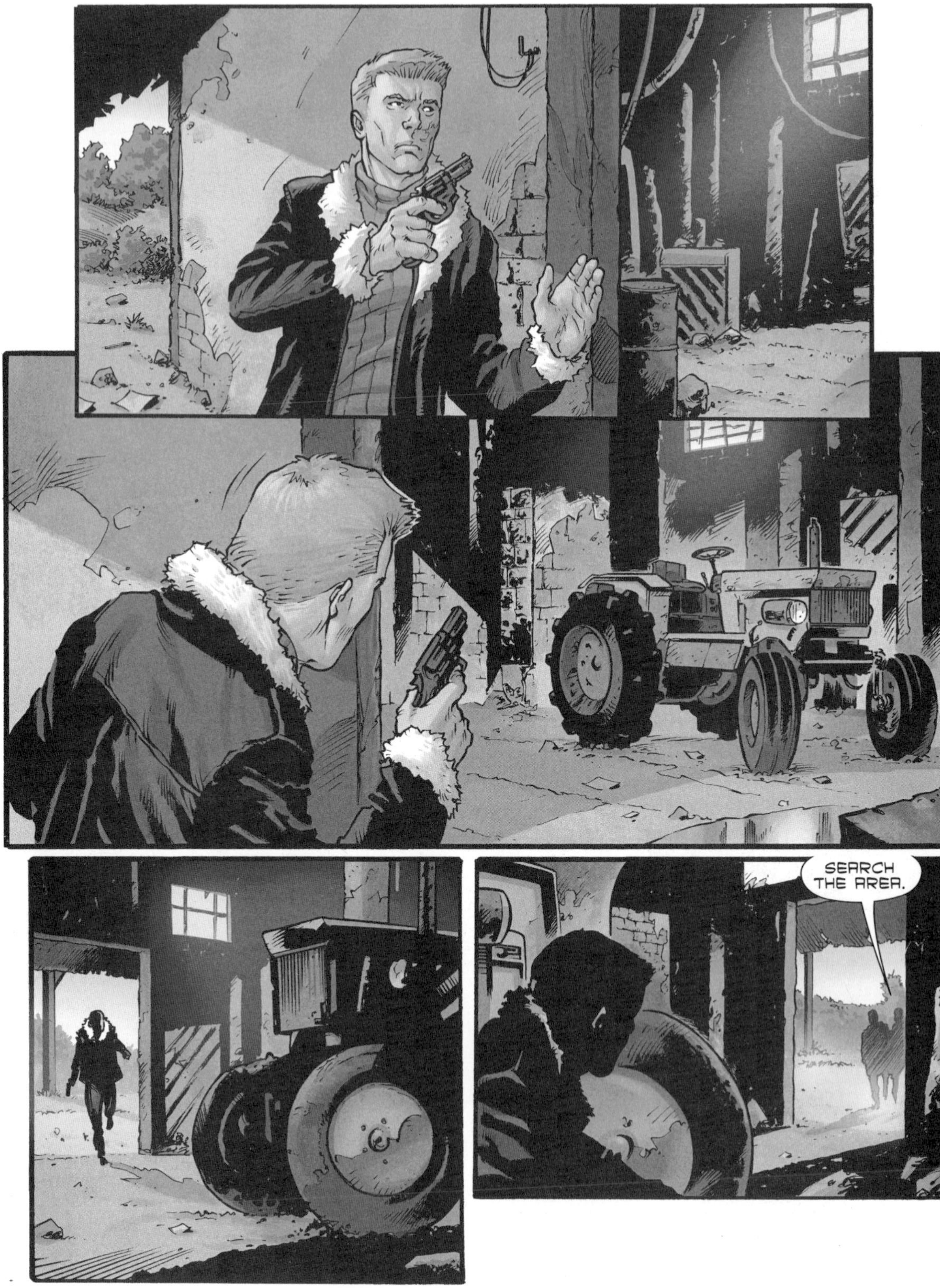
SEARCH THE AREA.

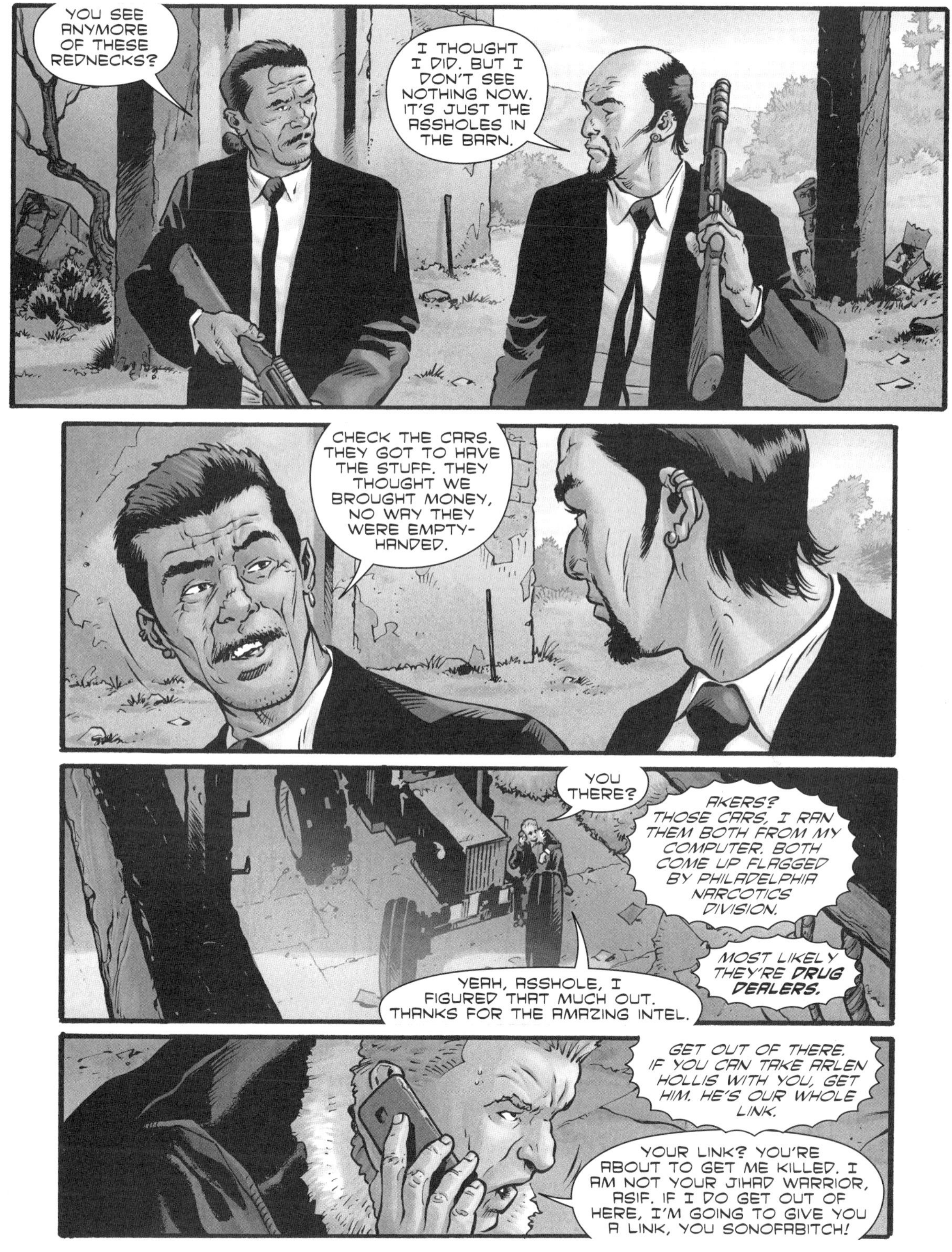
YOU SEE ANYMORE OF THESE REDNECKS?
I THOUGHT I DID. BUT I DON'T SEE NOTHING NOW. IT'S JUST THE ASSHOLES IN THE BARN.
CHECK THE CARS. THEY GOT TO HAVE THE STUFF. THEY THOUGHT WE BROUGHT MONEY, NO WAY THEY WERE EMPTY-HANDED.
YOU THERE?
AKERS? THOSE CARS, I RAN THEM BOTH FROM MY COMPUTER. BOTH COME UP FLAGGED BY PHILADELPHIA NARCOTICS DIVISION.
MOST LIKELY THEY'RE DRUG DEALERS.
YEAH, ASSHOLE, I FIGURED THAT MUCH OUT. THANKS FOR THE AMAZING INTEL.
GET OUT OF THERE. IF YOU CAN TAKE ARLEN HOLLIS WITH YOU, GET HIM. HE'S OUR WHOLE LINK.
YOUR LINK? YOU'RE ABOUT TO GET ME KILLED. I AM NOT YOUR JIHAD WARRIOR, ASIF. IF I DO GET OUT OF HERE, I'M GOING TO GIVE YOU A LINK, YOU SONOFABITCH!

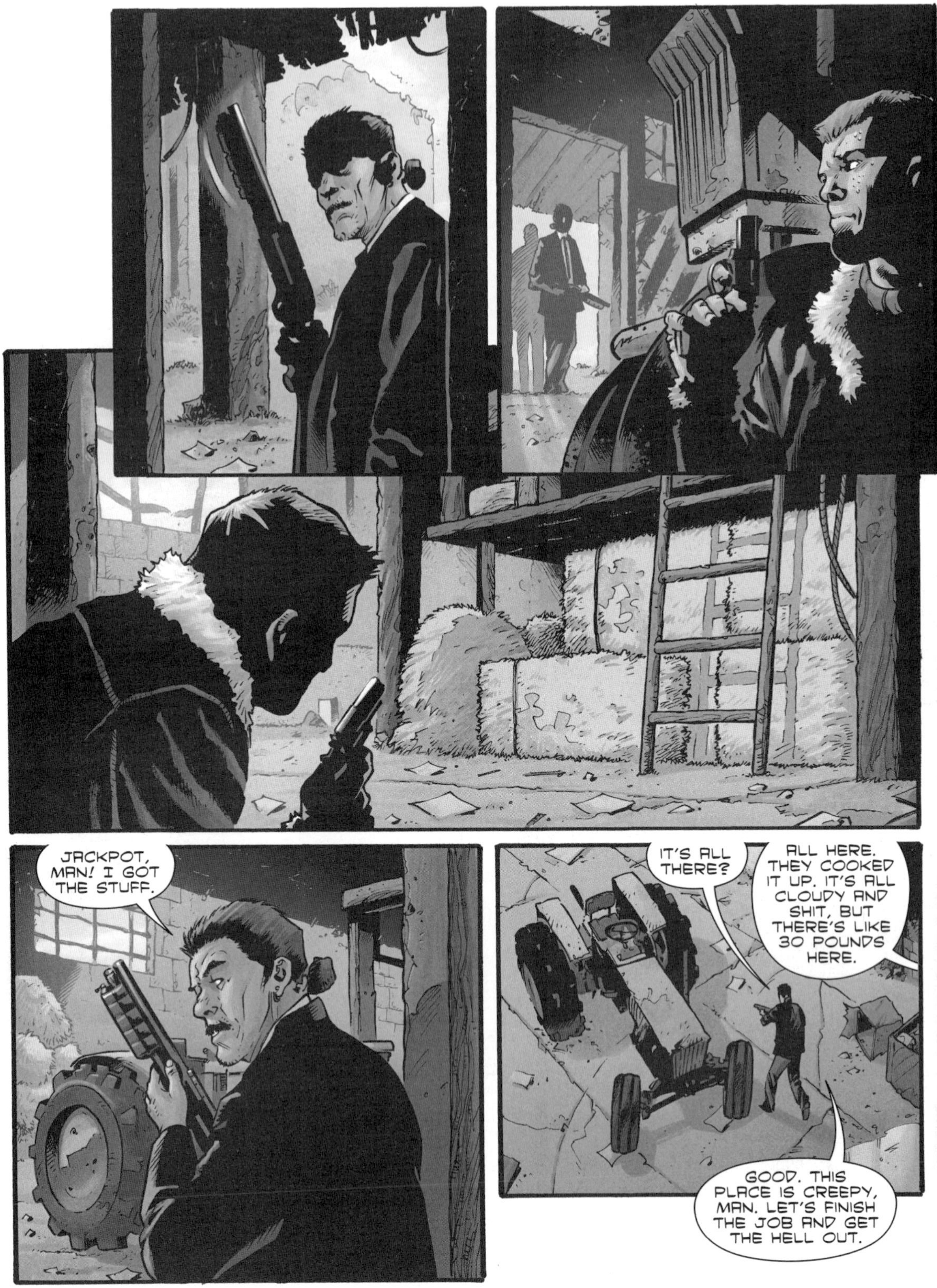
JACKPOT, MAN! I GOT THE STUFF.
IT'S ALL THERE?
ALL HERE. THEY COOKED IT UP. IT'S ALL CLOUDY AND SHIT, BUT THERE'S LIKE 30 POUNDS HERE.
GOOD. THIS PLACE IS CREEPY, MAN. LET'S FINISH THE JOB AND GET THE HELL OUT.

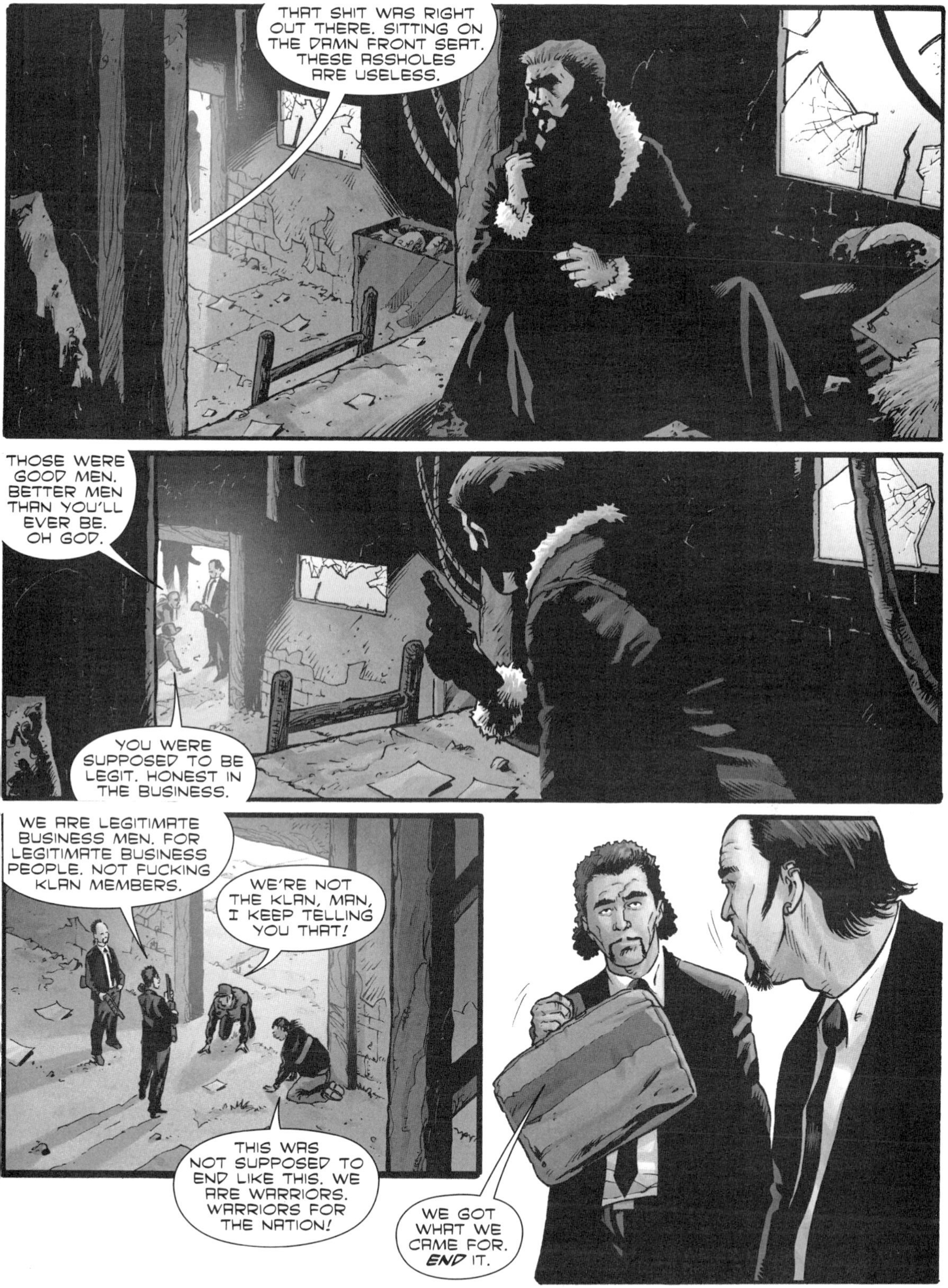

THAT SHIT WAS RIGHT OUT THERE. SITTING ON THE DAMN FRONT SEAT. THESE ASSHOLES ARE USELESS.
THOSE WERE GOOD MEN. BETTER MEN THAN YOU'LL EVER BE. OH GOD.
YOU WERE SUPPOSED TO BE LEGIT. HONEST IN THE BUSINESS.
WE ARE LEGITIMATE BUSINESS MEN. FOR LEGITIMATE BUSINESS PEOPLE. NOT FUCKING KLAN MEMBERS.
WE'RE NOT THE KLAN, MAN, I KEEP TELLING YOU THAT!
THIS WAS NOT SUPPOSED TO END LIKE THIS. WE ARE WARRIORS. WARRIORS FOR THE NATION!
WE GOT WHAT WE CAME FOR. END IT.

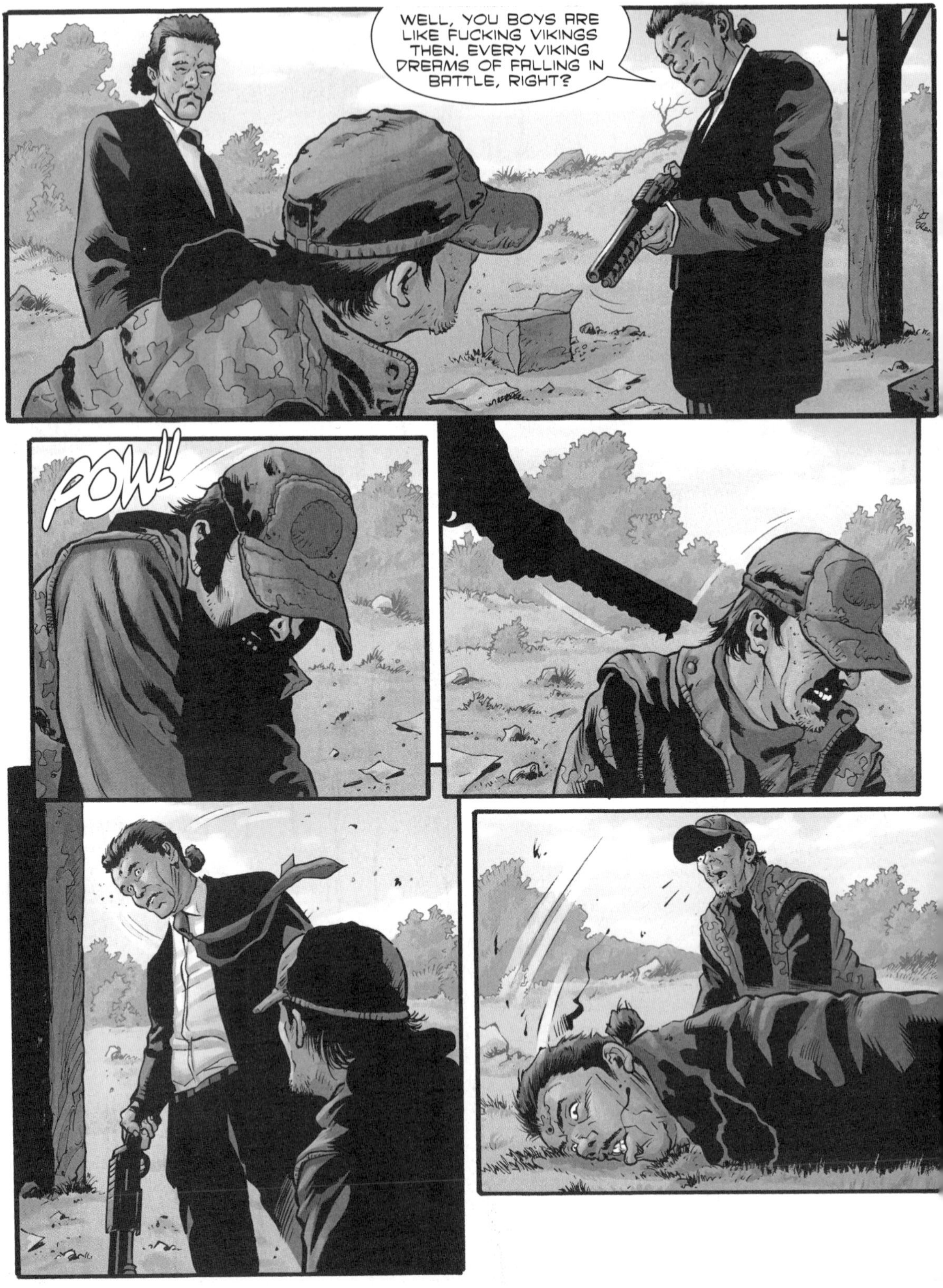
WELL, YOU BOYS ARE LIKE FUCKING VIKINGS THEN. EVERY VIKING DREAMS OF FALLING IN BATTLE, RIGHT?
POW!!

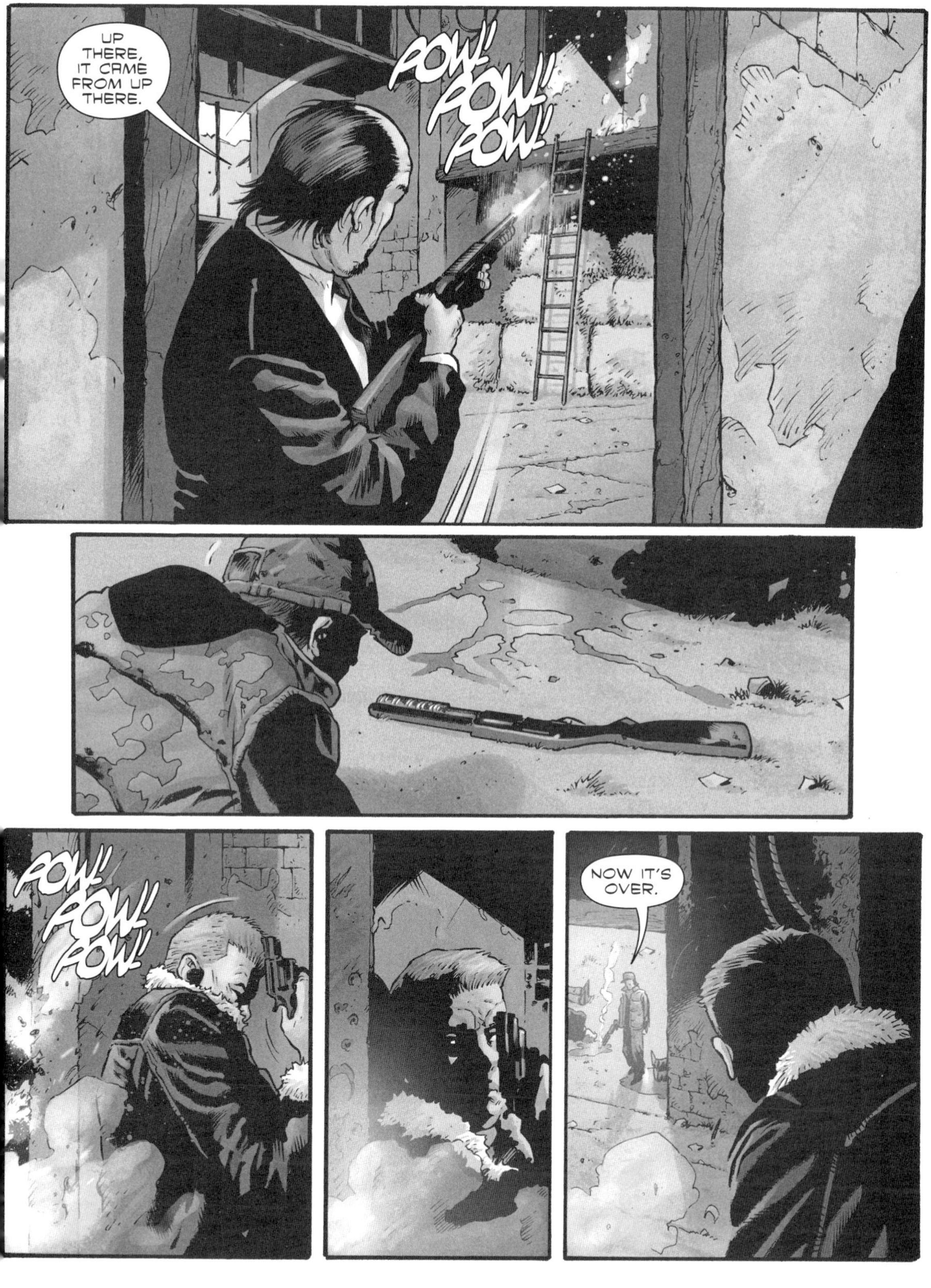
UP THERE, IT CAME FROM UP THERE.
POW! POW! POW!
POW! POW! POW!
NOW IT'S OVER.

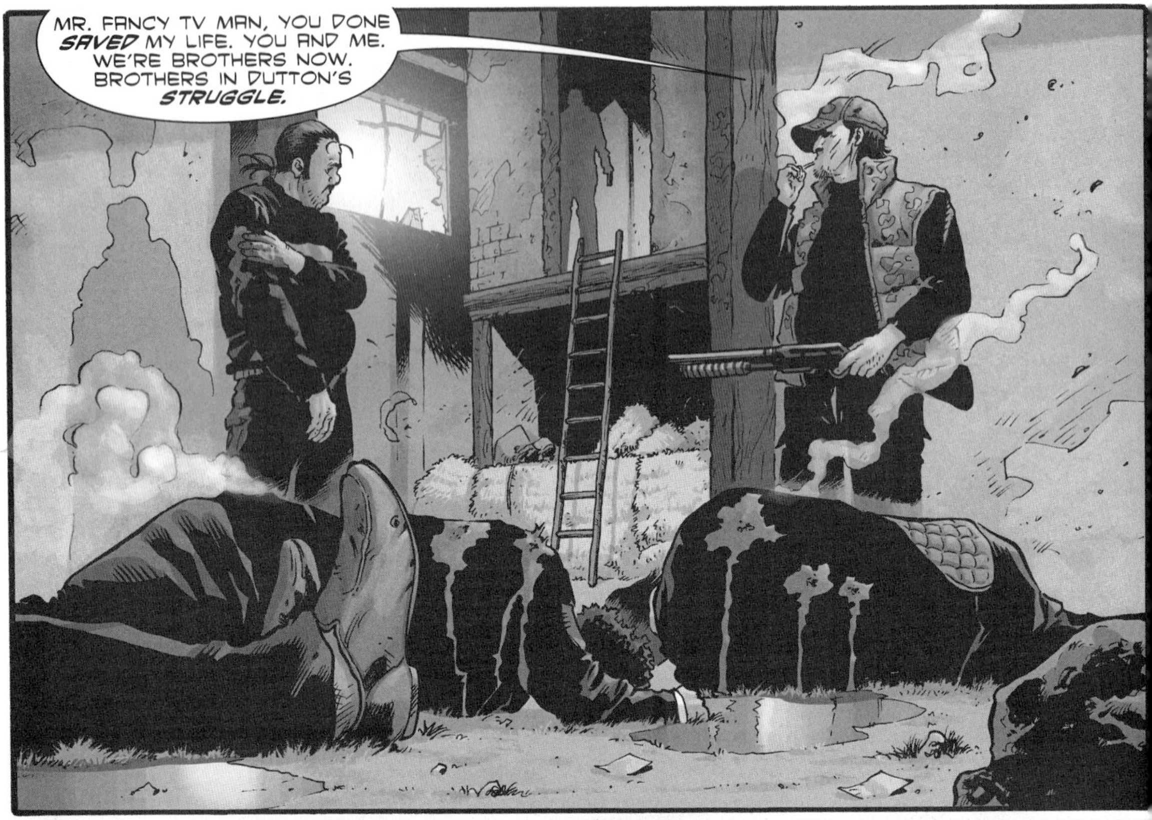
MR. FANCY TV MAN, YOU DONE SAVED MY LIFE. YOU AND ME. WE'RE BROTHERS NOW. BROTHERS IN DUTTON'S STRUGGLE.

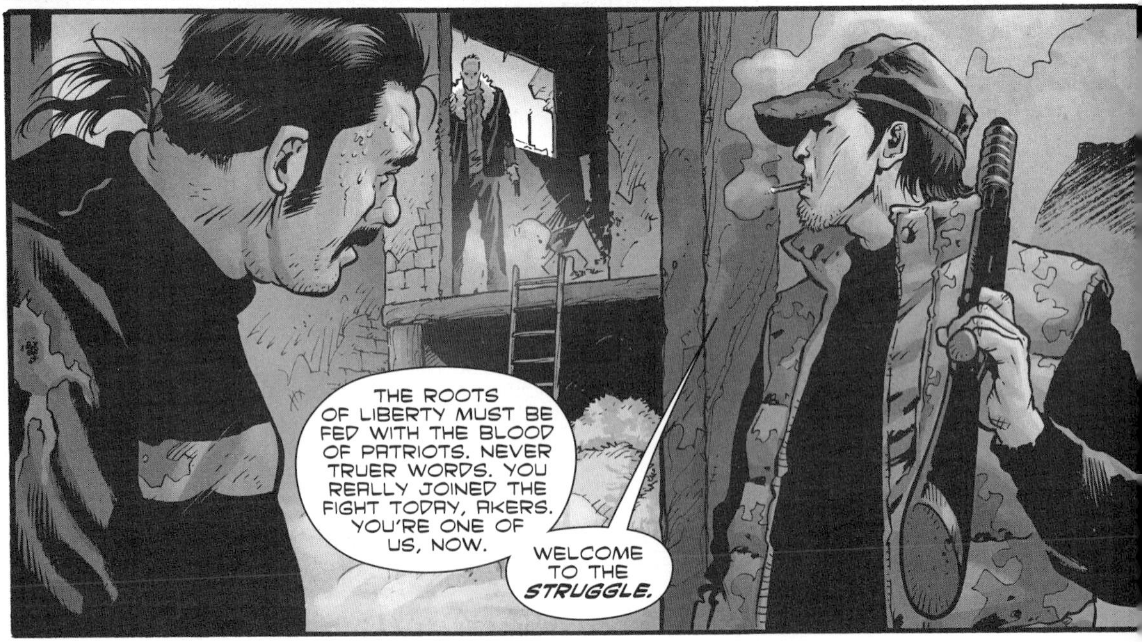
THE ROOTS OF LIBERTY MUST BE FED WITH THE BLOOD OF PATRIOTS. NEVER TRUER WORDS. YOU REALLY JOINED THE FIGHT TODAY, AKERS. YOU'RE ONE OF US, NOW.
WELCOME TO THE STRUGGLE.

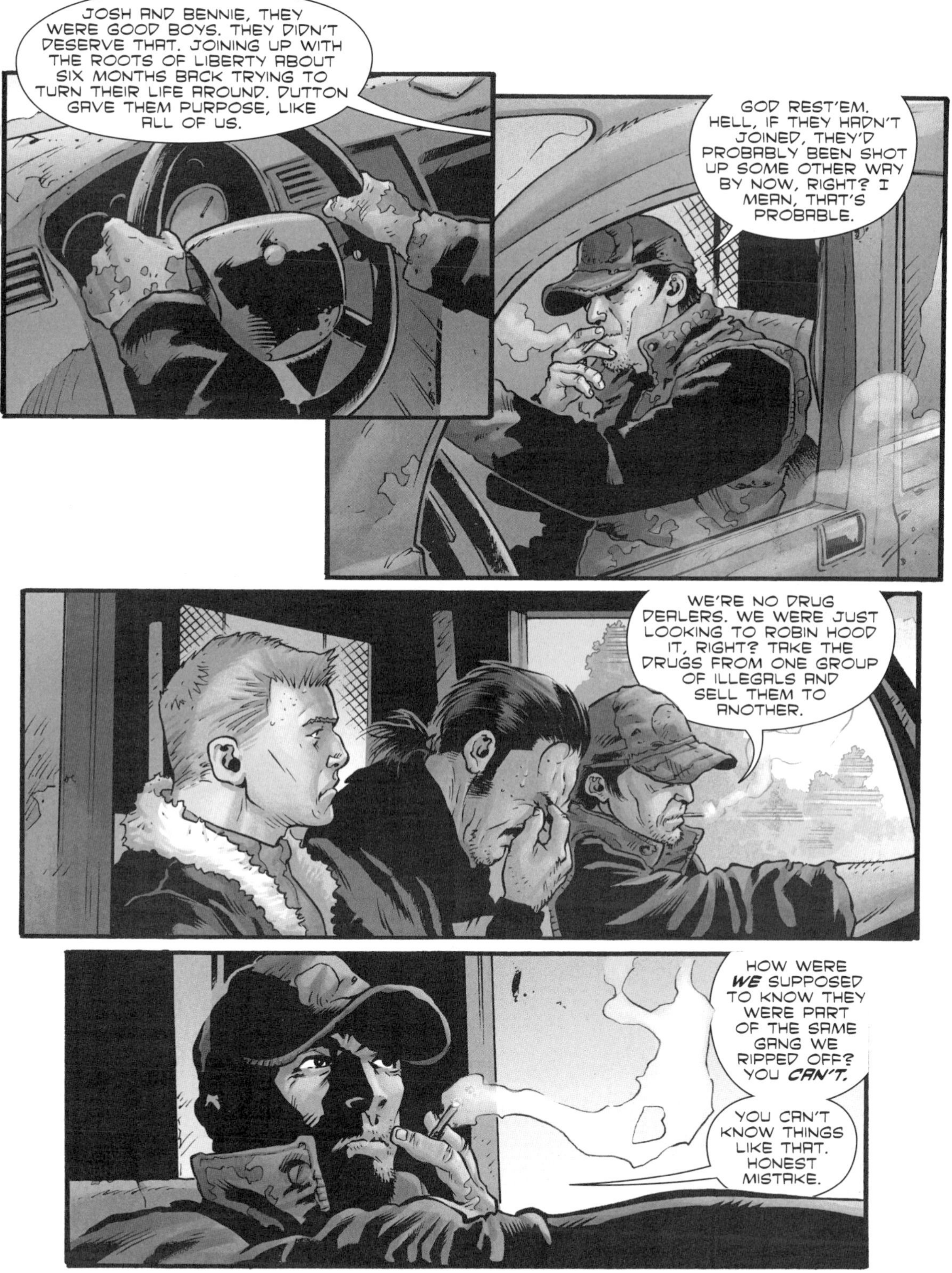
JOSH AND BENNIE, THEY WERE GOOD BOYS. THEY DIDN'T DESERVE THAT. JOINING UP WITH THE ROOTS OF LIBERTY ABOUT SIX MONTHS BACK TRYING TO TURN THEIR LIFE AROUND. DUTTON GAVE THEM PURPOSE, LIKE ALL OF US.
GOD REST'EM. HELL, IF THEY HADN'T JOINED, THEY'D PROBABLY BEEN SHOT UP SOME OTHER WAY BY NOW, RIGHT? I MEAN, THAT'S PROBABLE.
WE'RE NO DRUG DEALERS. WE WERE JUST LOOKING TO ROBIN HOOD IT, RIGHT? TAKE THE DRUGS FROM ONE GROUP OF ILLEGALS AND SELL THEM TO ANOTHER.
HOW WERE ***WE*** SUPPOSED TO KNOW THEY WERE PART OF THE SAME GANG WE RIPPED OFF? YOU ***CAN'T.***
YOU CAN'T KNOW THINGS LIKE THAT. HONEST MISTAKE.

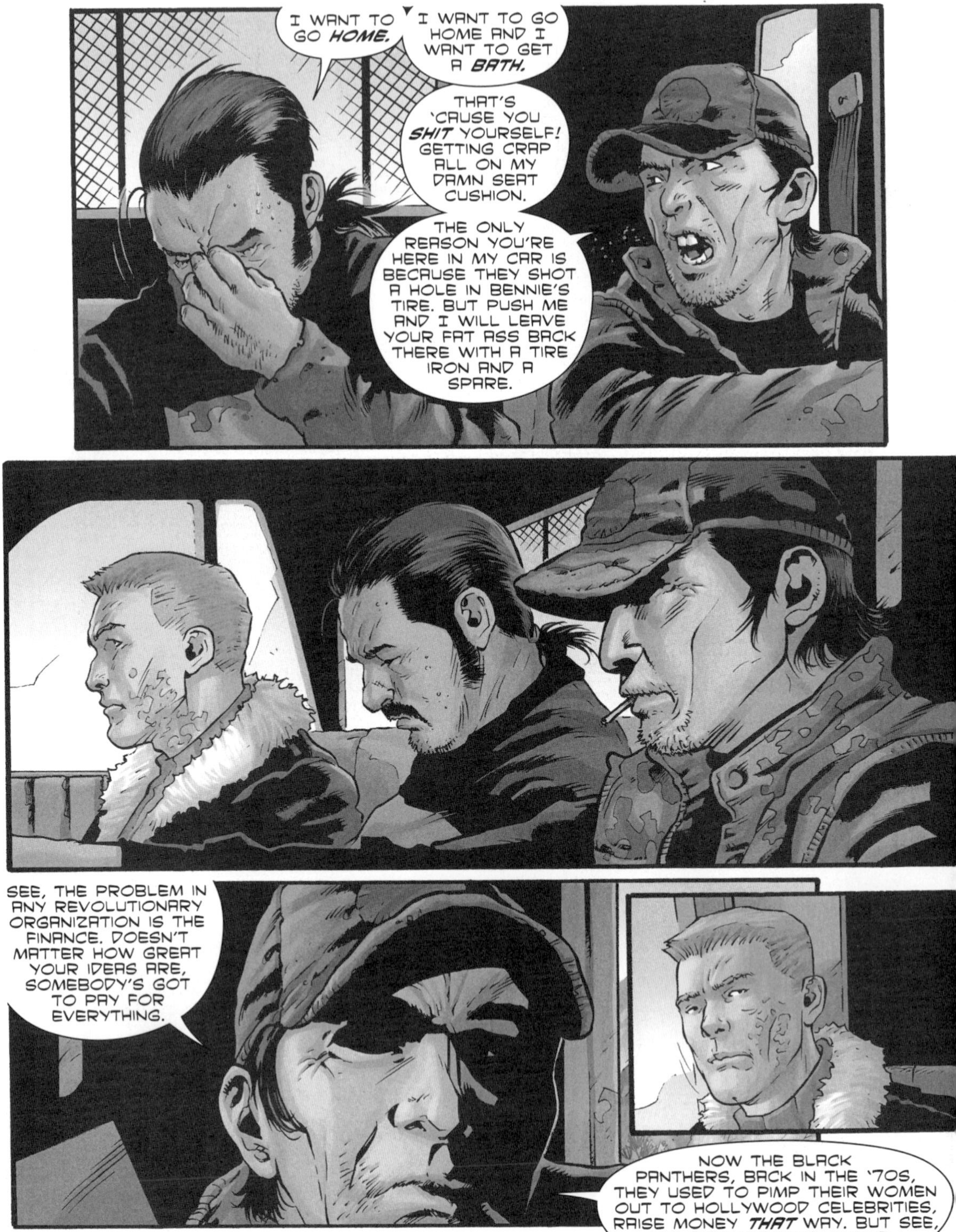
I WANT TO GO HOME.
I WANT TO GO HOME AND I WANT TO GET A BATH.
THAT'S 'CAUSE YOU SHIT YOURSELF! GETTING CRAP ALL ON MY DAMN SEAT CUSHION.
THE ONLY REASON YOU'RE HERE IN MY CAR IS BECAUSE THEY SHOT A HOLE IN BENNIE'S TIRE. BUT PUSH ME AND I WILL LEAVE YOUR FAT ASS BACK THERE WITH A TIRE IRON AND A SPARE.
SEE, THE PROBLEM IN ANY REVOLUTIONARY ORGANIZATION IS THE FINANCE. DOESN'T MATTER HOW GREAT YOUR IDEAS ARE, SOMEBODY'S GOT TO PAY FOR EVERYTHING.
NOW THE BLACK PANTHERS, BACK IN THE '70S, THEY USED TO PIMP THEIR WOMEN OUT TO HOLLYWOOD CELEBRITIES, RAISE MONEY THAT WAY. BUT SEE, WE RESPECT OUR WOMEN TOO MUCH.

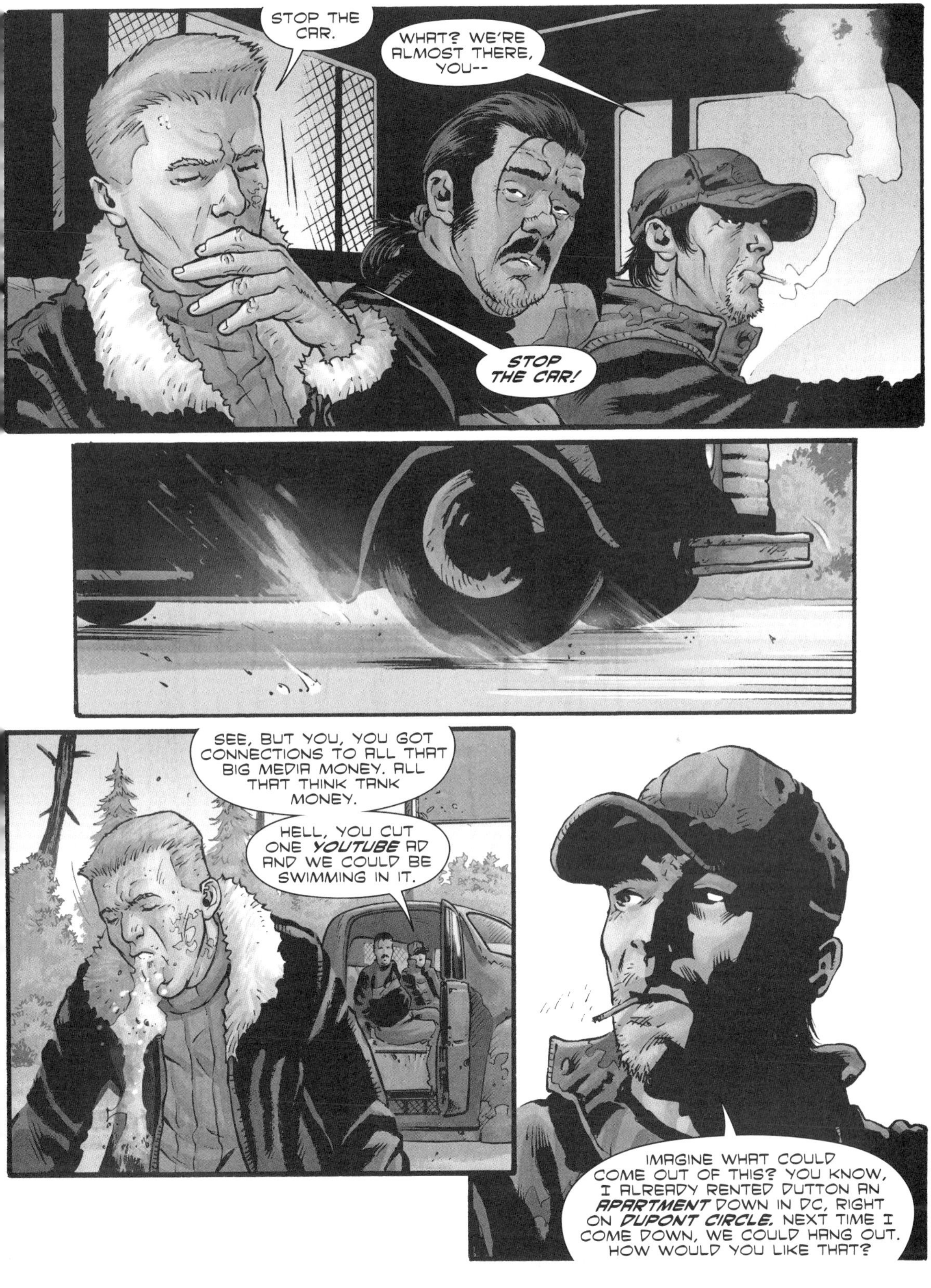

STOP THE CAR.
WHAT? WE'RE ALMOST THERE, YOU--
STOP THE CAR!
SEE, BUT YOU, YOU GOT CONNECTIONS TO ALL THAT BIG MEDIA MONEY. ALL THAT THINK TANK MONEY.
HELL, YOU CUT ONE YOUTUBE AD AND WE COULD BE SWIMMING IN IT.
IMAGINE WHAT COULD COME OUT OF THIS? YOU KNOW, I ALREADY RENTED DUTTON AN APARTMENT DOWN IN DC, RIGHT ON DUPONT CIRCLE. NEXT TIME I COME DOWN, WE COULD HANG OUT. HOW WOULD YOU LIKE THAT?

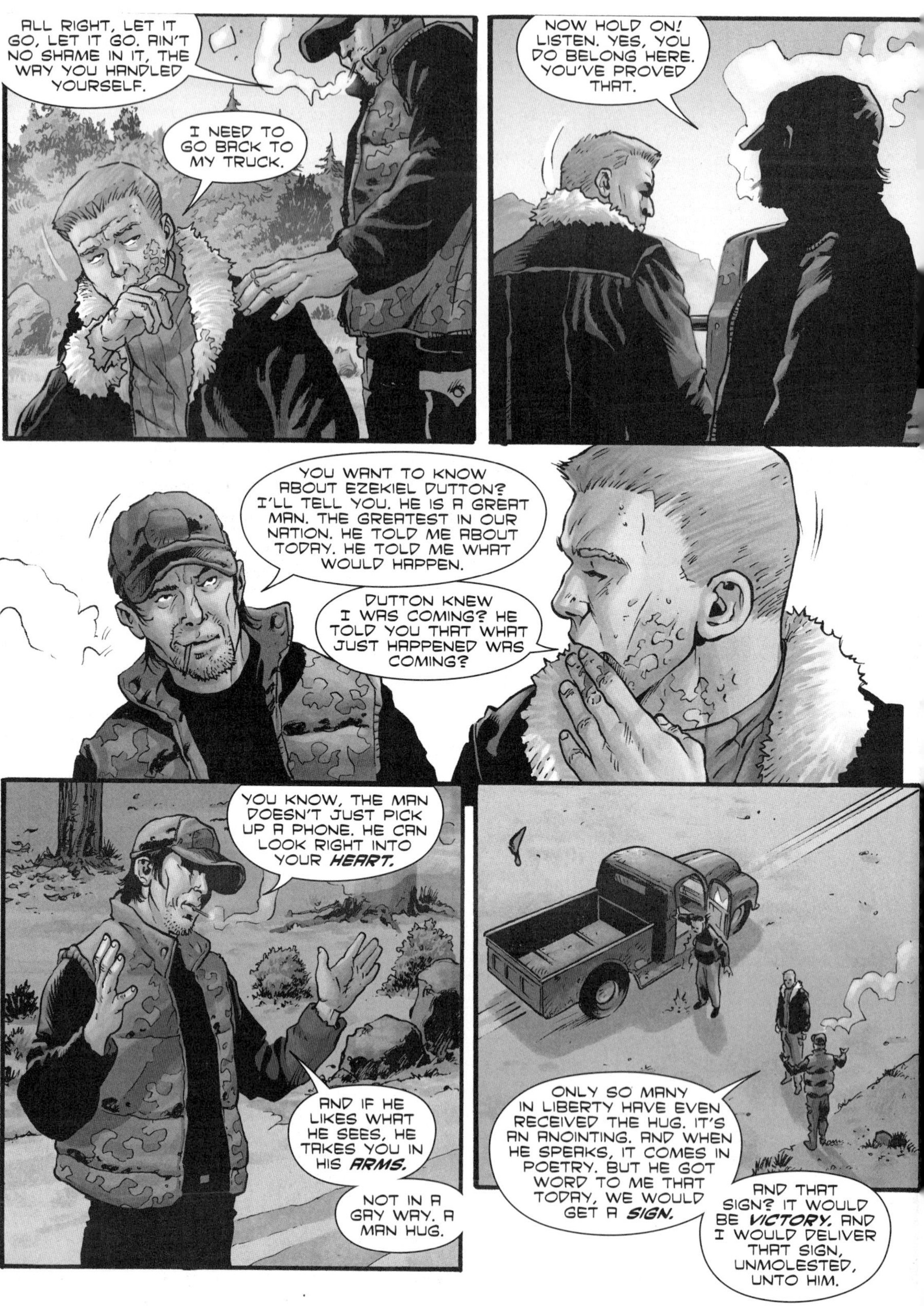
ALL RIGHT, LET IT GO, LET IT GO. AIN'T NO SHAME IN IT, THE WAY YOU HANDLED YOURSELF.
I NEED TO GO BACK TO MY TRUCK.
NOW HOLD ON! LISTEN. YES, YOU DO BELONG HERE. YOU'VE PROVED THAT.
YOU WANT TO KNOW ABOUT EZEKIEL DUTTON? I'LL TELL YOU. HE IS A GREAT MAN. THE GREATEST IN OUR NATION. HE TOLD ME ABOUT TODAY. HE TOLD ME WHAT WOULD HAPPEN.
DUTTON KNEW I WAS COMING? HE TOLD YOU THAT WHAT JUST HAPPENED WAS COMING?
YOU KNOW, THE MAN DOESN'T JUST PICK UP A PHONE. HE CAN LOOK RIGHT INTO YOUR *HEART.*
AND IF HE LIKES WHAT HE SEES, HE TAKES YOU IN HIS *ARMS.*
NOT IN A GAY WAY. A MAN HUG.
ONLY SO MANY IN LIBERTY HAVE EVEN RECEIVED THE HUG. IT'S AN ANOINTING. AND WHEN HE SPEAKS, IT COMES IN POETRY. BUT HE GOT WORD TO ME THAT TODAY, WE WOULD GET A *SIGN.*
AND THAT SIGN? IT WOULD BE *VICTORY.* AND I WOULD DELIVER THAT SIGN, UNMOLESTED, UNTO HIM.

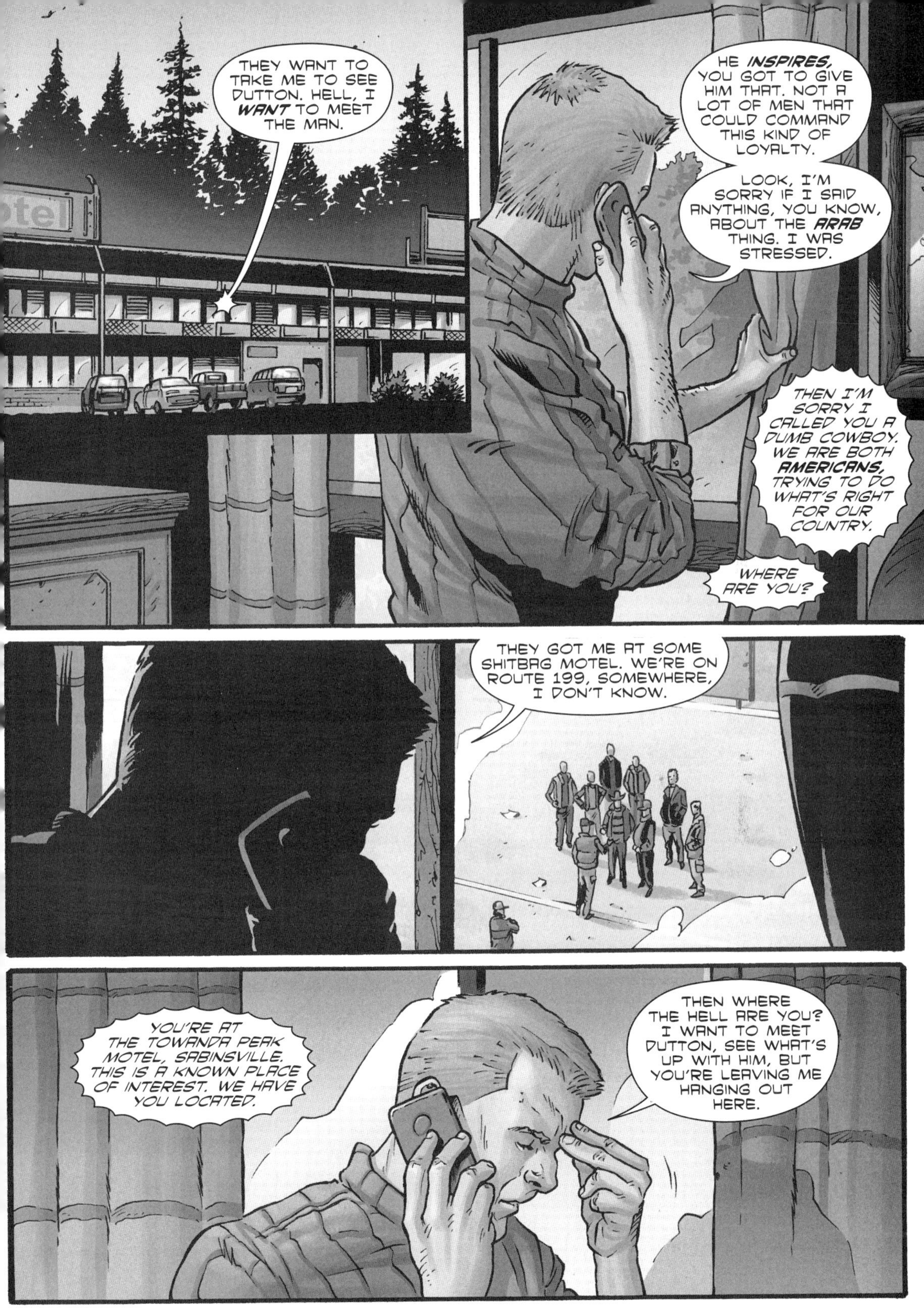
THEY WANT TO TAKE ME TO SEE DUTTON. HELL, I WANT TO MEET THE MAN.
HE INSPIRES, YOU GOT TO GIVE HIM THAT. NOT A LOT OF MEN THAT COULD COMMAND THIS KIND OF LOYALTY.
LOOK, I'M SORRY IF I SAID ANYTHING, YOU KNOW, ABOUT THE ARAB THING. I WAS STRESSED.
THEN I'M SORRY I CALLED YOU A DUMB COWBOY. WE ARE BOTH AMERICANS, TRYING TO DO WHAT'S RIGHT FOR OUR COUNTRY.
WHERE ARE YOU?
THEY GOT ME AT SOME SHITBAG MOTEL. WE'RE ON ROUTE 199, SOMEWHERE, I DON'T KNOW.
YOU'RE AT THE TOWANDA PEAK MOTEL, SABINSVILLE. THIS IS A KNOWN PLACE OF INTEREST. WE HAVE YOU LOCATED.
THEN WHERE THE HELL ARE YOU? I WANT TO MEET DUTTON, SEE WHAT'S UP WITH HIM, BUT YOU'RE LEAVING ME HANGING OUT HERE.

BUT LISTEN TO ME, AKERS. I NEED YOU. I...COULD NOT HAVE GOTTEN THIS FAR. YOU...YOU'RE DOING SO WELL.

YEAH, BUT YOU'RE SCREWING UP. YOU WANTED ME TO MEET WITH DUTTON, BUT YOU DROPPED ME IN WITH HIS CRAZY BROTHER-IN-LAW. NOT THE SAME THING.

FIVE MEN ARE DEAD, THAT'S HOW WELL I'M DOING. I SHOT SOMEONE. I'VE NEVER SHOT ANYONE IN MY LIFE.

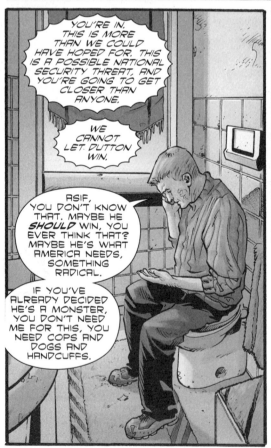

YOU'RE IN. THIS IS MORE THAN WE COULD HAVE HOPED FOR. THIS IS A POSSIBLE NATIONAL SECURITY THREAT, AND YOU'RE GOING TO GET CLOSER THAN ANYONE.

WE CANNOT LET DUTTON WIN.

ASIF, YOU DON'T KNOW THAT. MAYBE HE *SHOULD* WIN, YOU EVER THINK THAT? MAYBE HE'S WHAT AMERICA NEEDS, SOMETHING RADICAL.

IF YOU'VE ALREADY DECIDED HE'S A MONSTER, YOU DON'T NEED ME FOR THIS, YOU NEED COPS AND DOGS AND HANDCUFFS.

THAT OTHER CAR FROM THE ROOTS OF LIBERTY? THEY LEFT IT AT THE SCENE AT THE BARN. IT WAS SEARCHED 20 MINUTES AGO.

THESE GUYS AREN'T A THREAT TO THE NATION, THEY'RE A THREAT TO THEMSELVES AND EVERYONE AROUND THEM. THEY'RE HANGERS-ON. WANNA-BES. THEY DON'T TELL ME ANYTHING ABOUT DUTTON HIMSELF.

THEY FOUND THE *BODIES*. DO YOU WANT TO HEAR WHAT *ELSE* THEY FOUND?

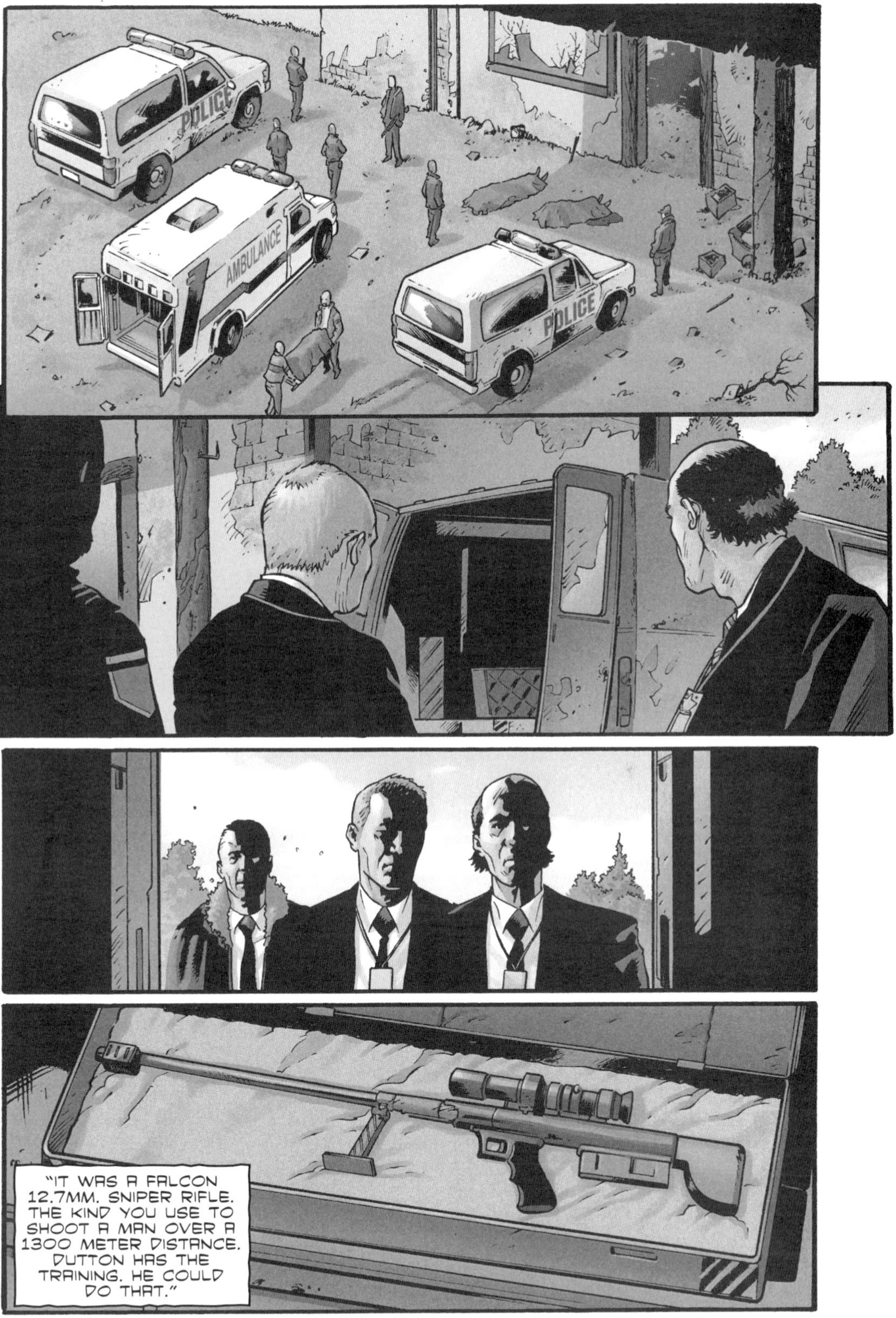
POLICE
AMBULANCE
POLICE
"IT WAS A FALCON 12.7MM. SNIPER RIFLE. THE KIND YOU USE TO SHOOT A MAN OVER A 1300 METER DISTANCE. DUTTON HAS THE TRAINING. HE COULD DO THAT."

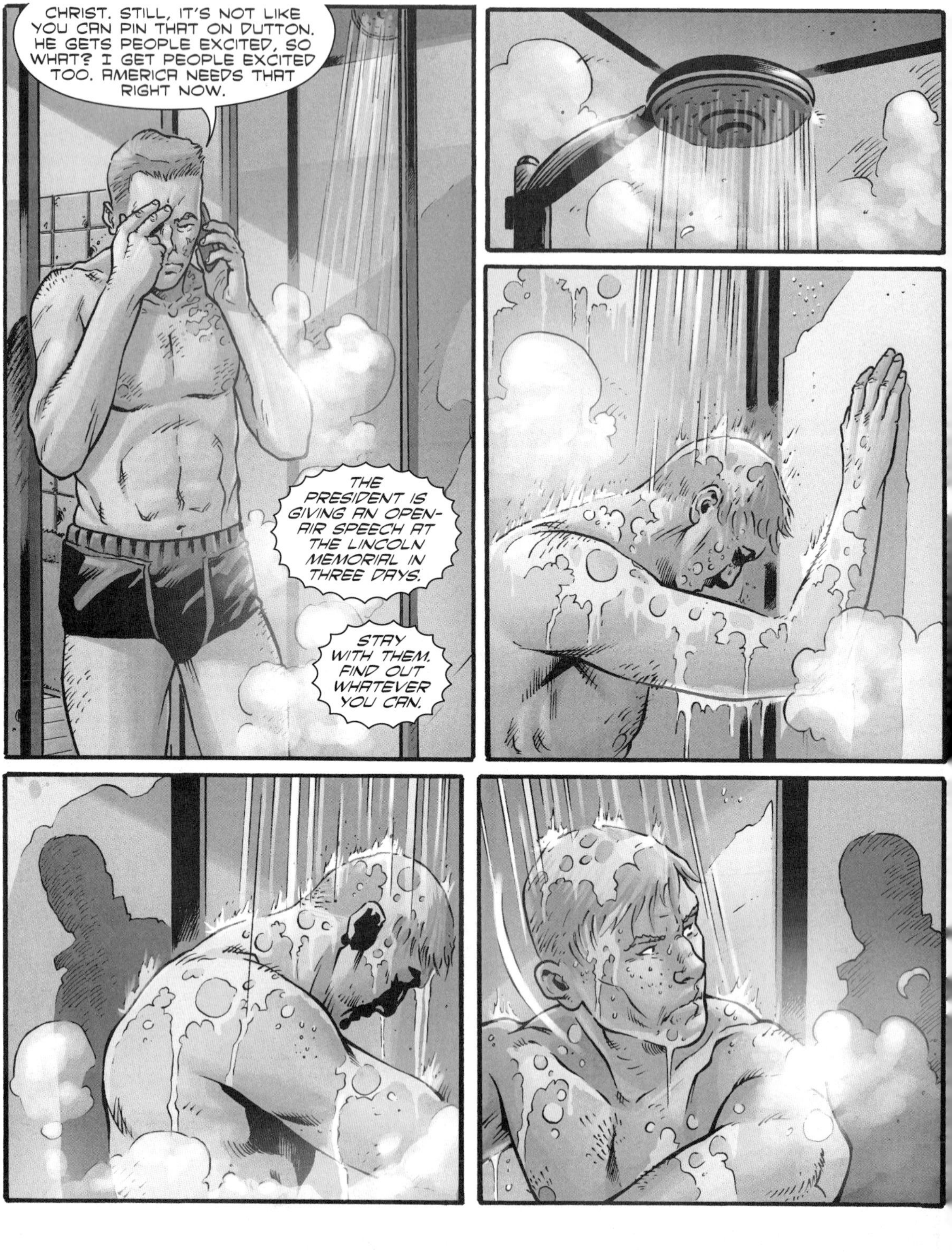
CHRIST. STILL, IT'S NOT LIKE YOU CAN PIN THAT ON DUTTON. HE GETS PEOPLE EXCITED, SO WHAT? I GET PEOPLE EXCITED TOO. AMERICA NEEDS THAT RIGHT NOW.
THE PRESIDENT IS GIVING AN OPEN-AIR SPEECH AT THE LINCOLN MEMORIAL IN THREE DAYS.
STAY WITH THEM. FIND OUT WHATEVER YOU CAN.

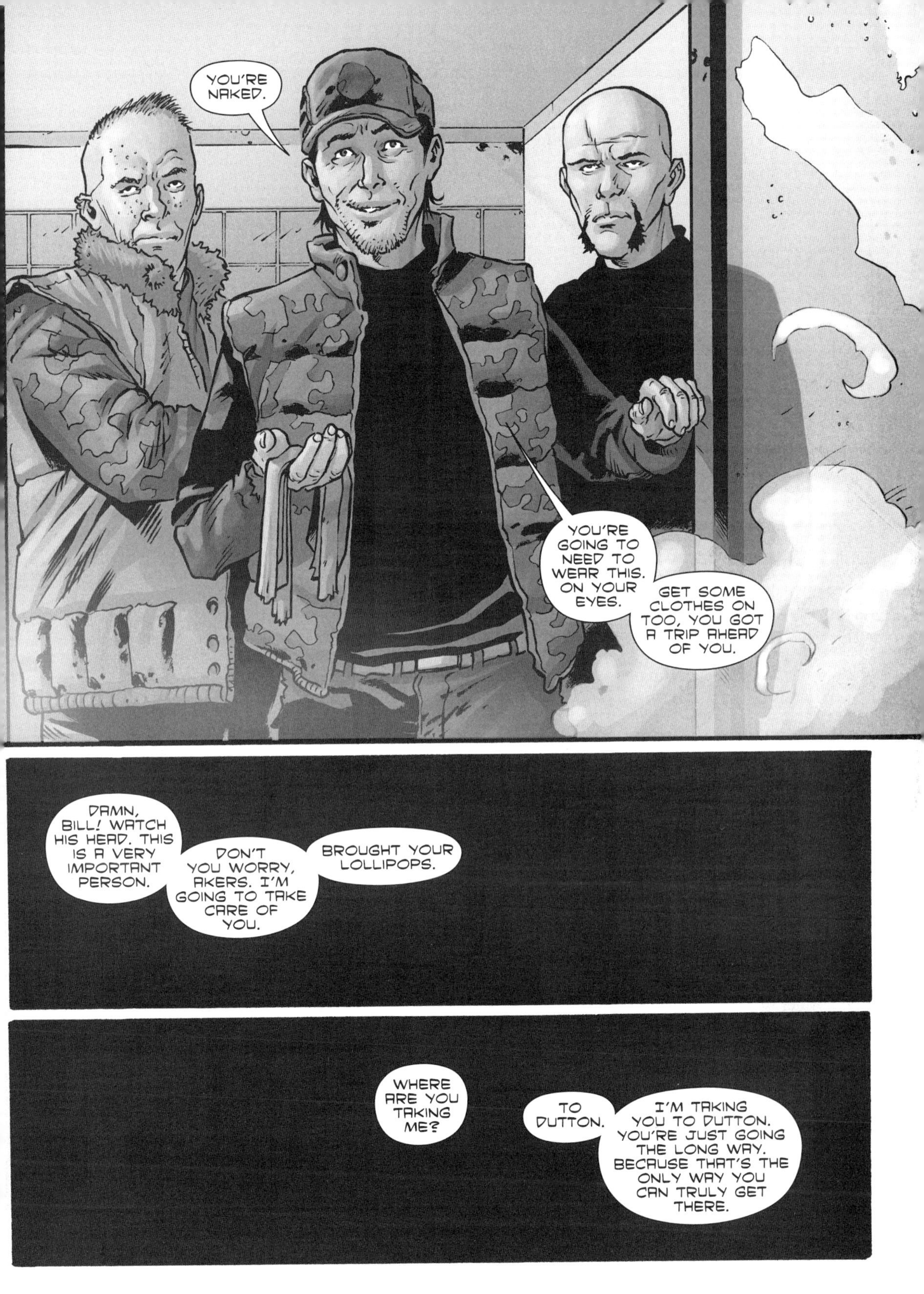
YOU'RE NAKED.
YOU'RE GOING TO NEED TO WEAR THIS. ON YOUR EYES.
GET SOME CLOTHES ON TOO, YOU GOT A TRIP AHEAD OF YOU.
DAMN, BILL! WATCH HIS HEAD. THIS IS A VERY IMPORTANT PERSON.
DON'T YOU WORRY, AKERS. I'M GOING TO TAKE CARE OF YOU.
BROUGHT YOUR LOLLIPOPS.
WHERE ARE YOU TAKING ME?
TO DUTTON.
I'M TAKING YOU TO DUTTON. YOU'RE JUST GOING THE LONG WAY. BECAUSE THAT'S THE ONLY WAY YOU CAN TRULY GET THERE.

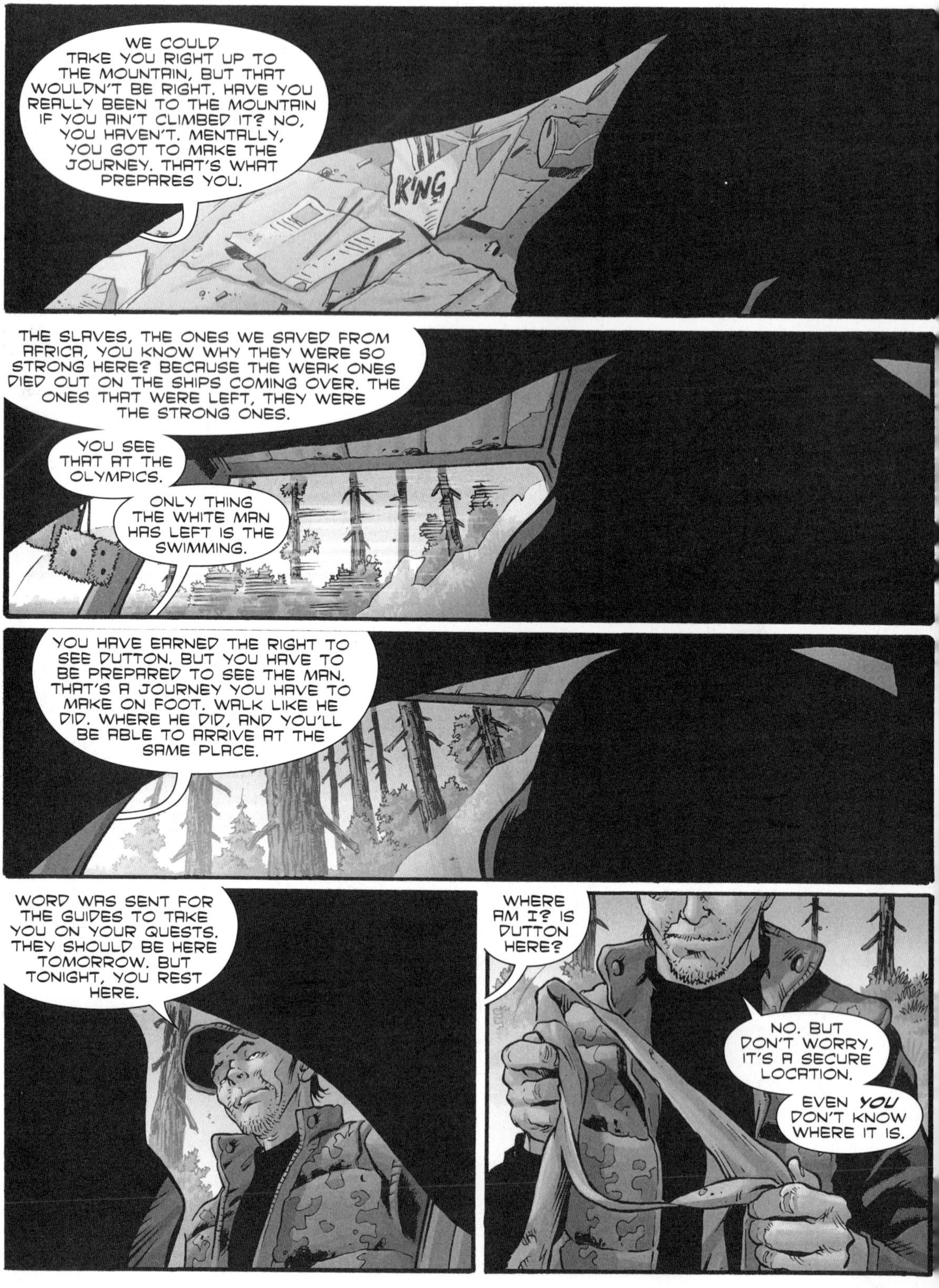
WE COULD TAKE YOU RIGHT UP TO THE MOUNTAIN, BUT THAT WOULDN'T BE RIGHT. HAVE YOU REALLY BEEN TO THE MOUNTAIN IF YOU AIN'T CLIMBED IT? NO, YOU HAVEN'T. MENTALLY, YOU GOT TO MAKE THE JOURNEY. THAT'S WHAT PREPARES YOU.
K'NG
THE SLAVES, THE ONES WE SAVED FROM AFRICA, YOU KNOW WHY THEY WERE SO STRONG HERE? BECAUSE THE WEAK ONES DIED OUT ON THE SHIPS COMING OVER. THE ONES THAT WERE LEFT, THEY WERE THE STRONG ONES.
YOU SEE THAT AT THE OLYMPICS.
ONLY THING THE WHITE MAN HAS LEFT IS THE SWIMMING.
YOU HAVE EARNED THE RIGHT TO SEE DUTTON. BUT YOU HAVE TO BE PREPARED TO SEE THE MAN. THAT'S A JOURNEY YOU HAVE TO MAKE ON FOOT. WALK LIKE HE DID. WHERE HE DID, AND YOU'LL BE ABLE TO ARRIVE AT THE SAME PLACE.
WORD WAS SENT FOR THE GUIDES TO TAKE YOU ON YOUR QUESTS. THEY SHOULD BE HERE TOMORROW. BUT TONIGHT, YOU REST HERE.
WHERE AM I? IS DUTTON HERE?
NO. BUT DON'T WORRY, IT'S A SECURE LOCATION.
EVEN YOU DON'T KNOW WHERE IT IS.

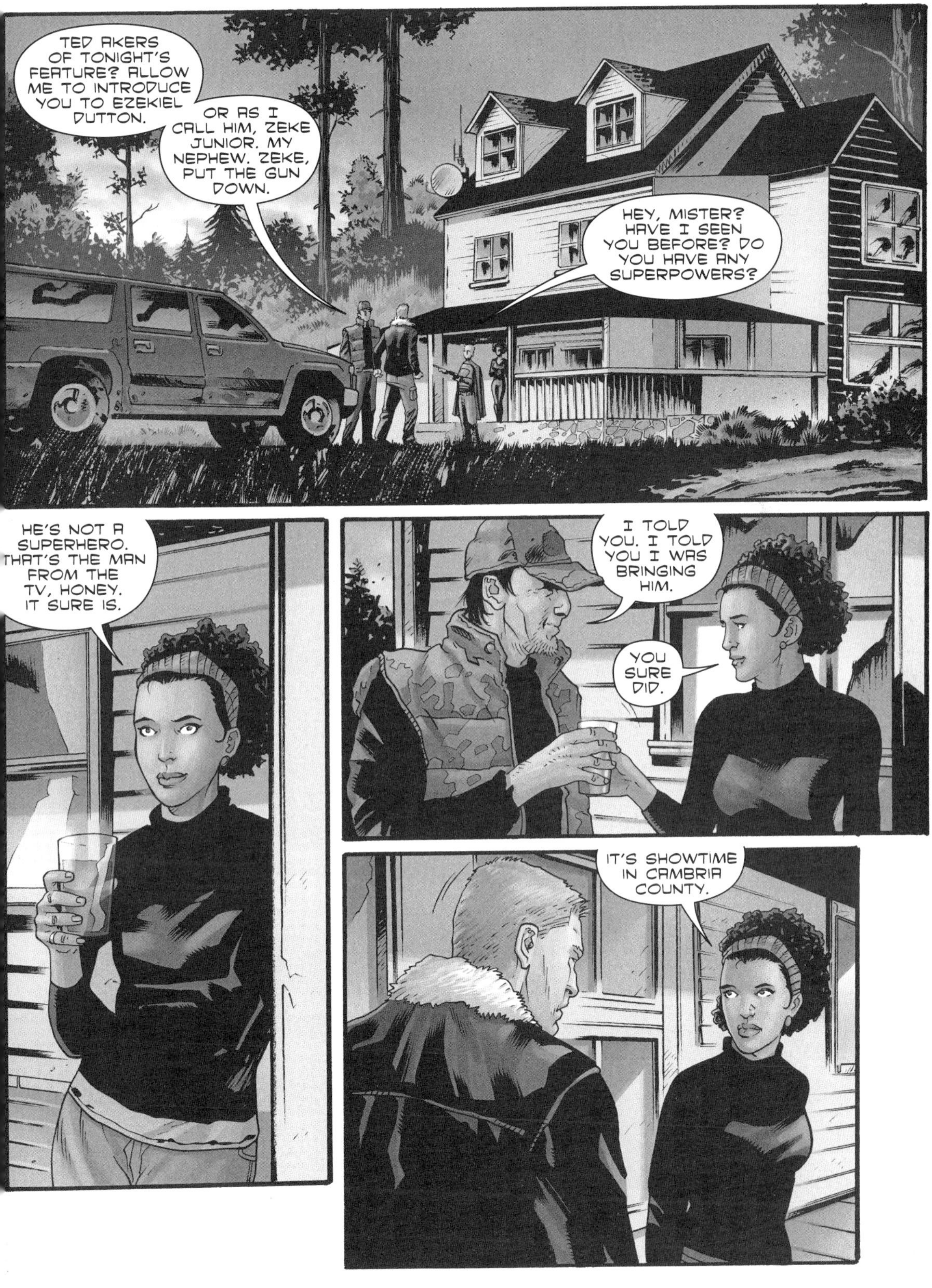
TED AKERS OF TONIGHT'S FEATURE? ALLOW ME TO INTRODUCE YOU TO EZEKIEL DUTTON.
OR AS I CALL HIM, ZEKE JUNIOR. MY NEPHEW. ZEKE, PUT THE GUN DOWN.
HEY, MISTER? HAVE I SEEN YOU BEFORE? DO YOU HAVE ANY SUPERPOWERS?
HE'S NOT A SUPERHERO. THAT'S THE MAN FROM THE TV, HONEY. IT SURE IS.
I TOLD YOU. I TOLD YOU I WAS BRINGING HIM.
YOU SURE DID.
IT'S SHOWTIME IN CAMBRIA COUNTY.

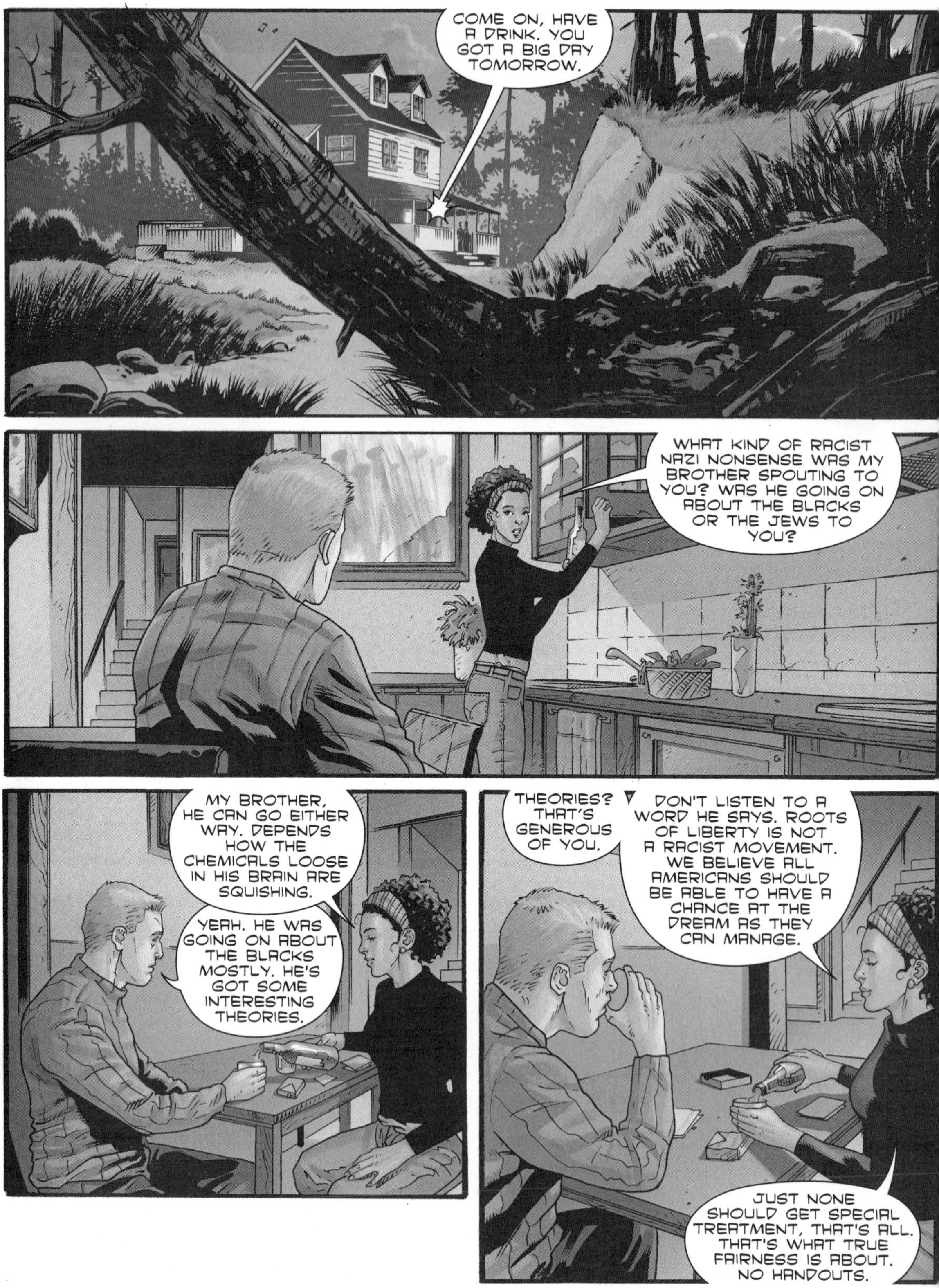
COME ON, HAVE A DRINK. YOU GOT A BIG DAY TOMORROW.
WHAT KIND OF RACIST NAZI NONSENSE WAS MY BROTHER SPOUTING TO YOU? WAS HE GOING ON ABOUT THE BLACKS OR THE JEWS TO YOU?
MY BROTHER, HE CAN GO EITHER WAY. DEPENDS HOW THE CHEMICALS LOOSE IN HIS BRAIN ARE SQUISHING.
YEAH. HE WAS GOING ON ABOUT THE BLACKS MOSTLY. HE'S GOT SOME INTERESTING THEORIES.
THEORIES? THAT'S GENEROUS OF YOU.
DON'T LISTEN TO A WORD HE SAYS. ROOTS OF LIBERTY IS NOT A RACIST MOVEMENT. WE BELIEVE ALL AMERICANS SHOULD BE ABLE TO HAVE A CHANCE AT THE DREAM AS THEY CAN MANAGE.
JUST NONE SHOULD GET SPECIAL TREATMENT, THAT'S ALL. THAT'S WHAT TRUE FAIRNESS IS ABOUT. NO HANDOUTS.

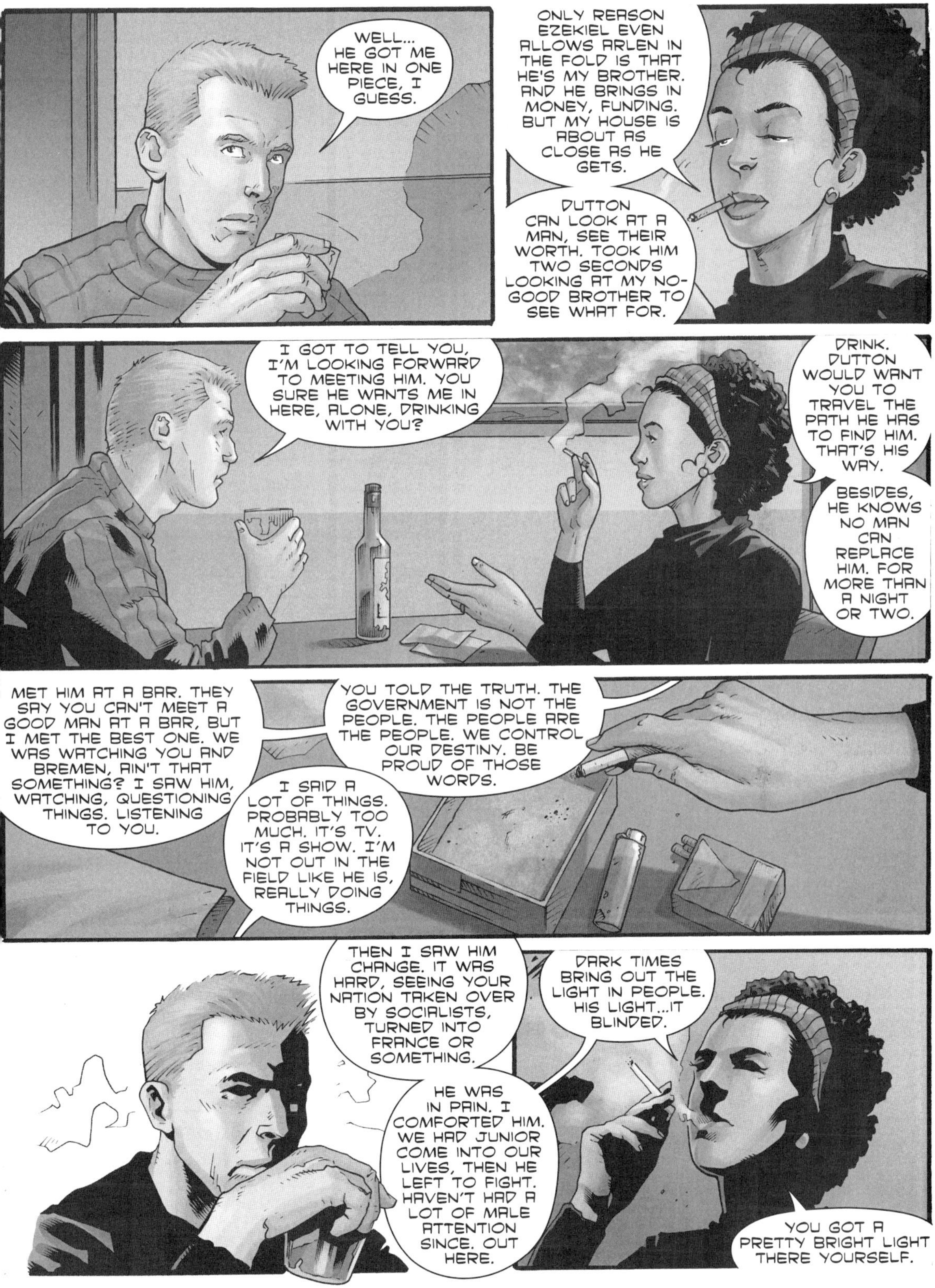
WELL... HE GOT ME HERE IN ONE PIECE, I GUESS.
ONLY REASON EZEKIEL EVEN ALLOWS ARLEN IN THE FOLD IS THAT HE'S MY BROTHER. AND HE BRINGS IN MONEY, FUNDING. BUT MY HOUSE IS ABOUT AS CLOSE AS HE GETS.
DUTTON CAN LOOK AT A MAN, SEE THEIR WORTH. TOOK HIM TWO SECONDS LOOKING AT MY NO-GOOD BROTHER TO SEE WHAT FOR.
I GOT TO TELL YOU, I'M LOOKING FORWARD TO MEETING HIM. YOU SURE HE WANTS ME IN HERE, ALONE, DRINKING WITH YOU?
DRINK. DUTTON WOULD WANT YOU TO TRAVEL THE PATH HE HAS TO FIND HIM. THAT'S HIS WAY.
BESIDES, HE KNOWS NO MAN CAN REPLACE HIM. FOR MORE THAN A NIGHT OR TWO.
MET HIM AT A BAR. THEY SAY YOU CAN'T MEET A GOOD MAN AT A BAR, BUT I MET THE BEST ONE. WE WAS WATCHING YOU AND BREMEN, AIN'T THAT SOMETHING? I SAW HIM, WATCHING, QUESTIONING THINGS. LISTENING TO YOU.
YOU TOLD THE TRUTH. THE GOVERNMENT IS NOT THE PEOPLE. THE PEOPLE ARE THE PEOPLE. WE CONTROL OUR DESTINY. BE PROUD OF THOSE WORDS.
I SAID A LOT OF THINGS. PROBABLY TOO MUCH. IT'S TV. IT'S A SHOW. I'M NOT OUT IN THE FIELD LIKE HE IS, REALLY DOING THINGS.
THEN I SAW HIM CHANGE. IT WAS HARD, SEEING YOUR NATION TAKEN OVER BY SOCIALISTS, TURNED INTO FRANCE OR SOMETHING.
DARK TIMES BRING OUT THE LIGHT IN PEOPLE. HIS LIGHT...IT BLINDED.
HE WAS IN PAIN. I COMFORTED HIM. WE HAD JUNIOR COME INTO OUR LIVES, THEN HE LEFT TO FIGHT. HAVEN'T HAD A LOT OF MALE ATTENTION SINCE. OUT HERE.
YOU GOT A PRETTY BRIGHT LIGHT THERE YOURSELF.

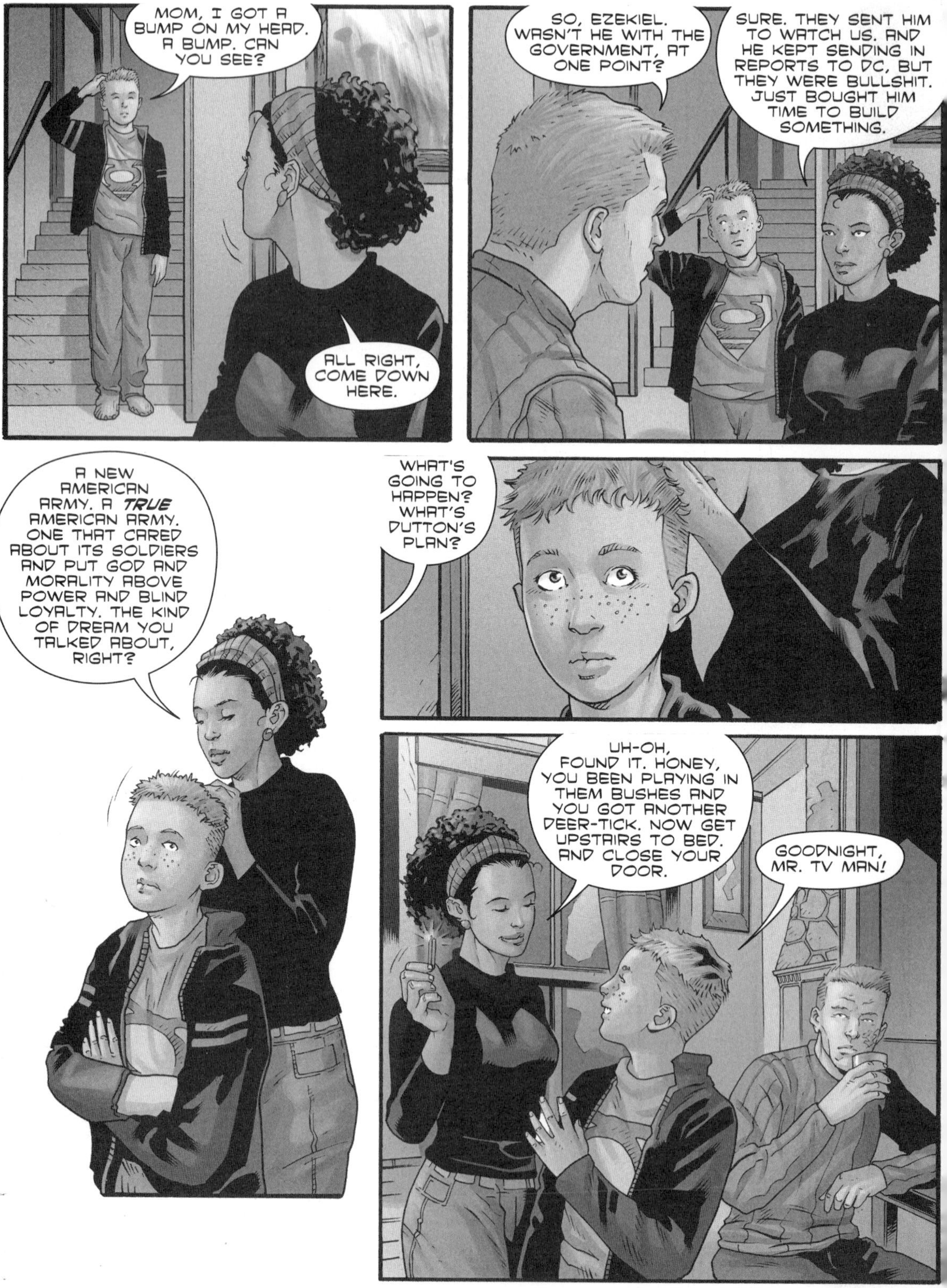
MOM, I GOT A BUMP ON MY HEAD. A BUMP. CAN YOU SEE?
ALL RIGHT, COME DOWN HERE.
SO, EZEKIEL. WASN'T HE WITH THE GOVERNMENT, AT ONE POINT?
SURE. THEY SENT HIM TO WATCH US. AND HE KEPT SENDING IN REPORTS TO DC, BUT THEY WERE BULLSHIT. JUST BOUGHT HIM TIME TO BUILD SOMETHING.
A NEW AMERICAN ARMY. A TRUE AMERICAN ARMY. ONE THAT CARED ABOUT ITS SOLDIERS AND PUT GOD AND MORALITY ABOVE POWER AND BLIND LOYALTY. THE KIND OF DREAM YOU TALKED ABOUT, RIGHT?
WHAT'S GOING TO HAPPEN? WHAT'S DUTTON'S PLAN?
UH-OH, FOUND IT. HONEY, YOU BEEN PLAYING IN THEM BUSHES AND YOU GOT ANOTHER DEER-TICK. NOW GET UPSTAIRS TO BED. AND CLOSE YOUR DOOR.
GOODNIGHT, MR. TV MAN!

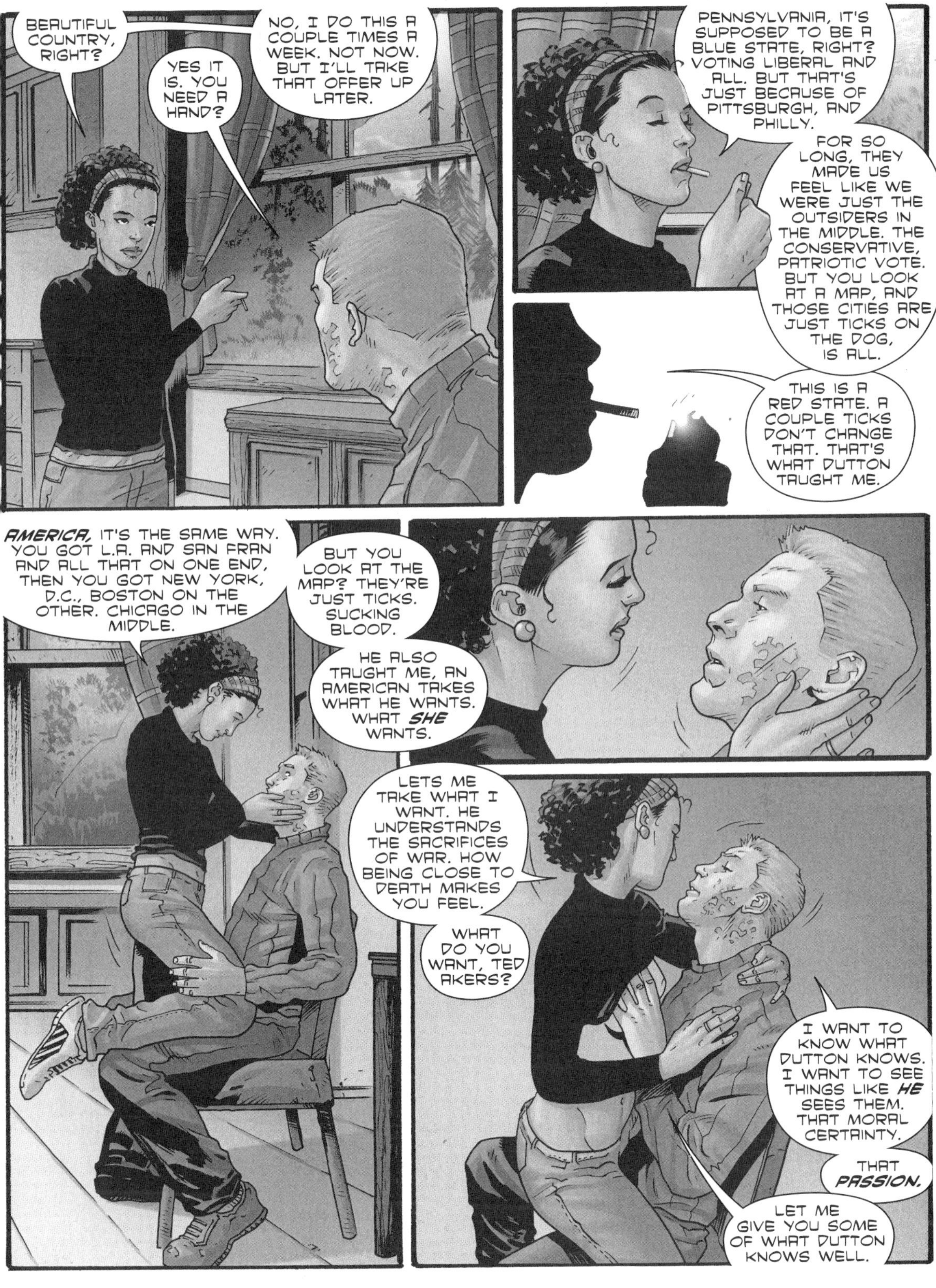
BEAUTIFUL COUNTRY, RIGHT?
YES IT IS. YOU NEED A HAND?
NO, I DO THIS A COUPLE TIMES A WEEK. NOT NOW. BUT I'LL TAKE THAT OFFER UP LATER.
PENNSYLVANIA, IT'S SUPPOSED TO BE A BLUE STATE, RIGHT? VOTING LIBERAL AND ALL. BUT THAT'S JUST BECAUSE OF PITTSBURGH, AND PHILLY.
FOR SO LONG, THEY MADE US FEEL LIKE WE WERE JUST THE OUTSIDERS IN THE MIDDLE. THE CONSERVATIVE, PATRIOTIC VOTE. BUT YOU LOOK AT A MAP, AND THOSE CITIES ARE JUST TICKS ON THE DOG, IS ALL.
THIS IS A RED STATE. A COUPLE TICKS DON'T CHANGE THAT. THAT'S WHAT DUTTON TAUGHT ME.
AMERICA, IT'S THE SAME WAY. YOU GOT L.A. AND SAN FRAN AND ALL THAT ON ONE END, THEN YOU GOT NEW YORK, D.C., BOSTON ON THE OTHER. CHICAGO IN THE MIDDLE.
BUT YOU LOOK AT THE MAP? THEY'RE JUST TICKS. SUCKING BLOOD.
HE ALSO TAUGHT ME, AN AMERICAN TAKES WHAT HE WANTS. WHAT SHE WANTS.
LETS ME TAKE WHAT I WANT. HE UNDERSTANDS THE SACRIFICES OF WAR. HOW BEING CLOSE TO DEATH MAKES YOU FEEL.
WHAT DO YOU WANT, TED AKERS?
I WANT TO KNOW WHAT DUTTON KNOWS. I WANT TO SEE THINGS LIKE HE SEES THEM. THAT MORAL CERTAINTY.
THAT PASSION.
LET ME GIVE YOU SOME OF WHAT DUTTON KNOWS WELL.

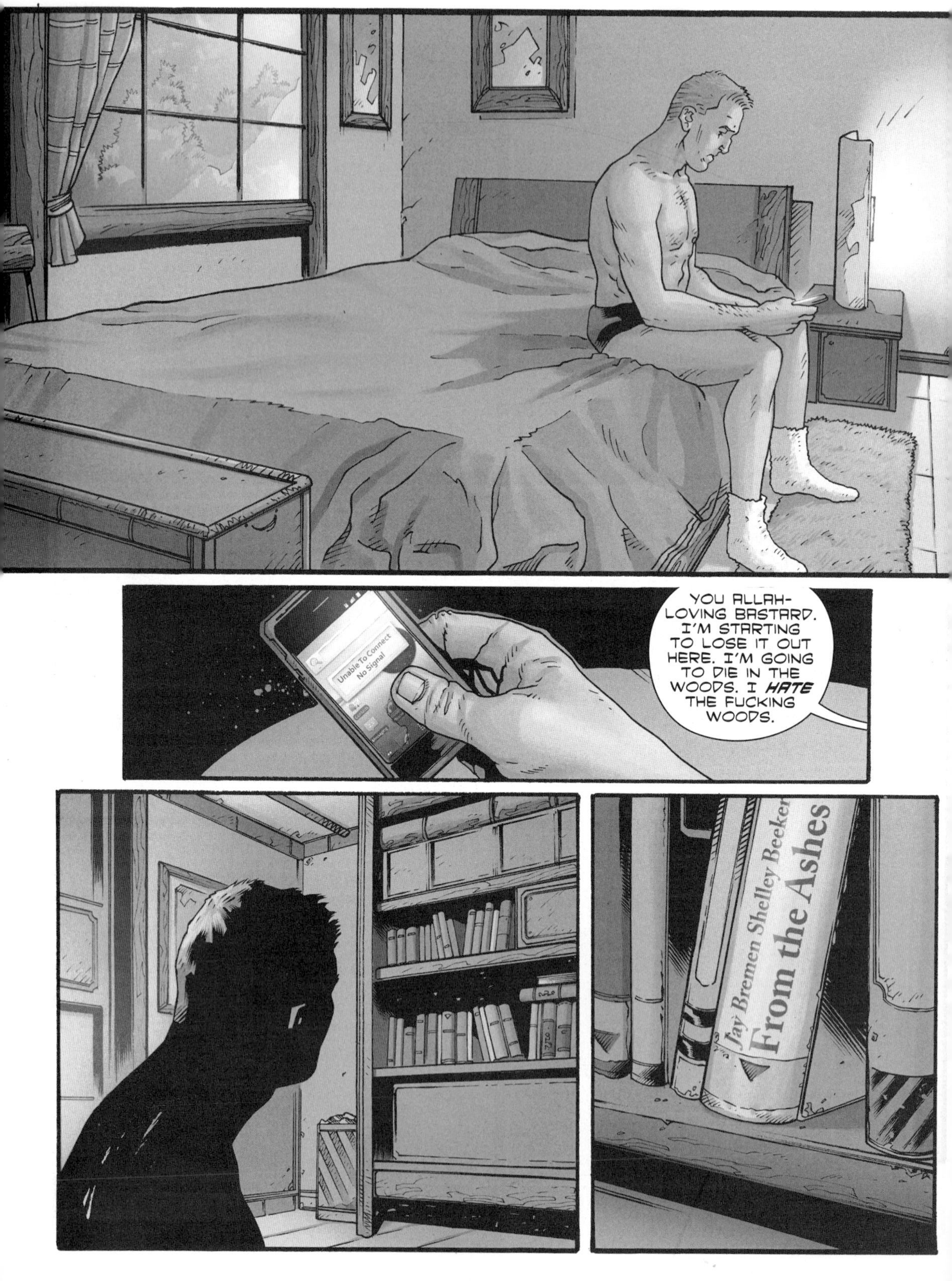
Unable To Connect
No Signal
YOU ALLAH-LOVING BASTARD. I'M STARTING TO LOSE IT OUT HERE. I'M GOING TO DIE IN THE WOODS. I *HATE* THE FUCKING WOODS.
Jay Bremen Shelley Beeker
From the Ashes

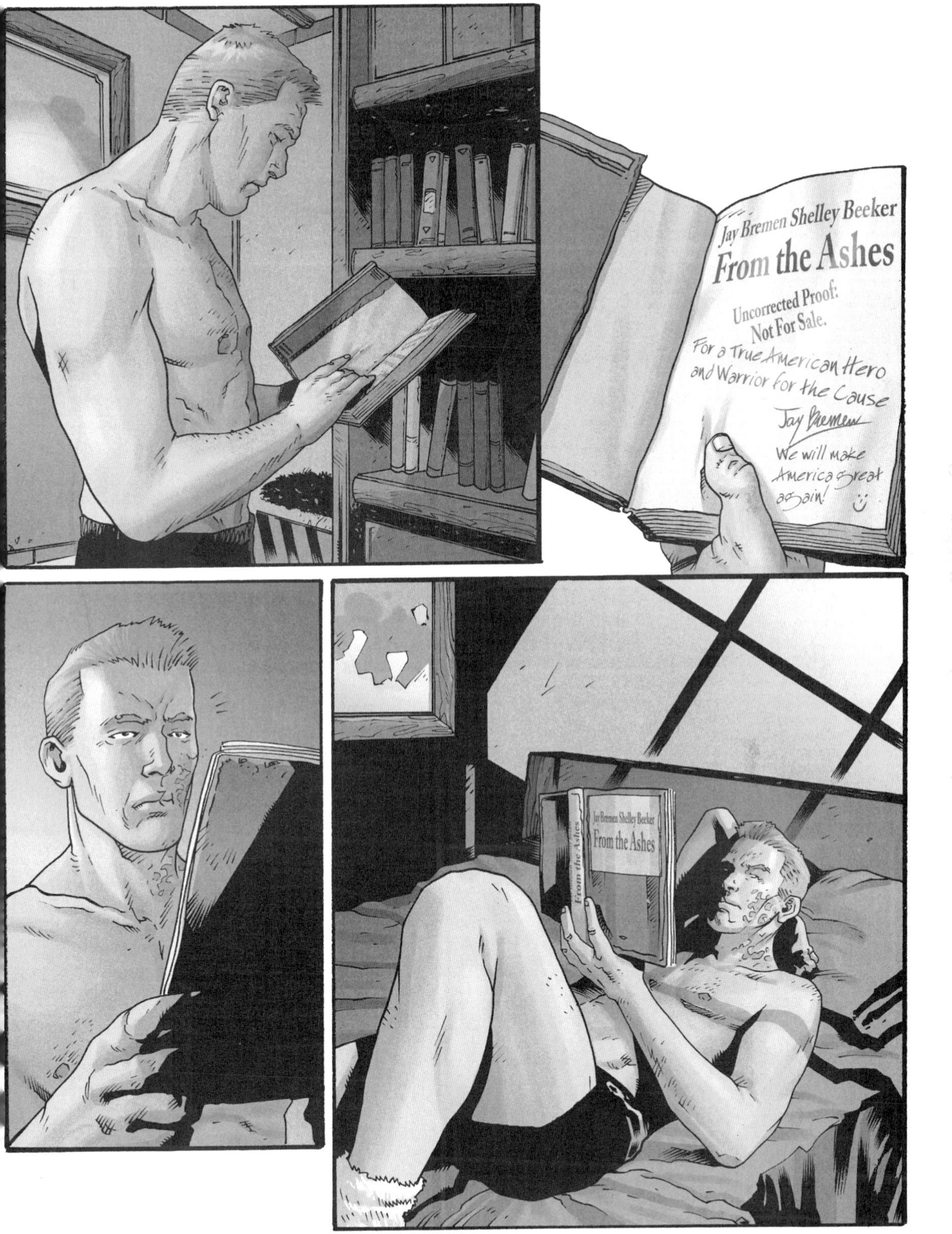
Jay Bremen Shelley Beeker
From the Ashes
Uncorrected Proof:
Not For Sale.
For a True American Hero
and Warrior for the Cause
Jay Bremen
We will make
America great
again!
Jay Bremen Shelley Beeker
From the Ashes
From the Ashes

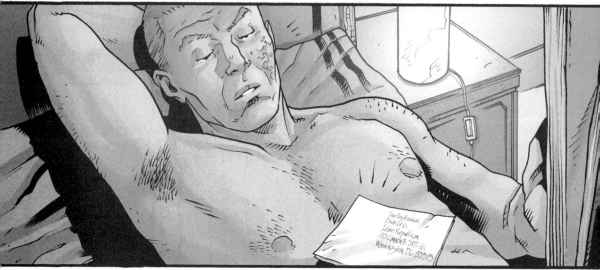

Shelley Becker,
District 6,
Idaho Republican
110 Cannon B. STE 6,
Washington, DC 20515

Shelley Becker,
District 6,
Idaho Republican
110 Cannon B. STE 6,
Washington, DC 20515

Thank you for your letters,
please accept this gift.
From the ashes,
we will build a
greater nation.

SB

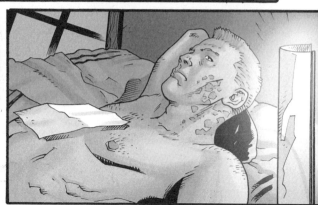

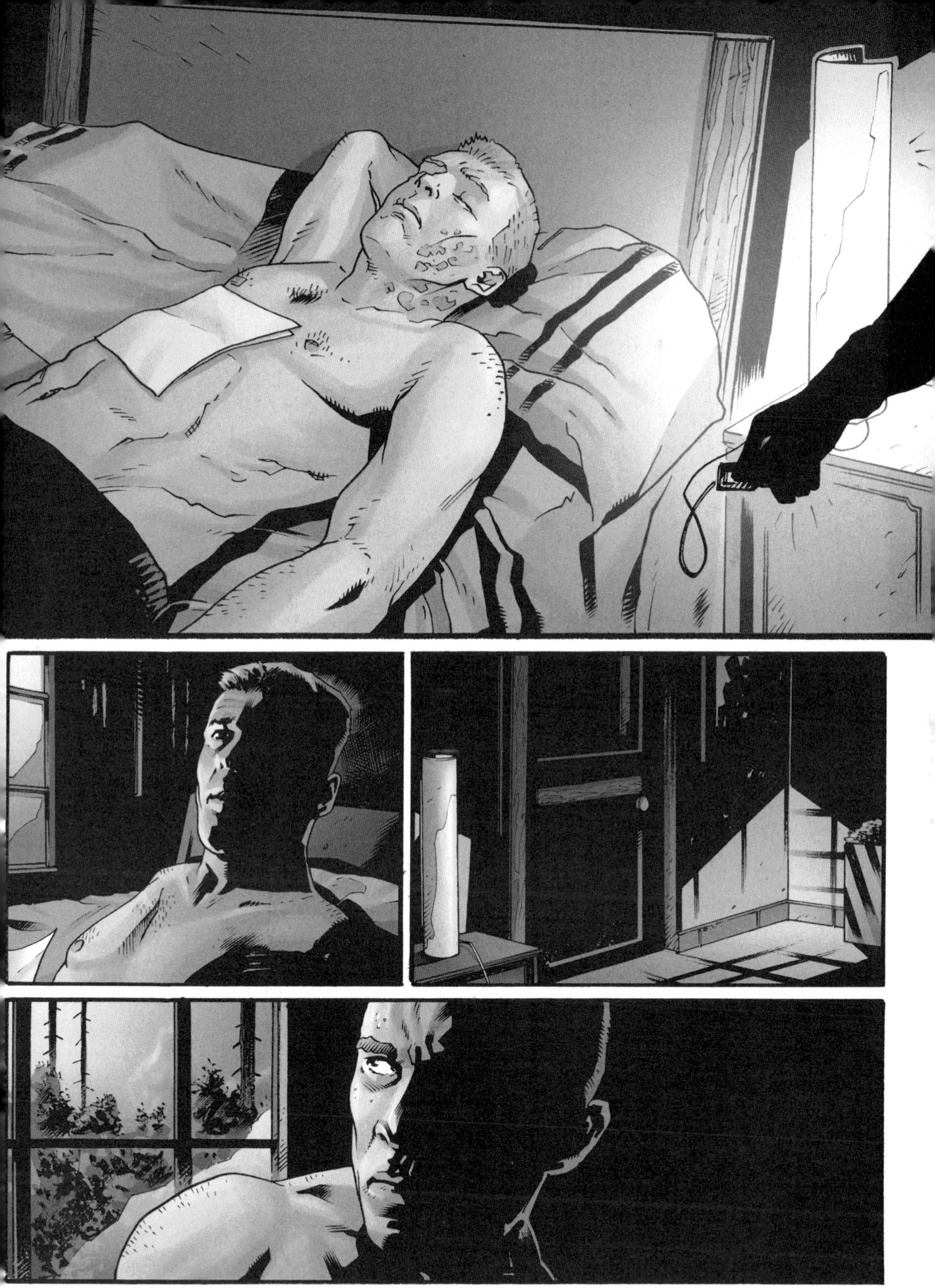

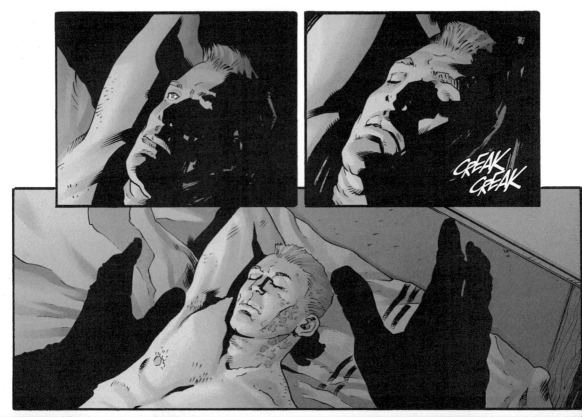

CREAK
CREAK

MMMMMPH!

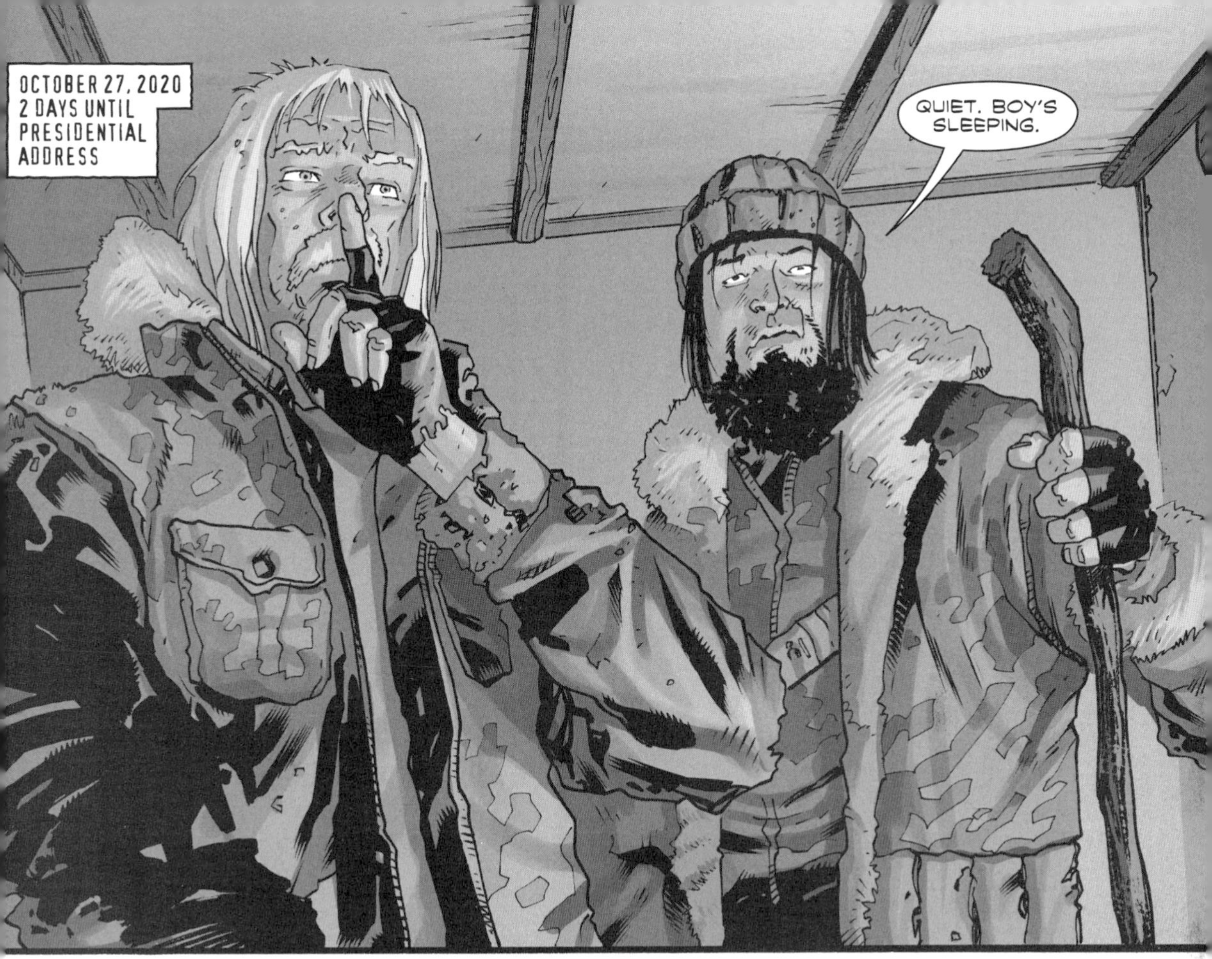
OCTOBER 27, 2020
2 DAYS UNTIL PRESIDENTIAL ADDRESS
QUIET. BOY'S SLEEPING.

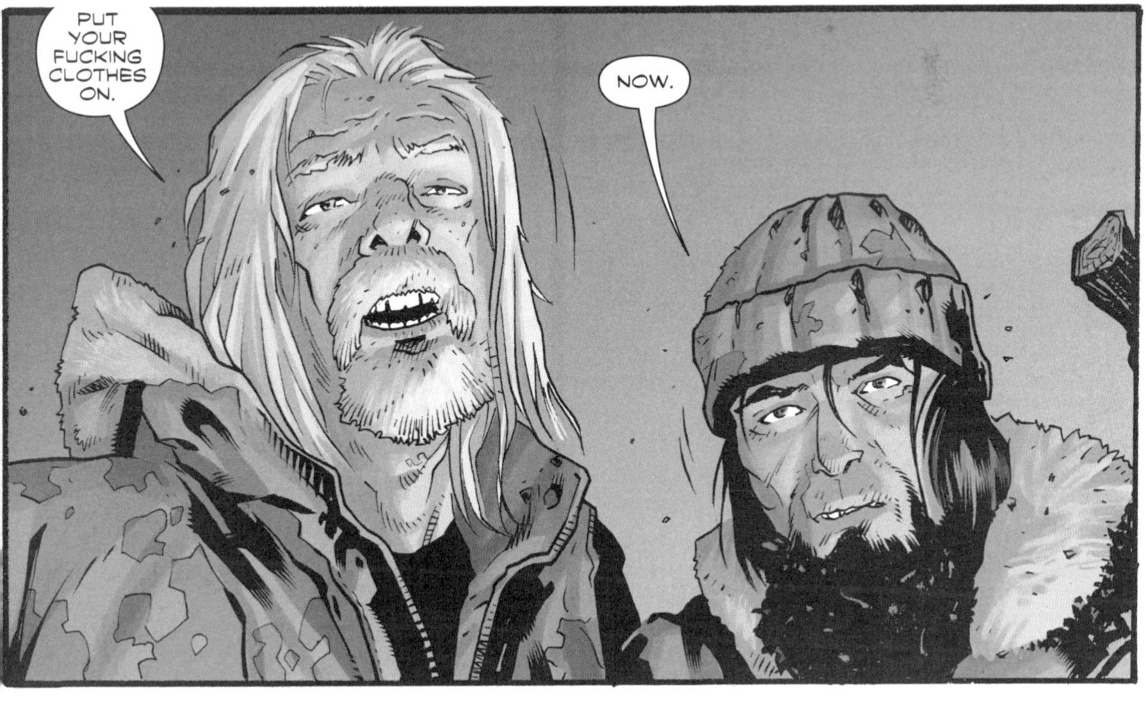
PUT YOUR FUCKING CLOTHES ON.
NOW.

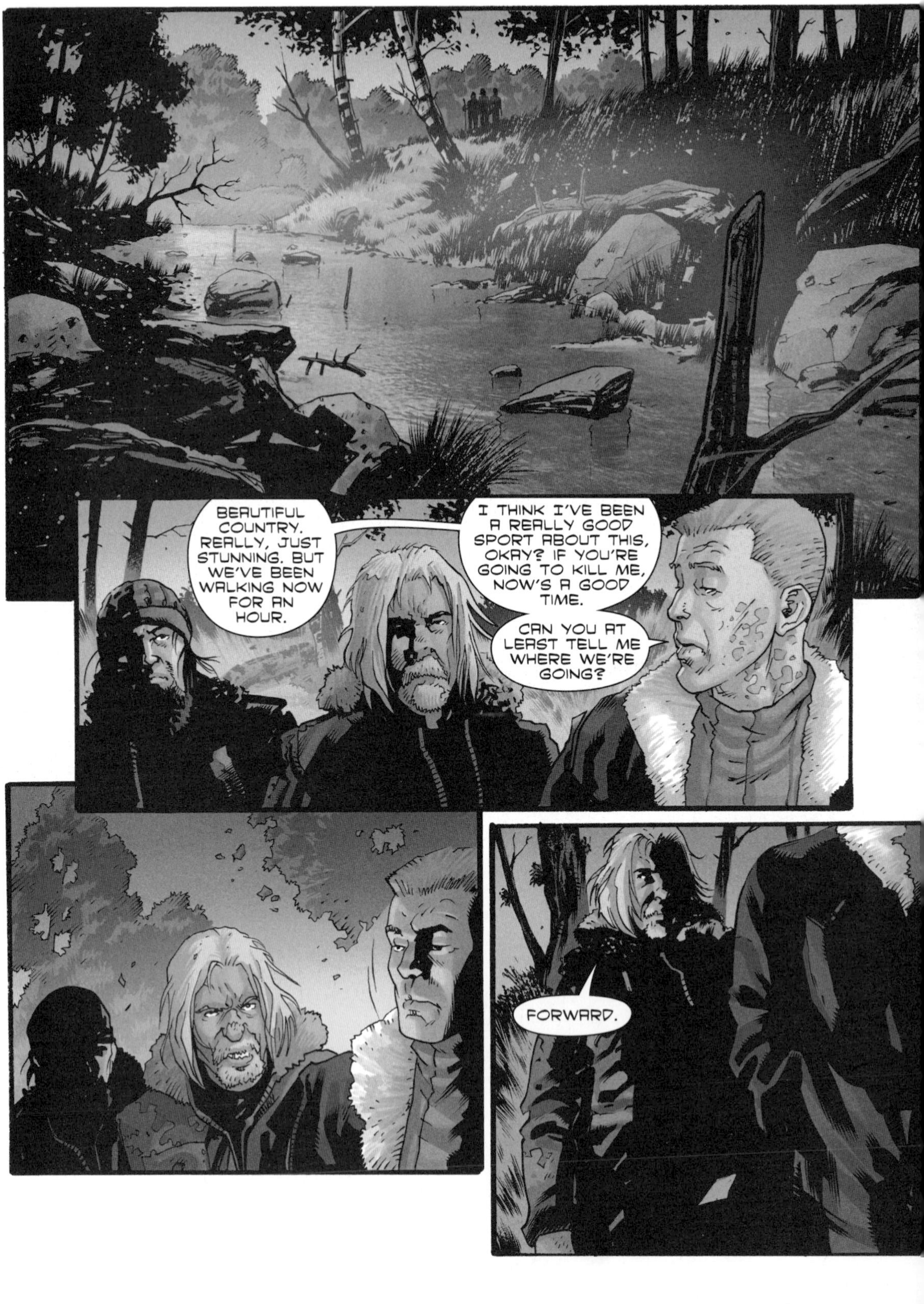
BEAUTIFUL COUNTRY. REALLY, JUST STUNNING. BUT WE'VE BEEN WALKING NOW FOR AN HOUR.
I THINK I'VE BEEN A REALLY GOOD SPORT ABOUT THIS, OKAY? IF YOU'RE GOING TO KILL ME, NOW'S A GOOD TIME.
CAN YOU AT LEAST TELL ME WHERE WE'RE GOING?
FORWARD.

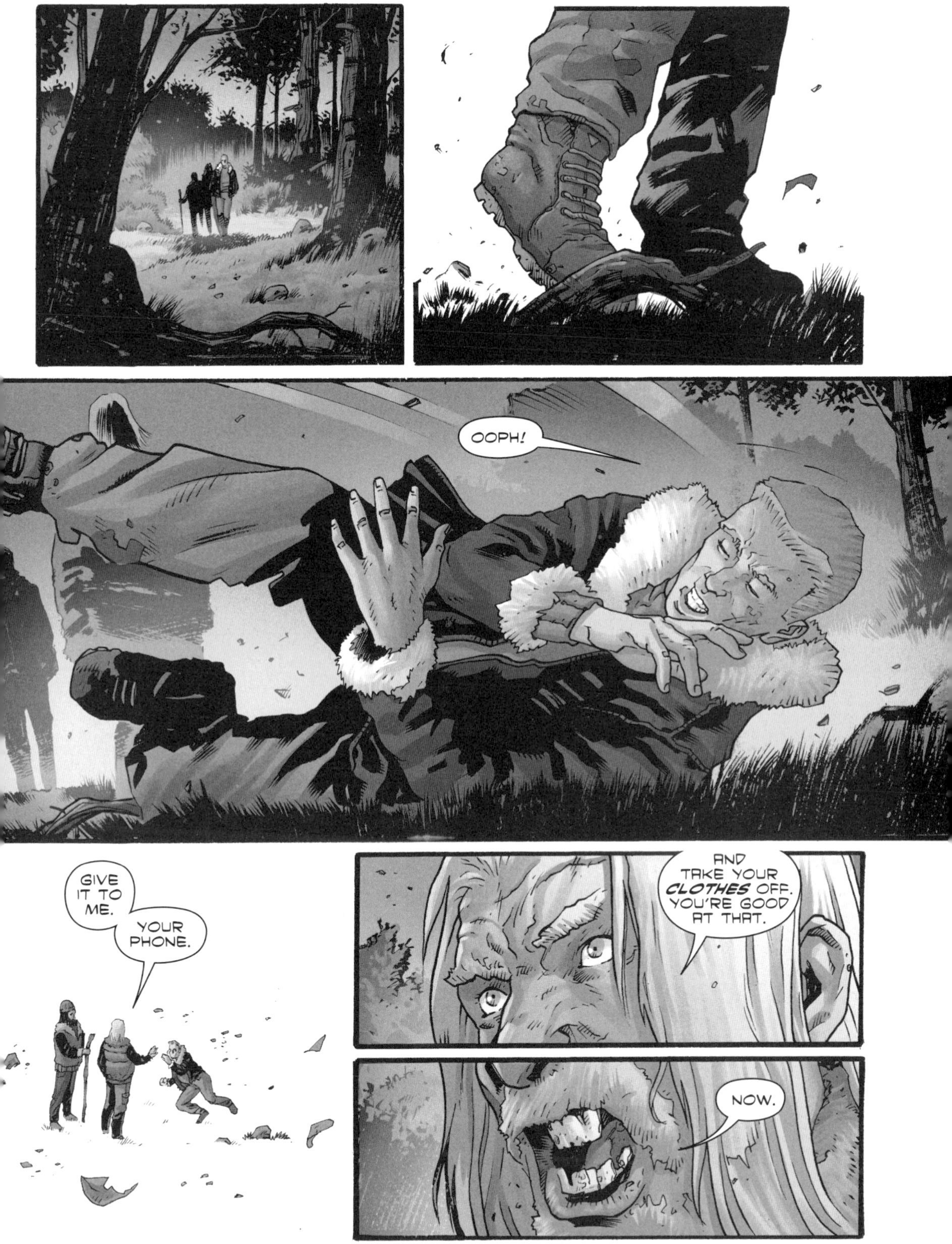
OOPH!
GIVE IT TO ME.
YOUR PHONE.
AND TAKE YOUR CLOTHES OFF. YOU'RE GOOD AT THAT.
NOW.

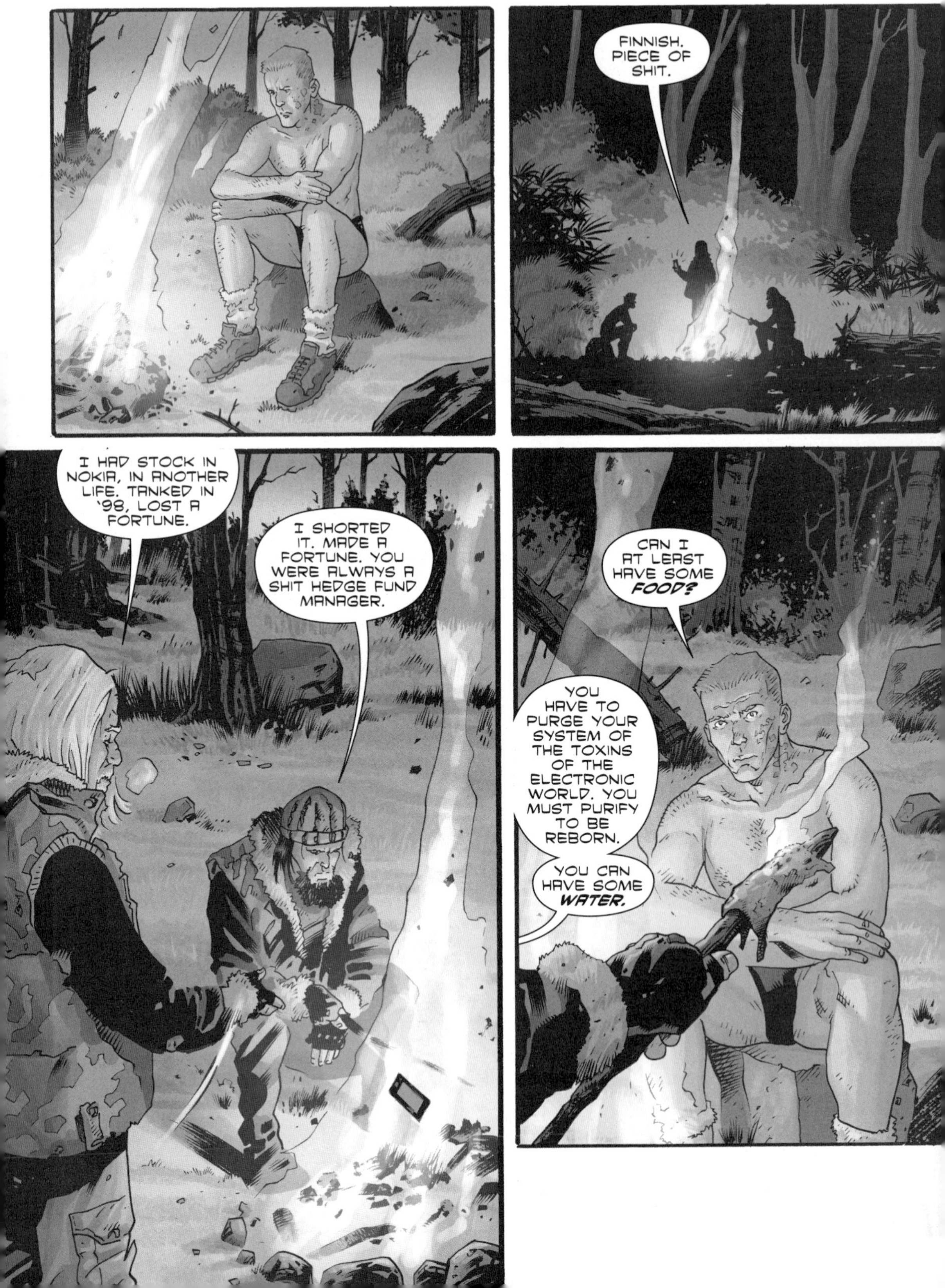
FINNISH. PIECE OF SHIT.
I HAD STOCK IN NOKIA, IN ANOTHER LIFE. TANKED IN '98, LOST A FORTUNE.
I SHORTED IT. MADE A FORTUNE. YOU WERE ALWAYS A SHIT HEDGE FUND MANAGER.
CAN I AT LEAST HAVE SOME FOOD?
YOU HAVE TO PURGE YOUR SYSTEM OF THE TOXINS OF THE ELECTRONIC WORLD. YOU MUST PURIFY TO BE REBORN.
YOU CAN HAVE SOME WATER.

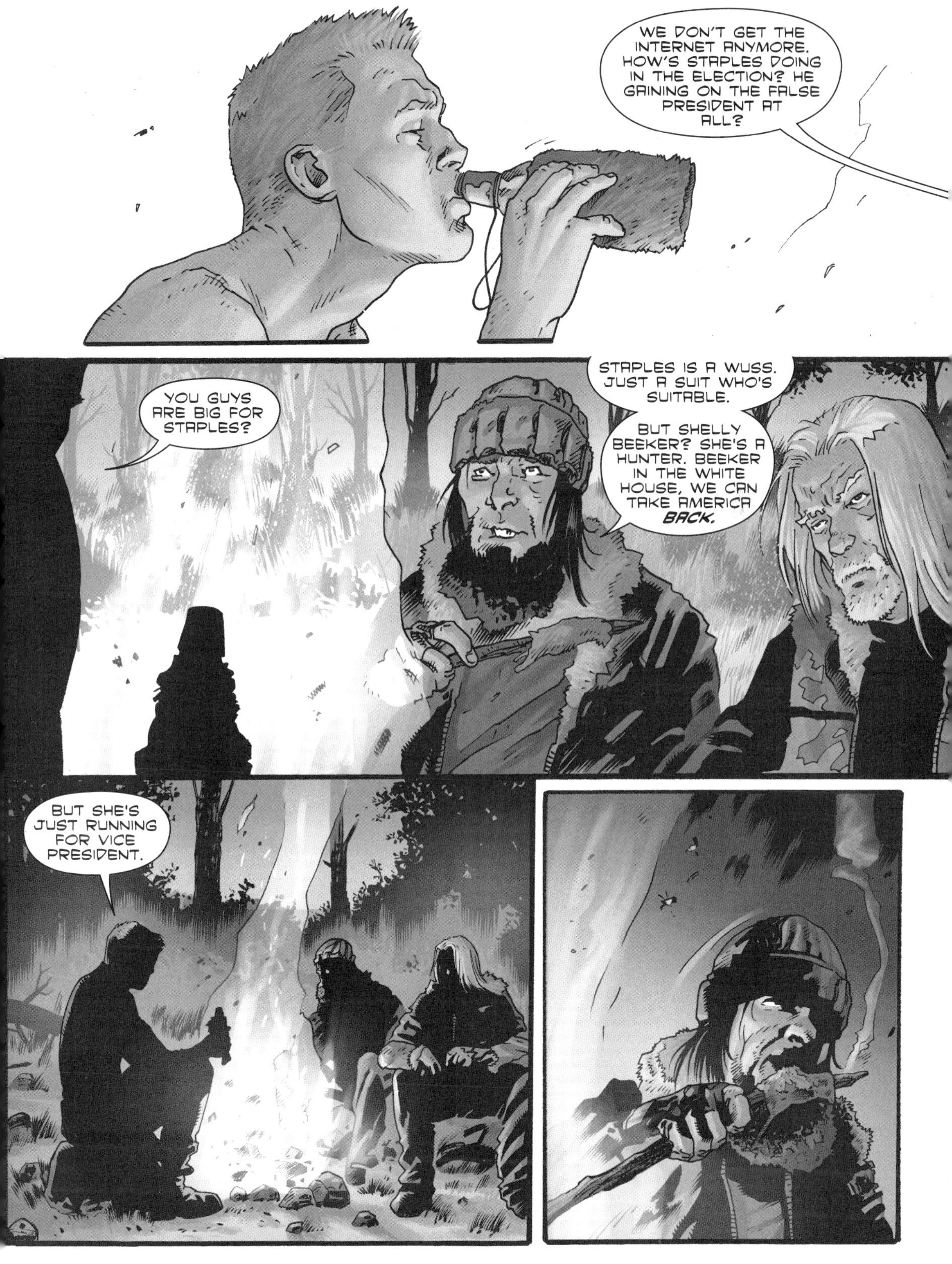
WE DON'T GET THE INTERNET ANYMORE. HOW'S STAPLES DOING IN THE ELECTION? HE GAINING ON THE FALSE PRESIDENT AT ALL?
YOU GUYS ARE BIG FOR STAPLES?
STAPLES IS A WUSS. JUST A SUIT WHO'S SUITABLE.
BUT SHELLY BEEKER? SHE'S A HUNTER. BEEKER IN THE WHITE HOUSE, WE CAN TAKE AMERICA ***BACK.***
BUT SHE'S JUST RUNNING FOR VICE PRESIDENT.

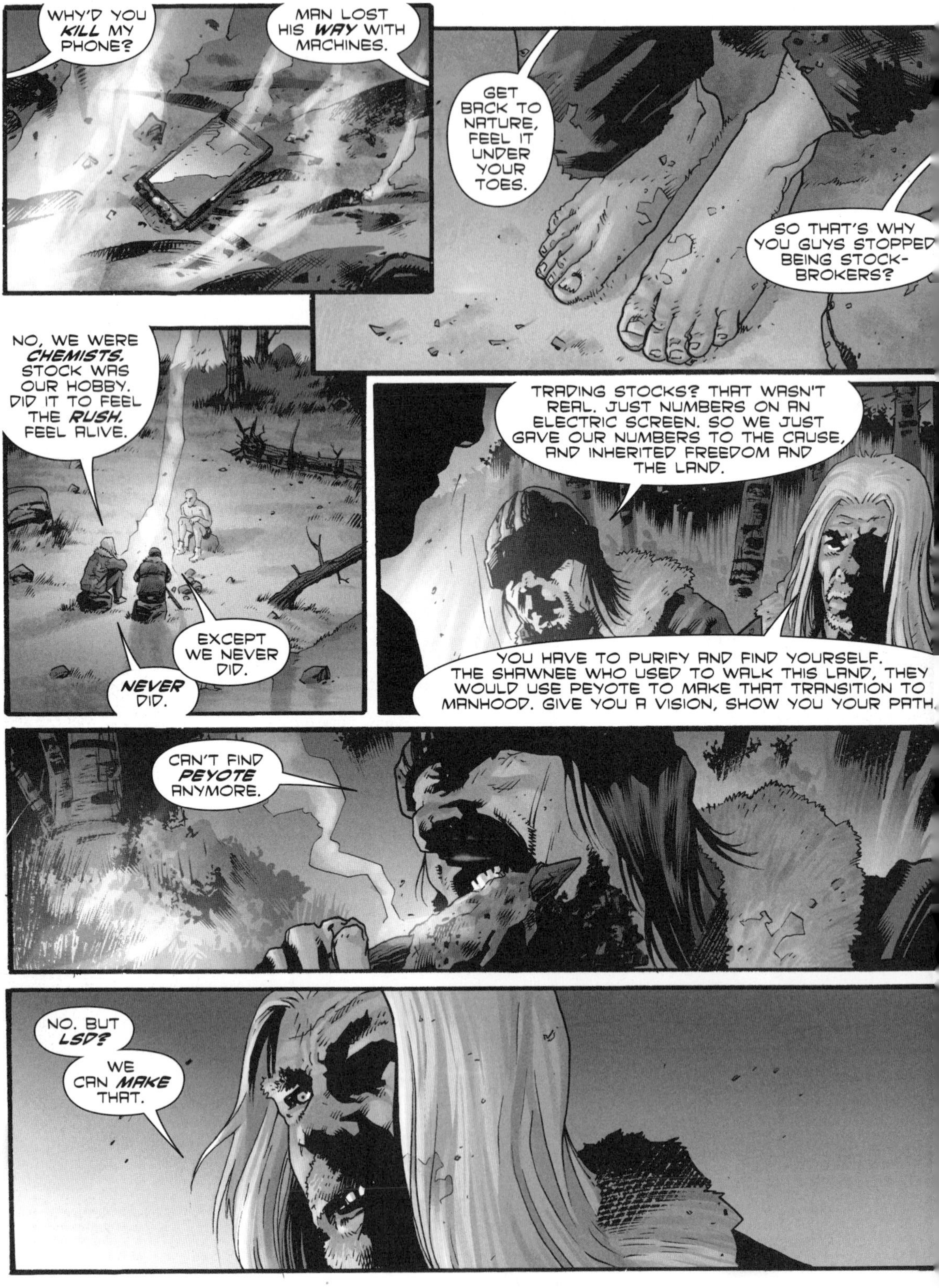
WHY'D YOU KILL MY PHONE?
MAN LOST HIS WAY WITH MACHINES.
GET BACK TO NATURE, FEEL IT UNDER YOUR TOES.
SO THAT'S WHY YOU GUYS STOPPED BEING STOCK-BROKERS?
NO, WE WERE CHEMISTS. STOCK WAS OUR HOBBY. DID IT TO FEEL THE RUSH. FEEL ALIVE.
EXCEPT WE NEVER DID.
NEVER DID.
TRADING STOCKS? THAT WASN'T REAL. JUST NUMBERS ON AN ELECTRIC SCREEN. SO WE JUST GAVE OUR NUMBERS TO THE CAUSE, AND INHERITED FREEDOM AND THE LAND.
YOU HAVE TO PURIFY AND FIND YOURSELF. THE SHAWNEE WHO USED TO WALK THIS LAND, THEY WOULD USE PEYOTE TO MAKE THAT TRANSITION TO MANHOOD. GIVE YOU A VISION, SHOW YOU YOUR PATH.
CAN'T FIND PEYOTE ANYMORE.
NO. BUT LSD?
WE CAN MAKE THAT.

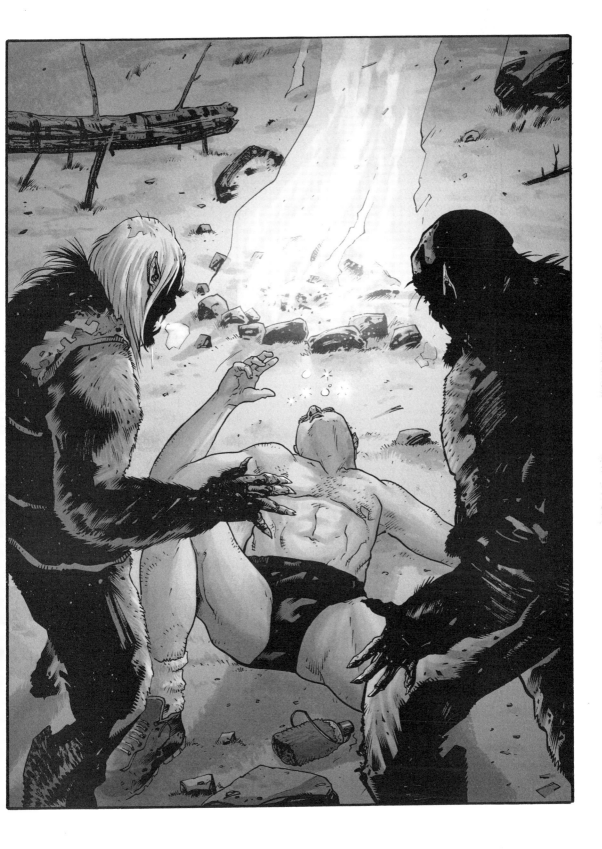

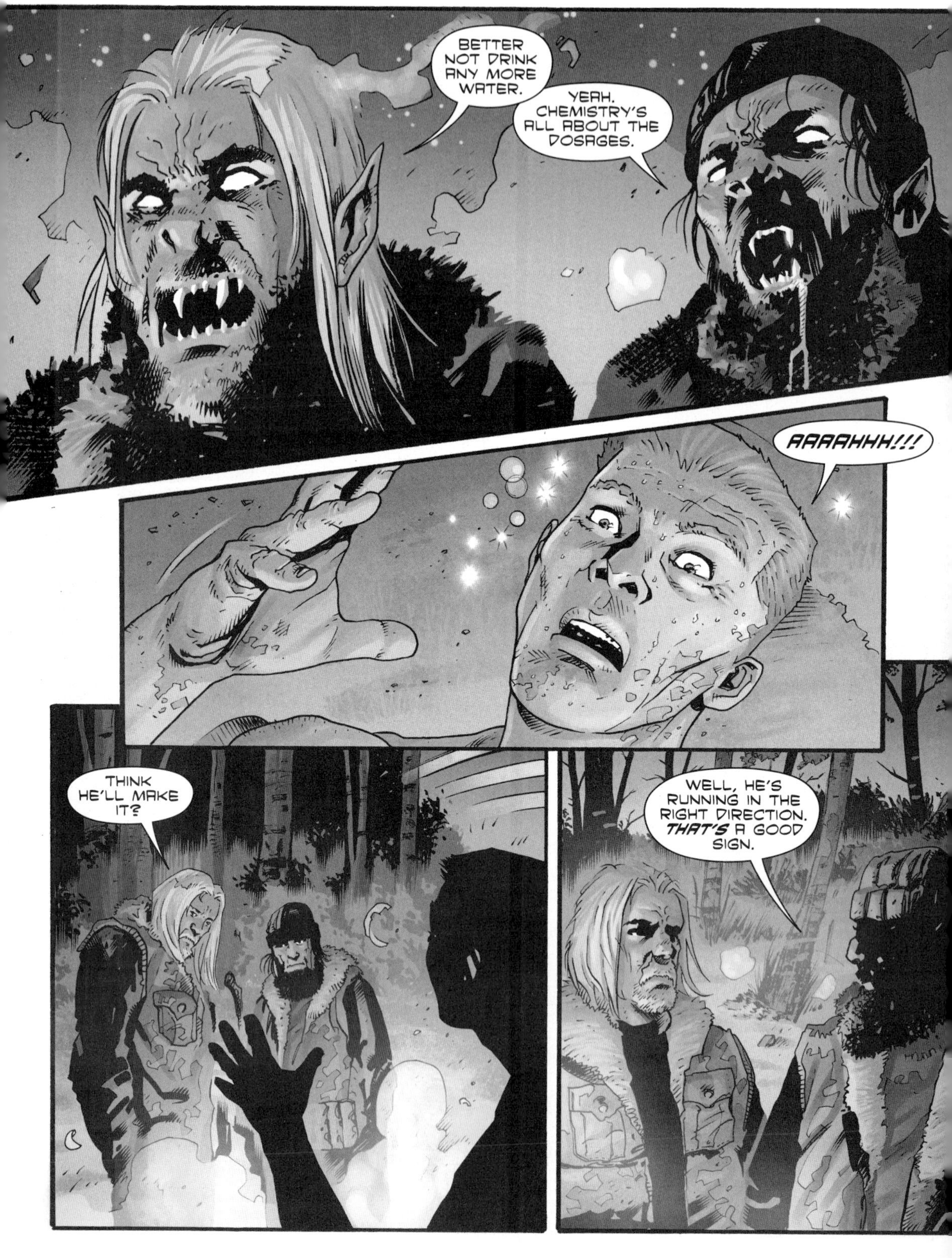
BETTER NOT DRINK ANY MORE WATER.
YEAH. CHEMISTRY'S ALL ABOUT THE DOSAGES.
AAAAHHH!!!
THINK HE'LL MAKE IT?
WELL, HE'S RUNNING IN THE RIGHT DIRECTION. *THAT'S* A GOOD SIGN.

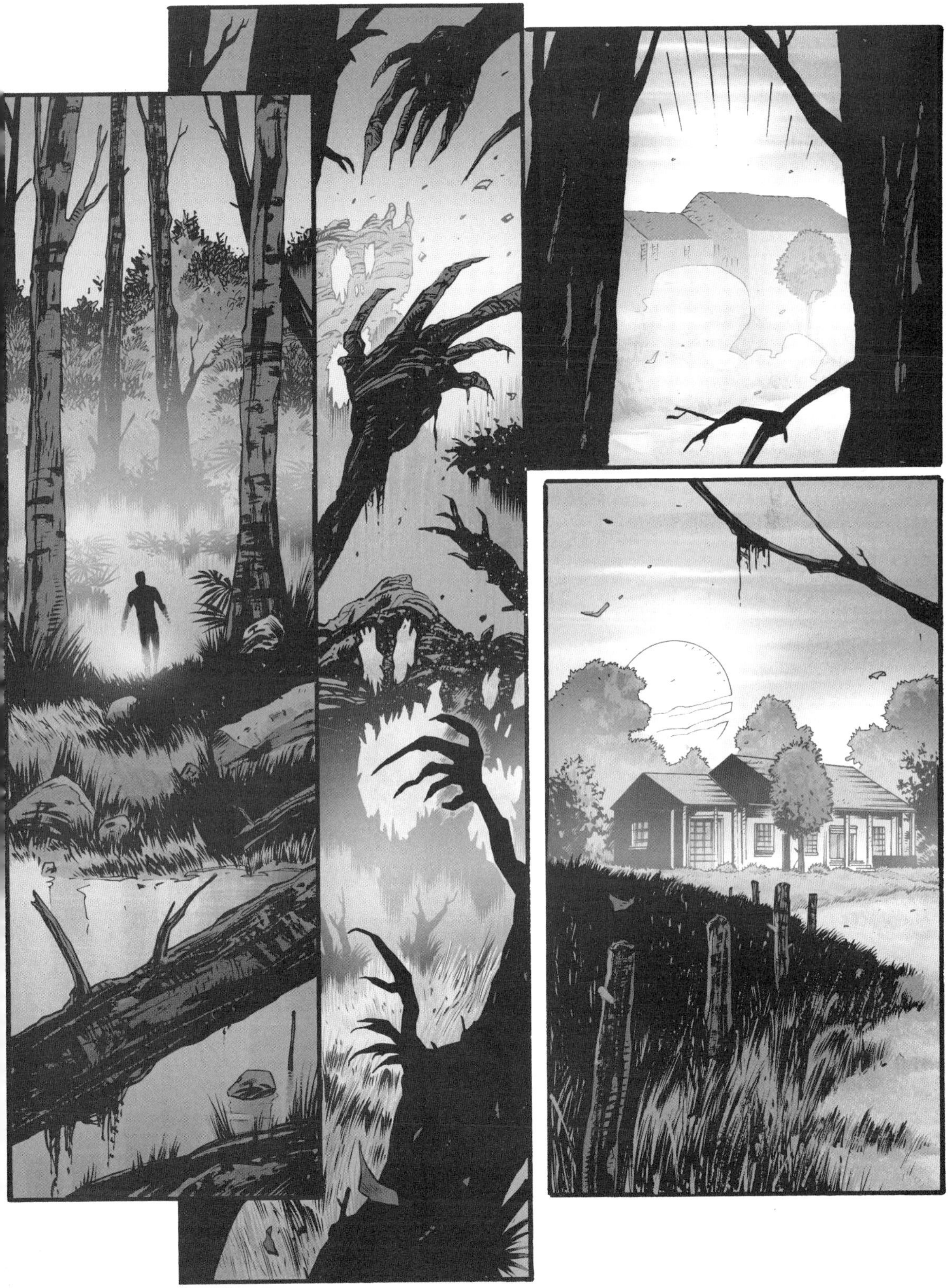

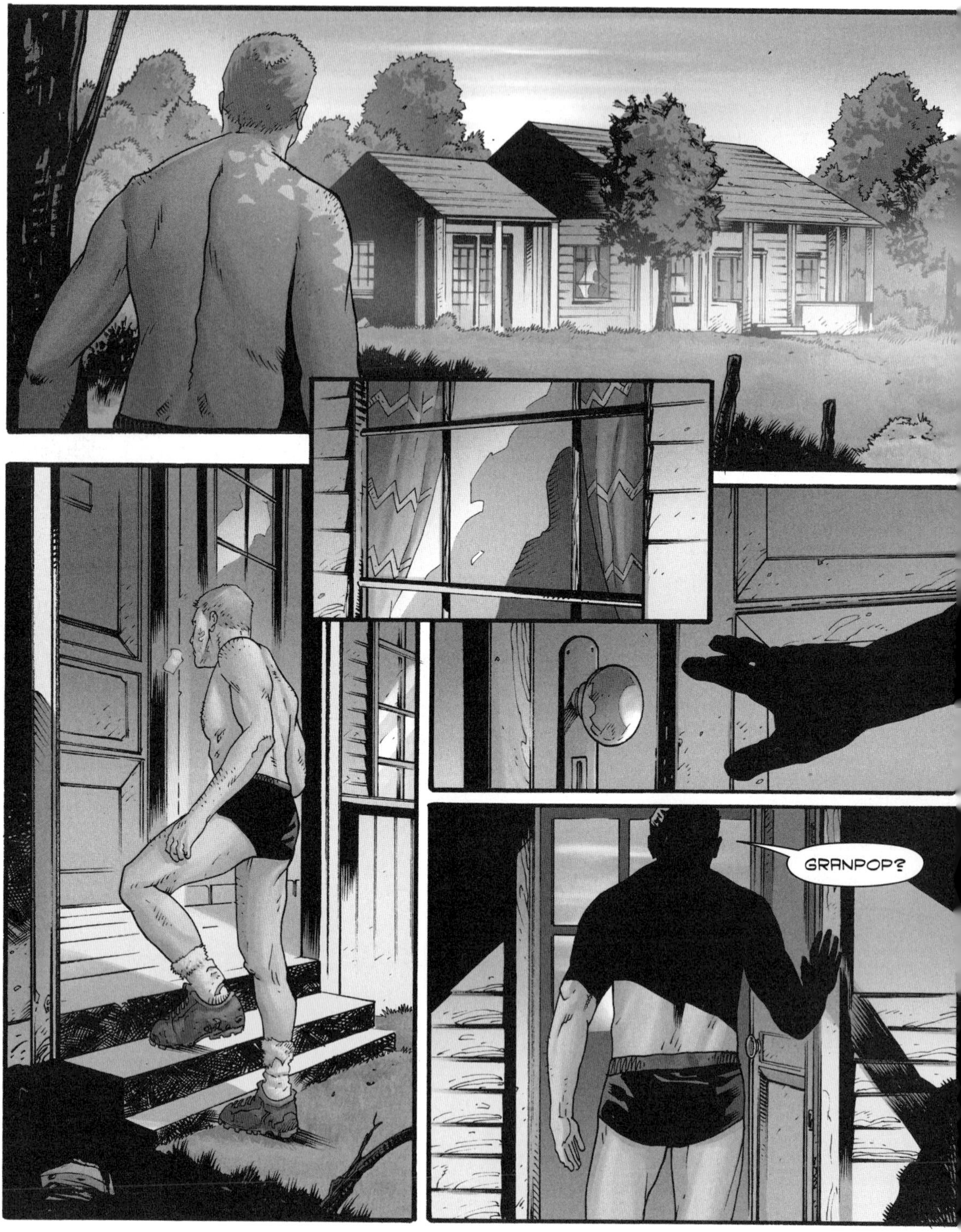
GRANPOP?

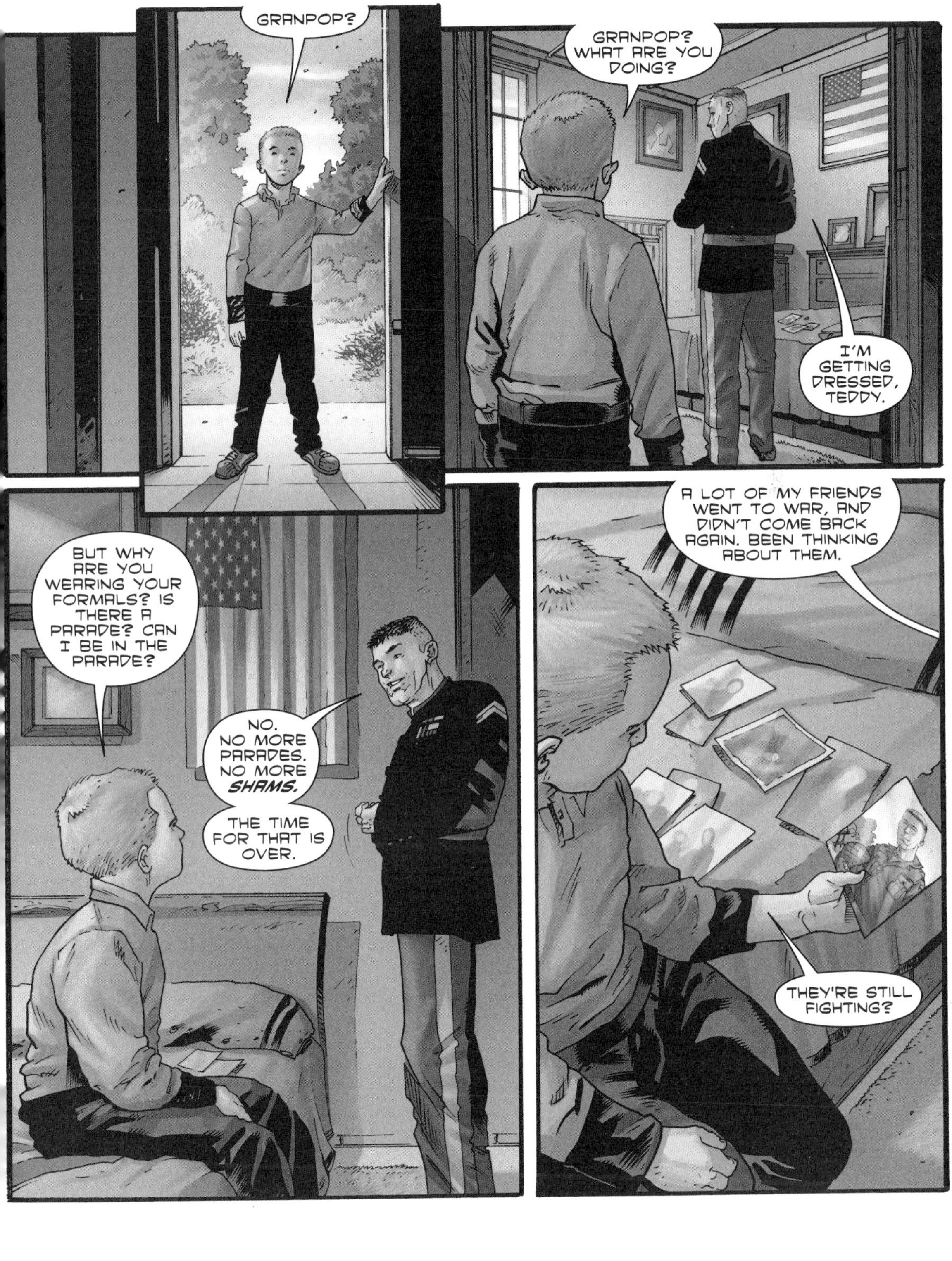
GRANPOP?
GRANPOP? WHAT ARE YOU DOING?
I'M GETTING DRESSED, TEDDY.
BUT WHY ARE YOU WEARING YOUR FORMALS? IS THERE A PARADE? CAN I BE IN THE PARADE?
NO. NO MORE PARADES. NO MORE SHAMS.
THE TIME FOR THAT IS OVER.
A LOT OF MY FRIENDS WENT TO WAR, AND DIDN'T COME BACK AGAIN. BEEN THINKING ABOUT THEM.
THEY'RE STILL FIGHTING?

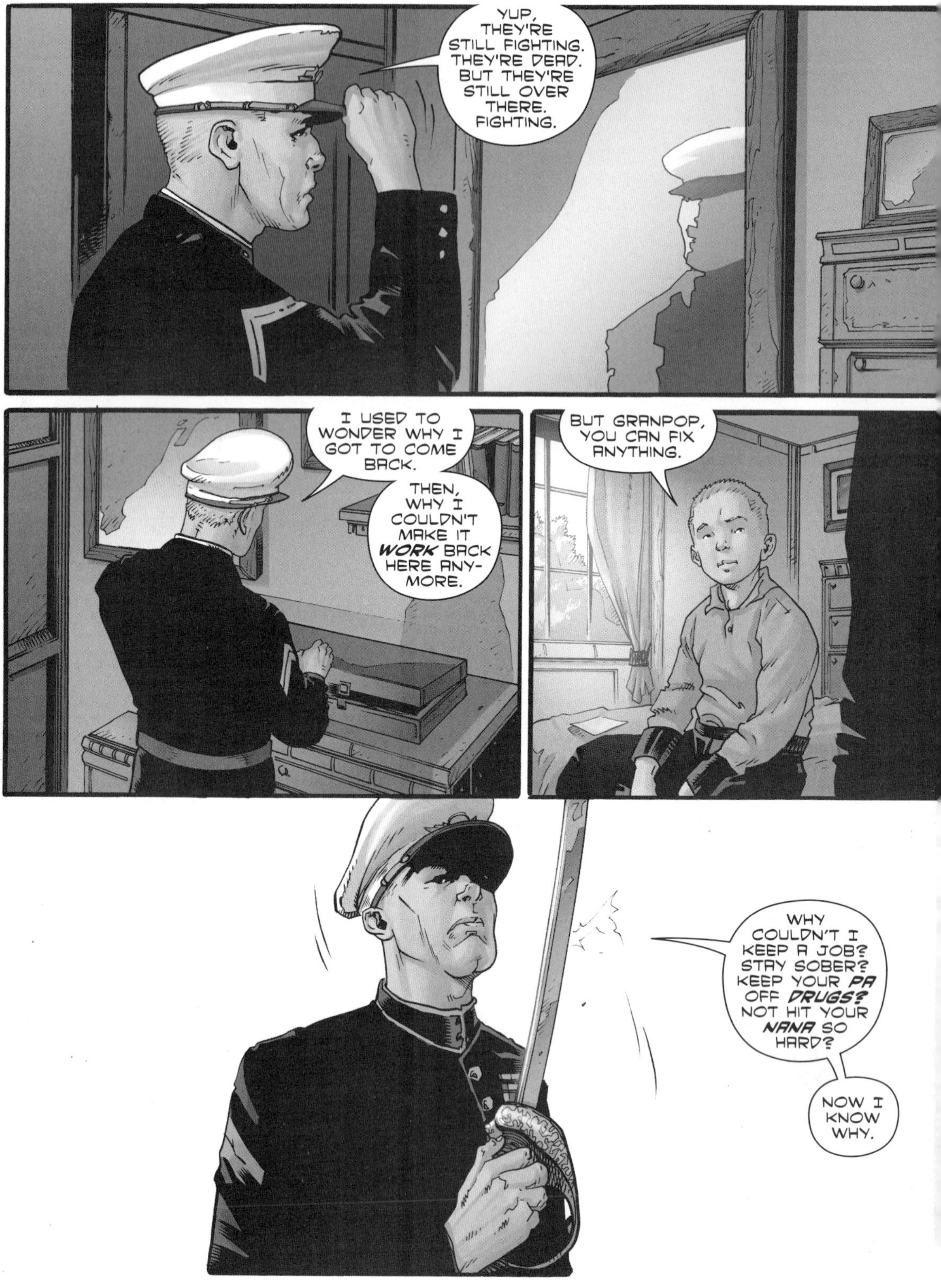
YUP, THEY'RE STILL FIGHTING. THEY'RE DEAD. BUT THEY'RE STILL OVER THERE. FIGHTING.
I USED TO WONDER WHY I GOT TO COME BACK.
THEN, WHY I COULDN'T MAKE IT WORK BACK HERE ANY-MORE.
BUT GRANPOP, YOU CAN FIX ANYTHING.
WHY COULDN'T I KEEP A JOB? STAY SOBER? KEEP YOUR PA OFF DRUGS? NOT HIT YOUR NANA SO HARD?
NOW I KNOW WHY.

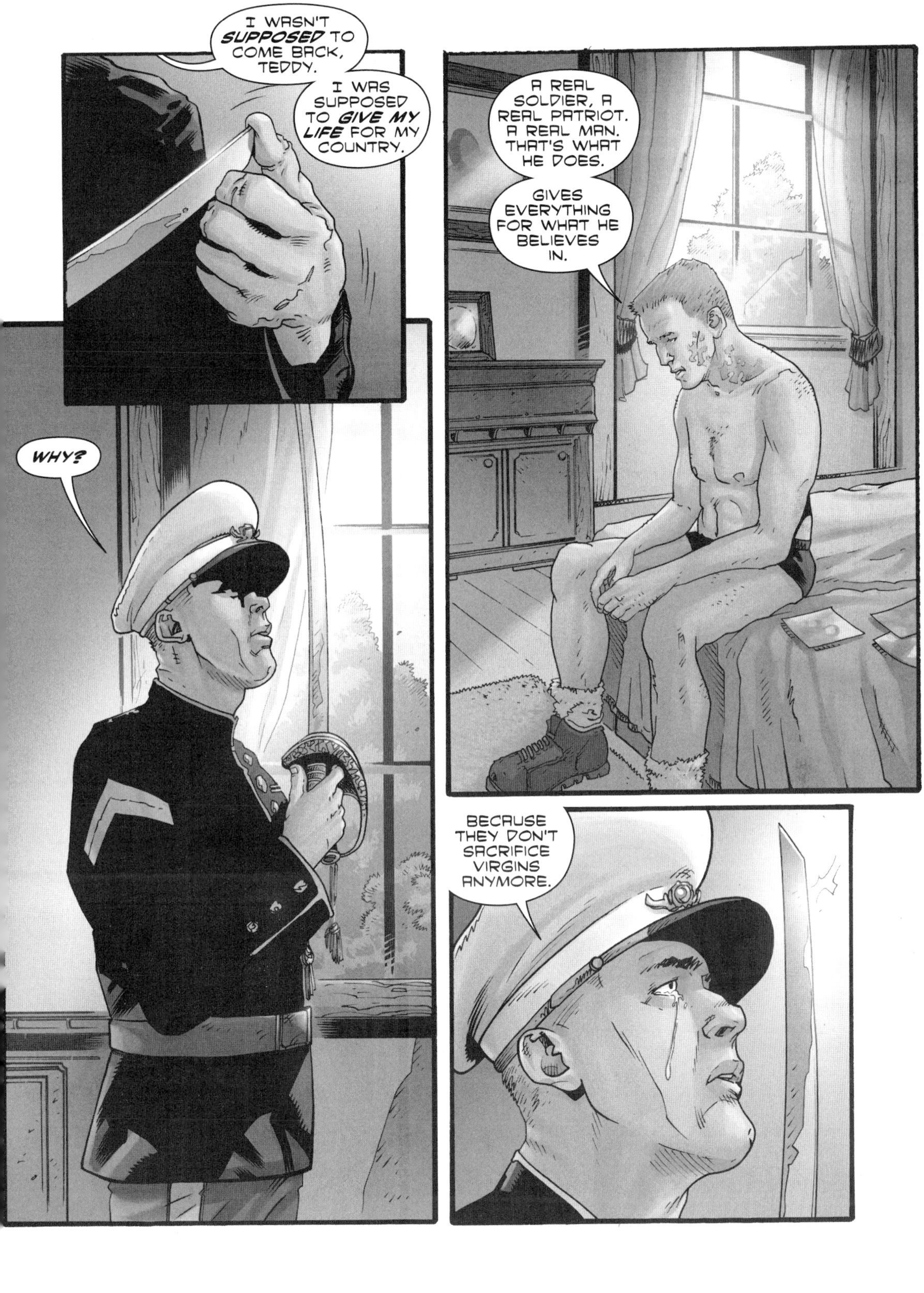
I WASN'T SUPPOSED TO COME BACK, TEDDY.
I WAS SUPPOSED TO GIVE MY LIFE FOR MY COUNTRY.
A REAL SOLDIER, A REAL PATRIOT. A REAL MAN. THAT'S WHAT HE DOES.
GIVES EVERYTHING FOR WHAT HE BELIEVES IN.
WHY?
BECAUSE THEY DON'T SACRIFICE VIRGINS ANYMORE.

GO OUT AND PLAY ON THE PORCH. YOUR MOTHER WILL BE HERE SOON TO PICK YOU UP. THAT'S AN *ORDER.*

BE A GOOD BOY.

BE A BETTER MAN.

UNNH!

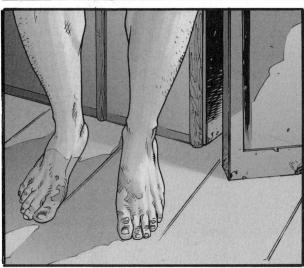

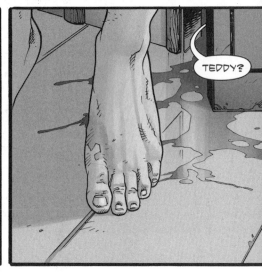

TEDDY?

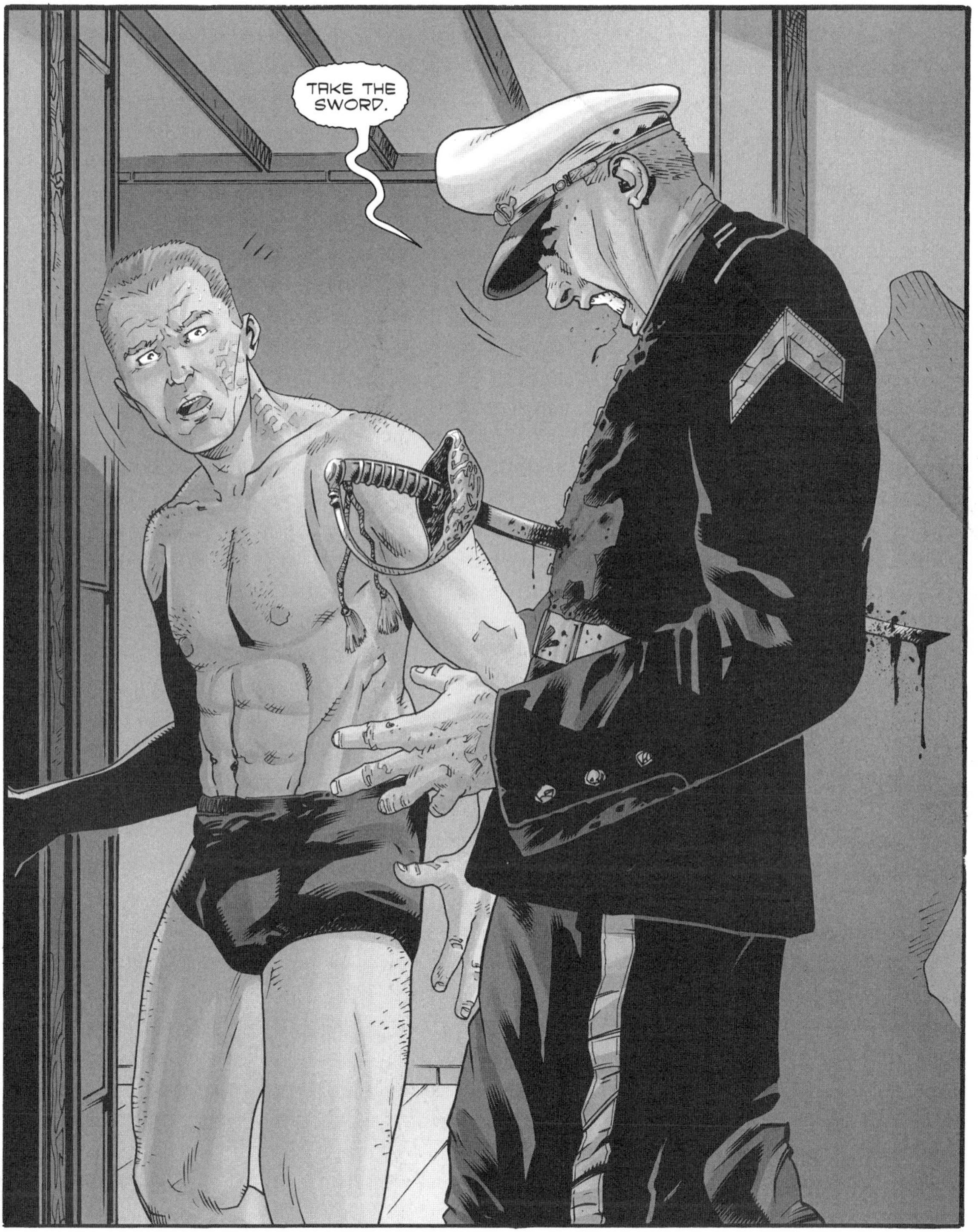
TAKE THE SWORD.

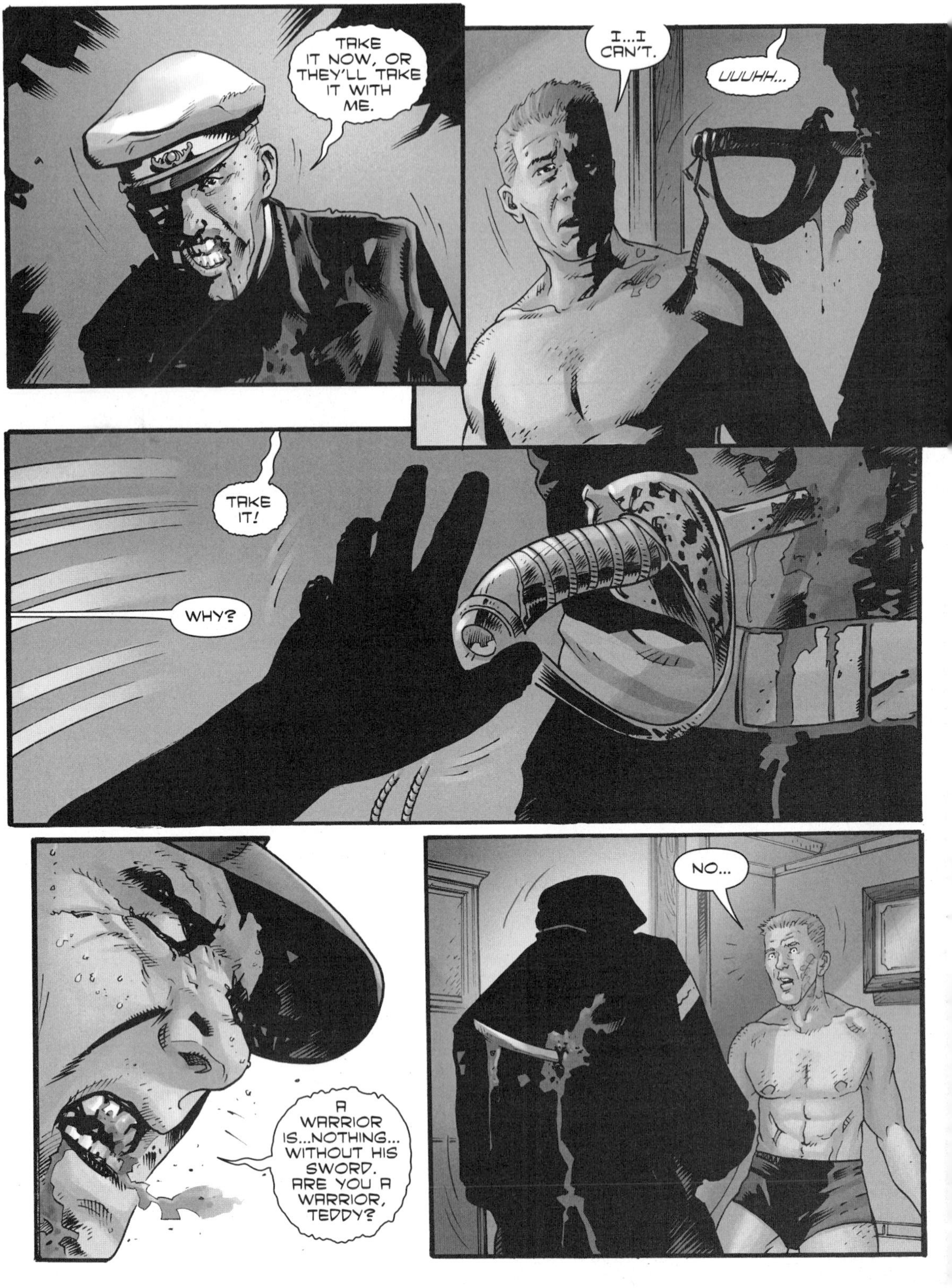
TAKE IT NOW, OR THEY'LL TAKE IT WITH ME.
I...I CAN'T.
UUUHH...
TAKE IT!
WHY?
A WARRIOR IS...NOTHING... WITHOUT HIS SWORD. ARE YOU A WARRIOR, TEDDY?
NO...

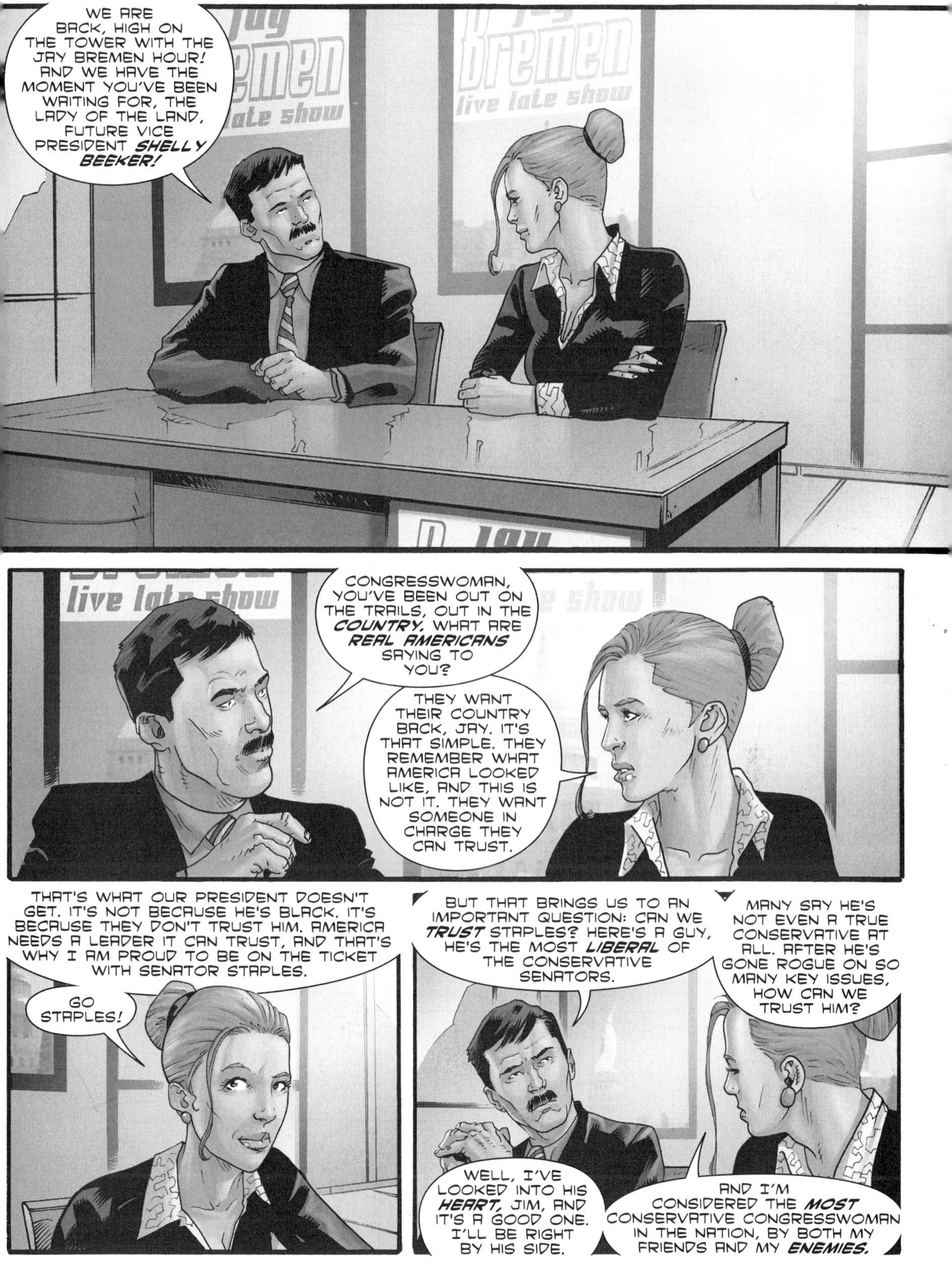
WE ARE BACK, HIGH ON THE TOWER WITH THE JAY BREMEN HOUR! AND WE HAVE THE MOMENT YOU'VE BEEN WAITING FOR, THE LADY OF THE LAND, FUTURE VICE PRESIDENT SHELLY BEEKER!
bremen live late show
CONGRESSWOMAN, YOU'VE BEEN OUT ON THE TRAILS, OUT IN THE COUNTRY. WHAT ARE REAL AMERICANS SAYING TO YOU?
THEY WANT THEIR COUNTRY BACK, JAY. IT'S THAT SIMPLE. THEY REMEMBER WHAT AMERICA LOOKED LIKE, AND THIS IS NOT IT. THEY WANT SOMEONE IN CHARGE THEY CAN TRUST.
THAT'S WHAT OUR PRESIDENT DOESN'T GET. IT'S NOT BECAUSE HE'S BLACK. IT'S BECAUSE THEY DON'T TRUST HIM. AMERICA NEEDS A LEADER IT CAN TRUST, AND THAT'S WHY I AM PROUD TO BE ON THE TICKET WITH SENATOR STAPLES.
GO STAPLES!
BUT THAT BRINGS US TO AN IMPORTANT QUESTION: CAN WE TRUST STAPLES? HERE'S A GUY, HE'S THE MOST LIBERAL OF THE CONSERVATIVE SENATORS.
MANY SAY HE'S NOT EVEN A TRUE CONSERVATIVE AT ALL. AFTER HE'S GONE ROGUE ON SO MANY KEY ISSUES, HOW CAN WE TRUST HIM?
WELL, I'VE LOOKED INTO HIS HEART, JIM, AND IT'S A GOOD ONE. I'LL BE RIGHT BY HIS SIDE.
AND I'M CONSIDERED THE MOST CONSERVATIVE CONGRESSWOMAN IN THE NATION, BY BOTH MY FRIENDS AND MY ENEMIES.

What do you make of this "coming together" speech by the President, this *grandstanding* at the Lincoln Memorial in two days?

Do you buy the liberal media line that he's *brave* to go out in this climate?

You want bravery, look at my candidate and yours, Senator Staples. He will be giving a speech about "reclaiming America's greatness" at the same time, in DC as well, at Square.

The liberal media are *ignoring* that.

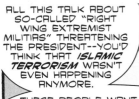

All this talk about so-called "right wing extremist militias" threatening the President--you'd think that *islamic terrorism* wasn't even happening anymore.

These people want to kill us all, but Senator Staples knows making himself available to the people in this campaign is more important than his own safety.

Staples is already behind in the polls. Some say he can't close the gap before the election. Many on the right say it was the wrong year to run a moderate, that *you* should be heading the ticket.

Don't you worry that the two speeches will be compared, that the President's speech will overshadow Senator Staples?

Lucifer has a golden tongue too, I'll remind you, Jim.

Oh boy, now the liberals are going to say I just called him the devil again, which of course I didn't. I've never seen *proof* he's the anti-christ. But you know what I mean.

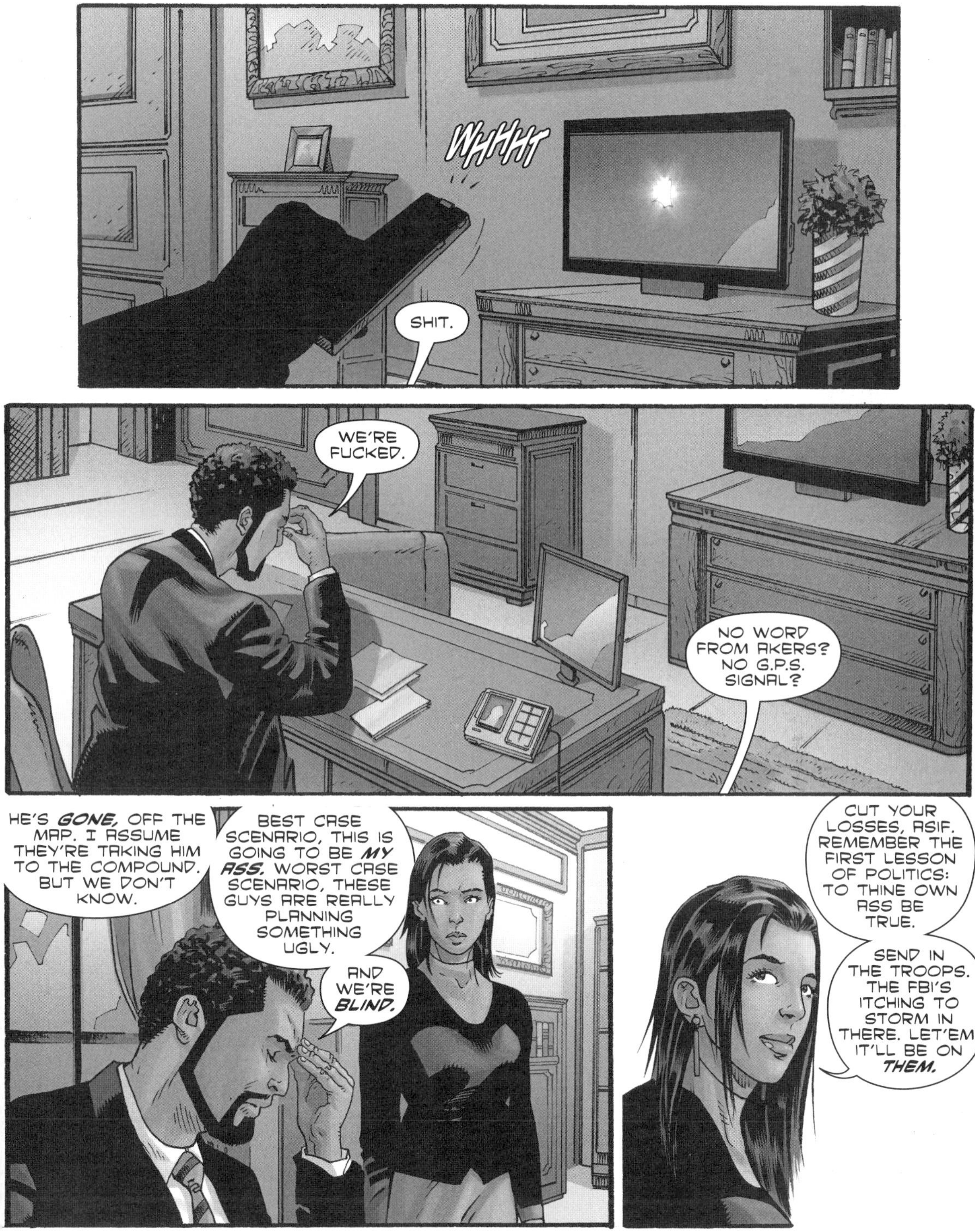
WHHHT
SHIT.
WE'RE FUCKED.
NO WORD FROM AKERS? NO G.P.S. SIGNAL?
HE'S GONE, OFF THE MAP. I ASSUME THEY'RE TAKING HIM TO THE COMPOUND. BUT WE DON'T KNOW.
BEST CASE SCENARIO, THIS IS GOING TO BE MY ASS. WORST CASE SCENARIO, THESE GUYS ARE REALLY PLANNING SOMETHING UGLY.
AND WE'RE BLIND.
CUT YOUR LOSSES, ASIF. REMEMBER THE FIRST LESSON OF POLITICS: TO THINE OWN ASS BE TRUE.
SEND IN THE TROOPS. THE FBI'S ITCHING TO STORM IN THERE. LET'EM. IT'LL BE ON THEM.

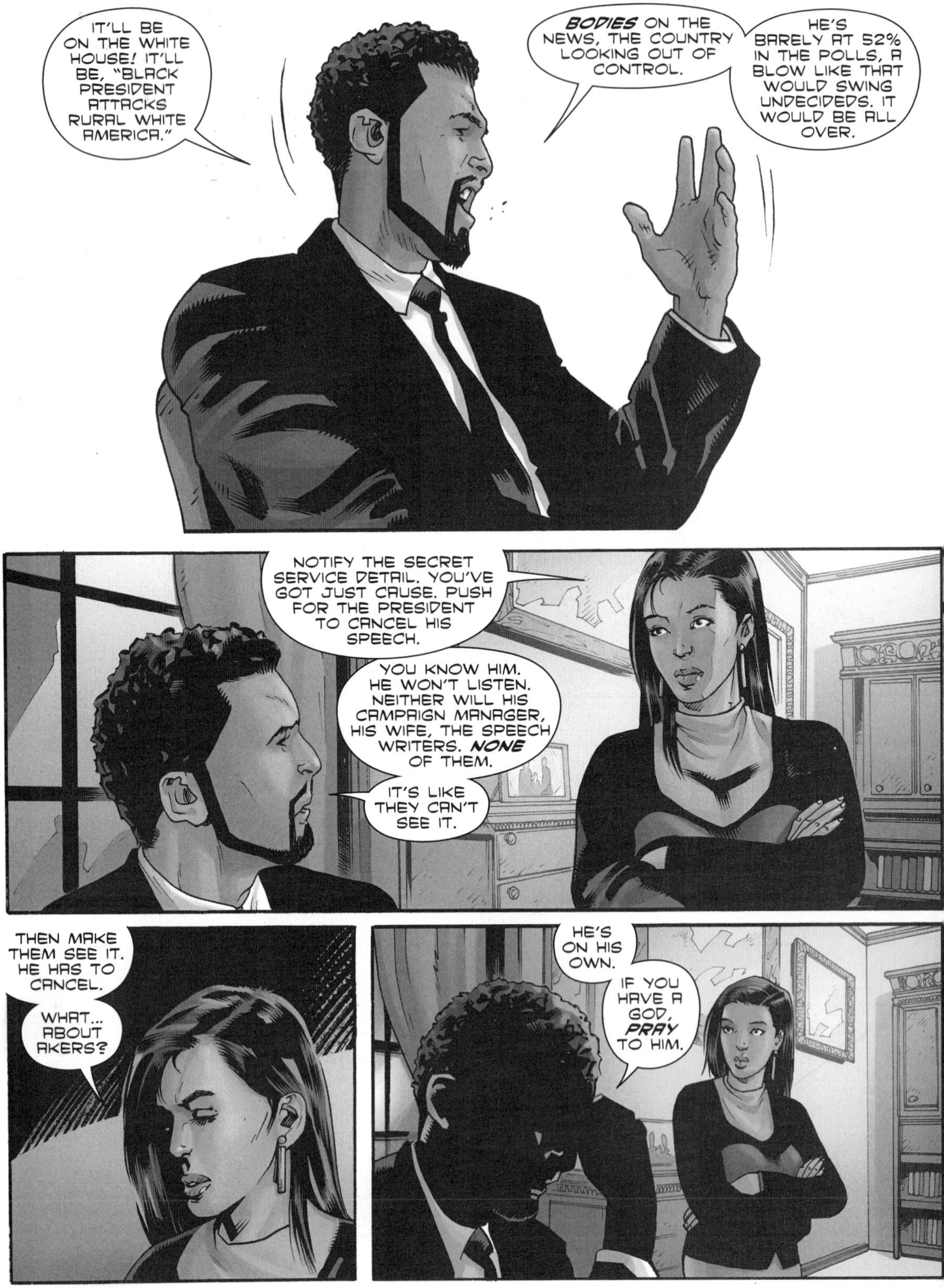
IT'LL BE ON THE WHITE HOUSE! IT'LL BE, "BLACK PRESIDENT ATTACKS RURAL WHITE AMERICA."
BODIES ON THE NEWS, THE COUNTRY LOOKING OUT OF CONTROL.
HE'S BARELY AT 52% IN THE POLLS, A BLOW LIKE THAT WOULD SWING UNDECIDEDS. IT WOULD BE ALL OVER.
NOTIFY THE SECRET SERVICE DETAIL. YOU'VE GOT JUST CAUSE. PUSH FOR THE PRESIDENT TO CANCEL HIS SPEECH.
YOU KNOW HIM. HE WON'T LISTEN. NEITHER WILL HIS CAMPAIGN MANAGER, HIS WIFE, THE SPEECH WRITERS. NONE OF THEM.
IT'S LIKE THEY CAN'T SEE IT.
THEN MAKE THEM SEE IT. HE HAS TO CANCEL.
WHAT... ABOUT AKERS?
HE'S ON HIS OWN.
IF YOU HAVE A GOD, PRAY TO HIM.

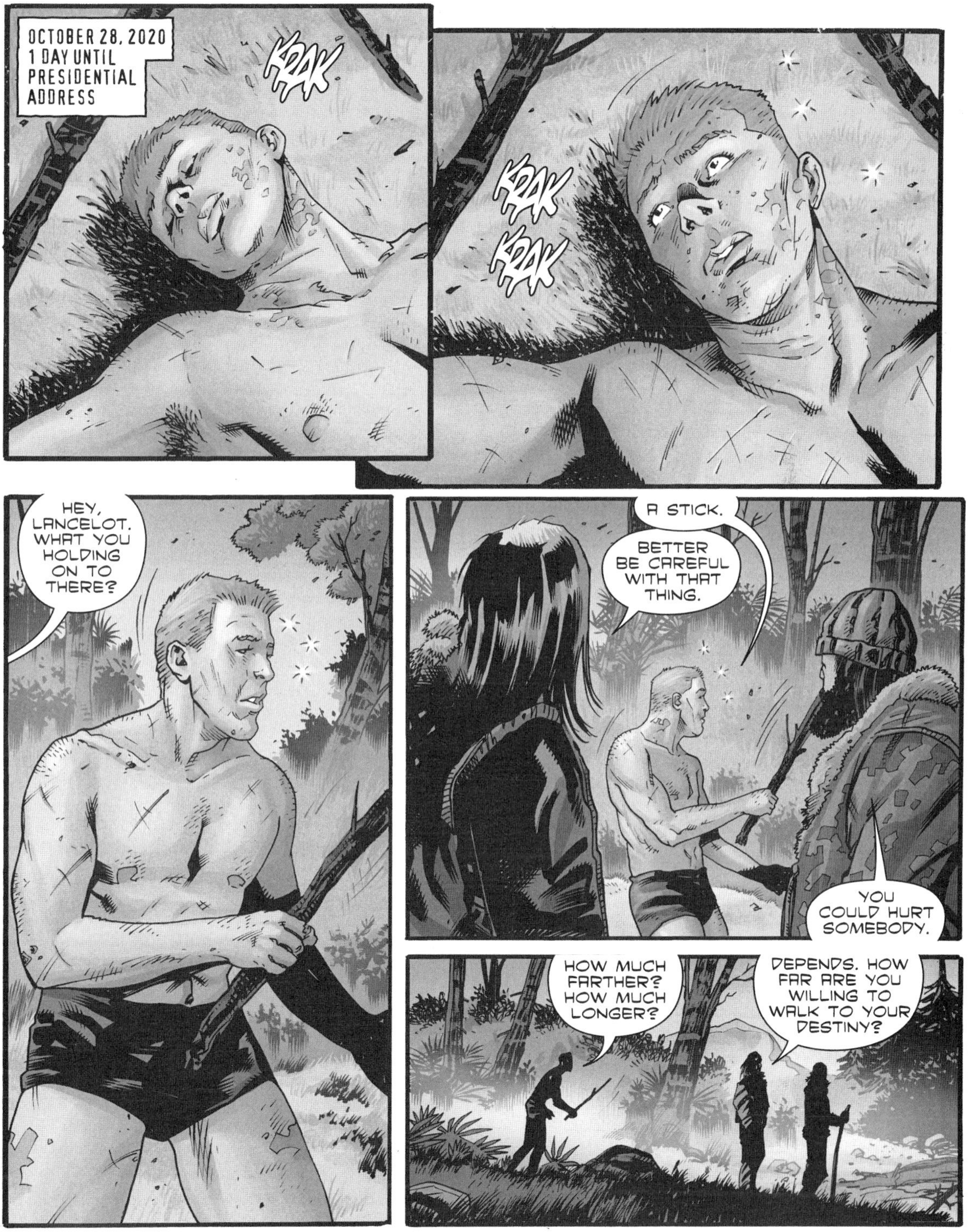
OCTOBER 28, 2020
1 DAY UNTIL PRESIDENTIAL ADDRESS
KRAK
KRAK
KRAK
HEY, LANCELOT. WHAT YOU HOLDING ON TO THERE?
A STICK.
BETTER BE CAREFUL WITH THAT THING.
YOU COULD HURT SOMEBODY.
HOW MUCH FARTHER? HOW MUCH LONGER?
DEPENDS. HOW FAR ARE YOU WILLING TO WALK TO YOUR DESTINY?

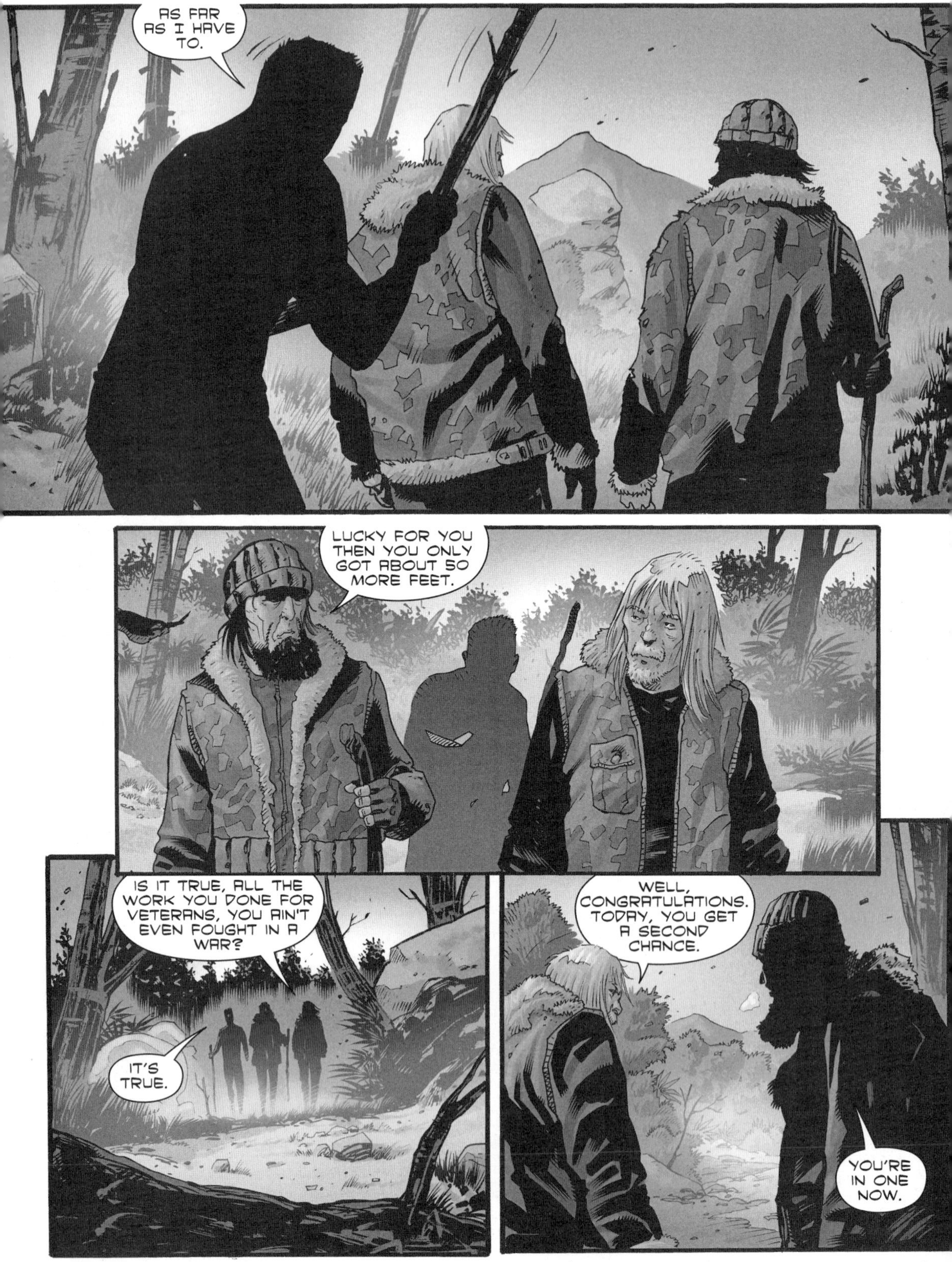
AS FAR AS I HAVE TO.
LUCKY FOR YOU THEN YOU ONLY GOT ABOUT 50 MORE FEET.
IS IT TRUE, ALL THE WORK YOU DONE FOR VETERANS, YOU AIN'T EVEN FOUGHT IN A WAR?
IT'S TRUE.
WELL, CONGRATULATIONS. TODAY, YOU GET A SECOND CHANCE.
YOU'RE IN ONE NOW.

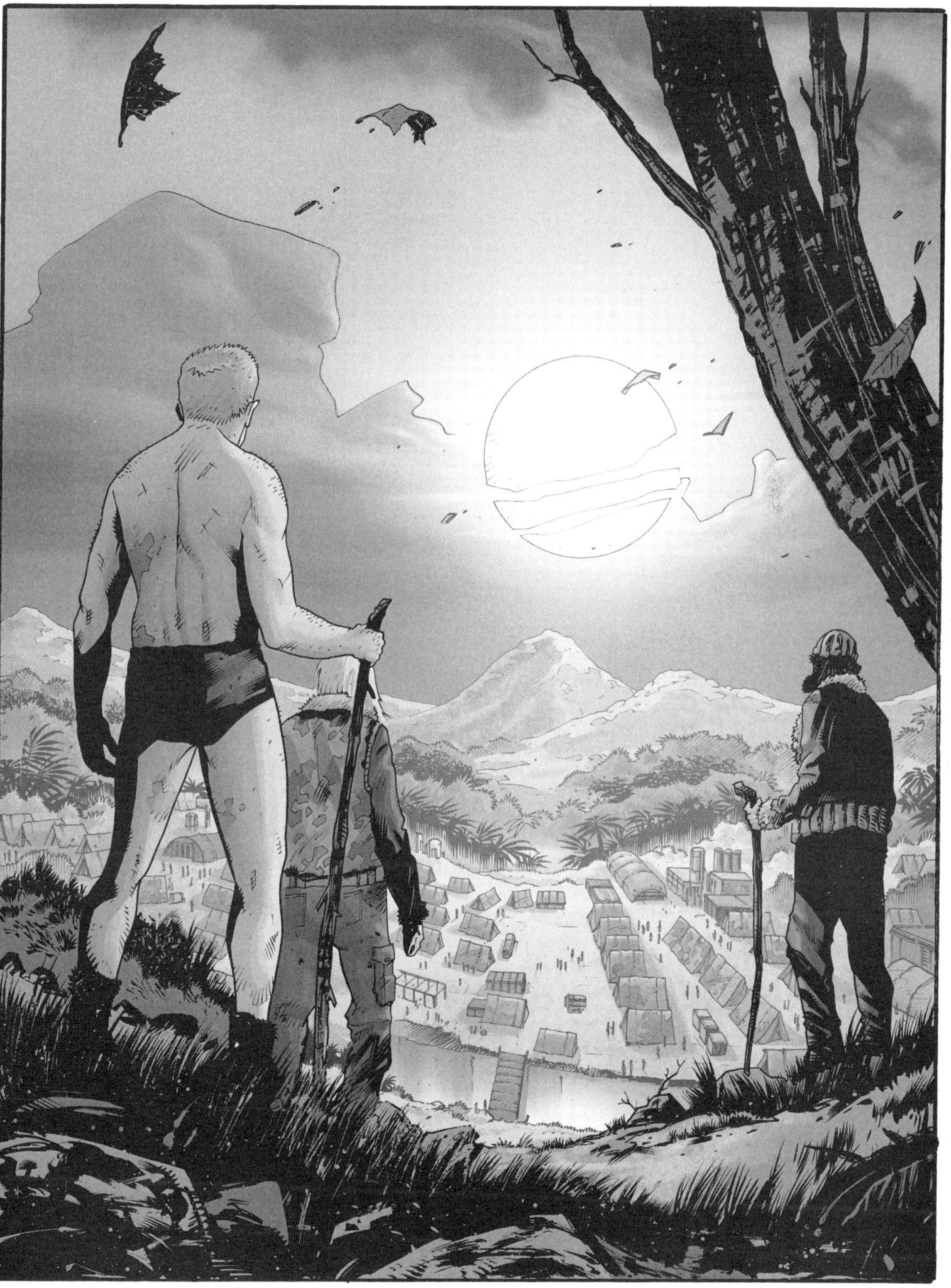

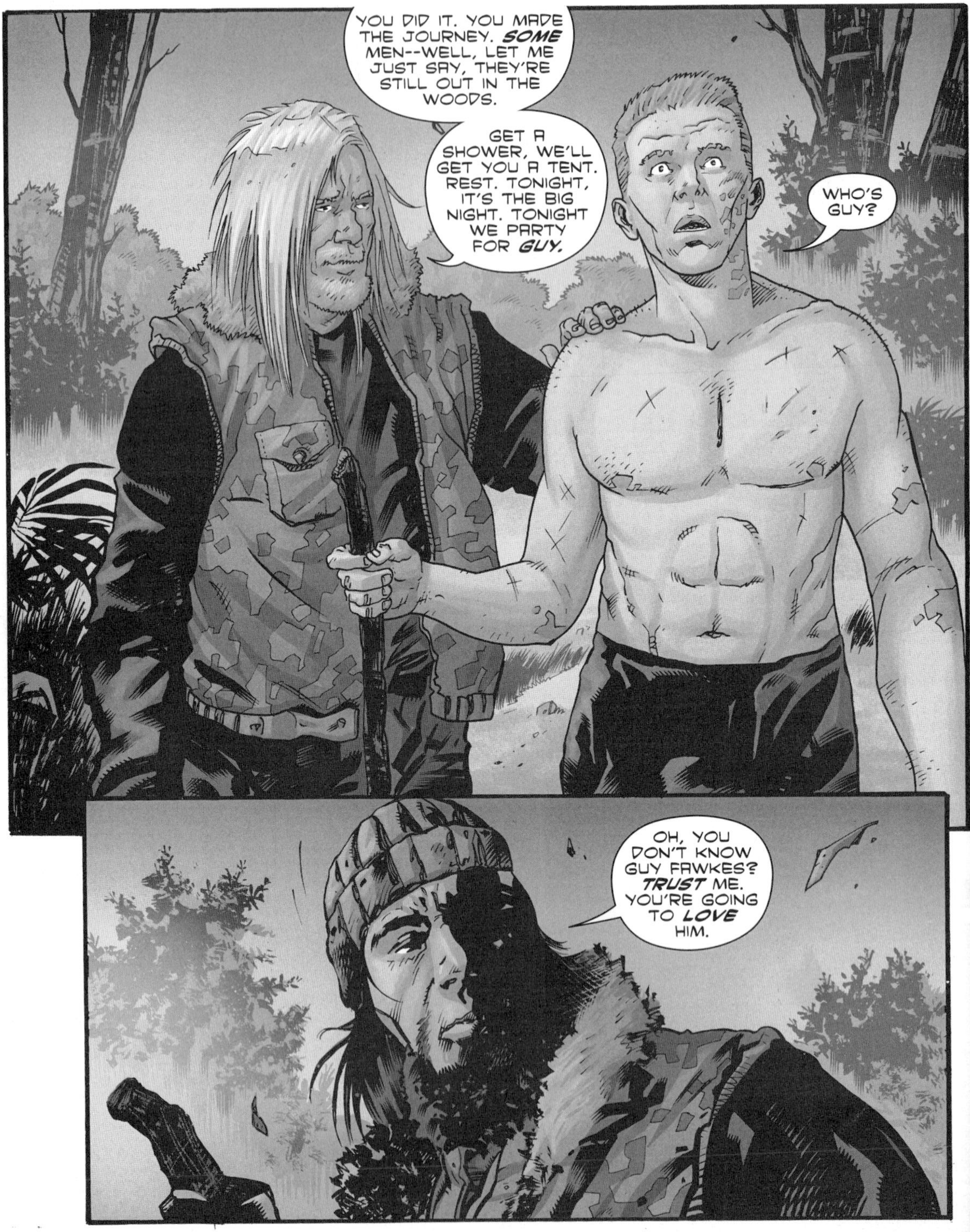
YOU DID IT. YOU MADE THE JOURNEY. *SOME* MEN--WELL, LET ME JUST SAY, THEY'RE STILL OUT IN THE WOODS.
GET A SHOWER, WE'LL GET YOU A TENT. REST. TONIGHT, IT'S THE BIG NIGHT. TONIGHT WE PARTY FOR *GUY.*
WHO'S GUY?
OH, YOU DON'T KNOW GUY FAWKES? *TRUST* ME. YOU'RE GOING TO *LOVE* HIM.

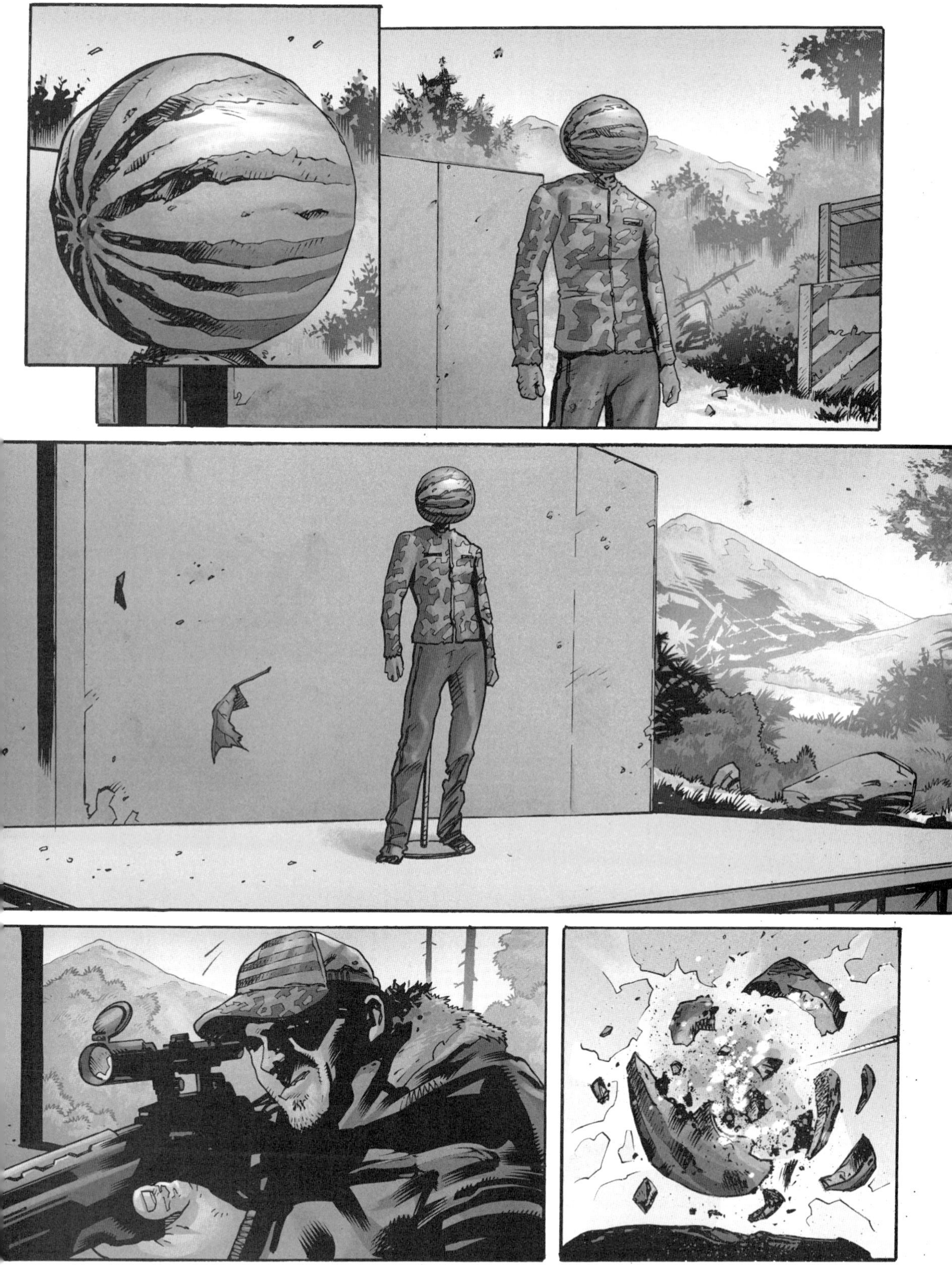

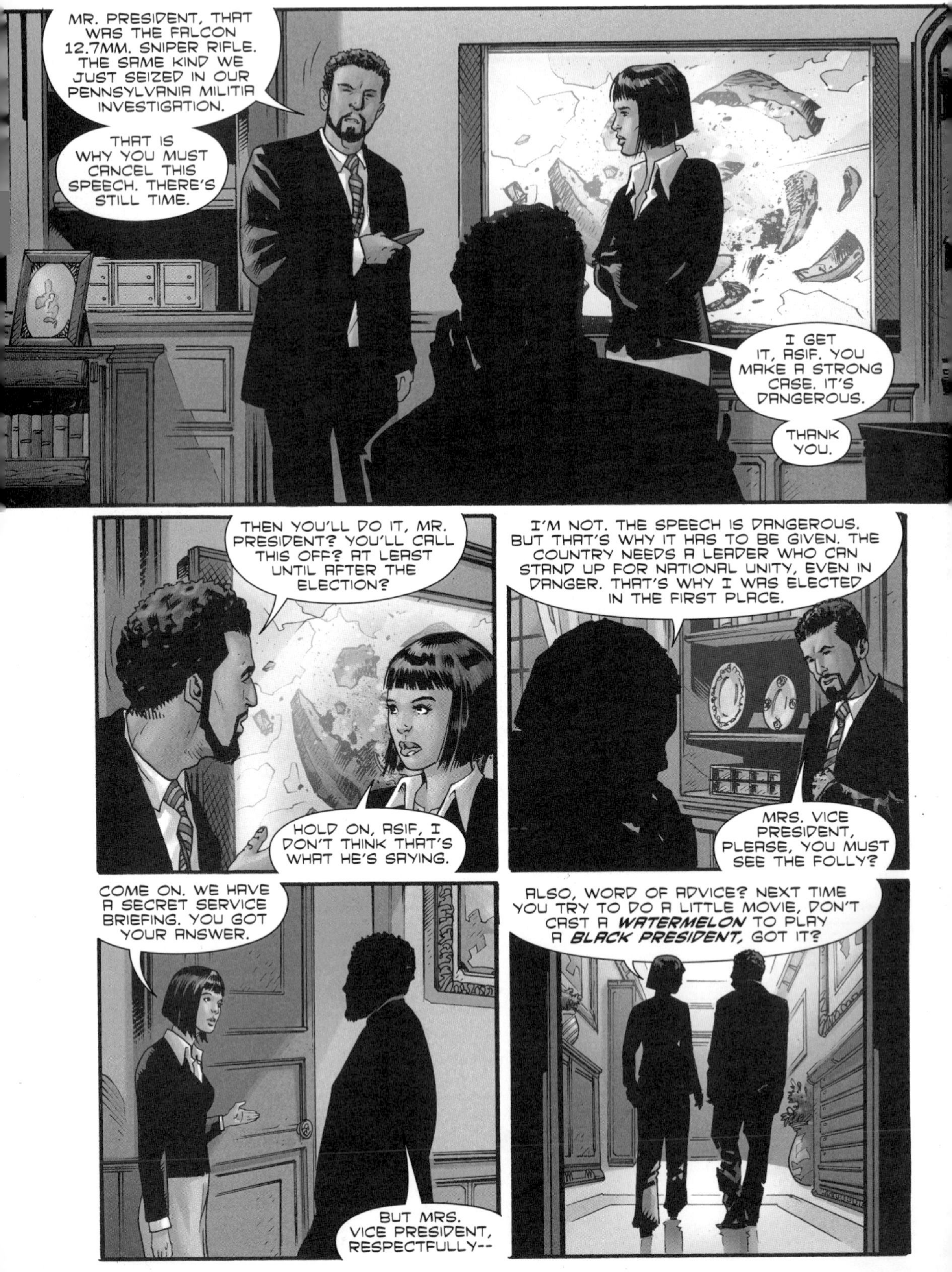
MR. PRESIDENT, THAT WAS THE FALCON 12.7MM. SNIPER RIFLE. THE SAME KIND WE JUST SEIZED IN OUR PENNSYLVANIA MILITIA INVESTIGATION.
THAT IS WHY YOU MUST CANCEL THIS SPEECH. THERE'S STILL TIME.
I GET IT, ASIF. YOU MAKE A STRONG CASE. IT'S DANGEROUS.
THANK YOU.
THEN YOU'LL DO IT, MR. PRESIDENT? YOU'LL CALL THIS OFF? AT LEAST UNTIL AFTER THE ELECTION?
HOLD ON, ASIF, I DON'T THINK THAT'S WHAT HE'S SAYING.
I'M NOT. THE SPEECH IS DANGEROUS. BUT THAT'S WHY IT HAS TO BE GIVEN. THE COUNTRY NEEDS A LEADER WHO CAN STAND UP FOR NATIONAL UNITY, EVEN IN DANGER. THAT'S WHY I WAS ELECTED IN THE FIRST PLACE.
MRS. VICE PRESIDENT, PLEASE, YOU MUST SEE THE FOLLY?
COME ON. WE HAVE A SECRET SERVICE BRIEFING. YOU GOT YOUR ANSWER.
BUT MRS. VICE PRESIDENT, RESPECTFULLY--
ALSO, WORD OF ADVICE? NEXT TIME YOU TRY TO DO A LITTLE MOVIE, DON'T CAST A ***WATERMELON*** TO PLAY A ***BLACK PRESIDENT,*** GOT IT?

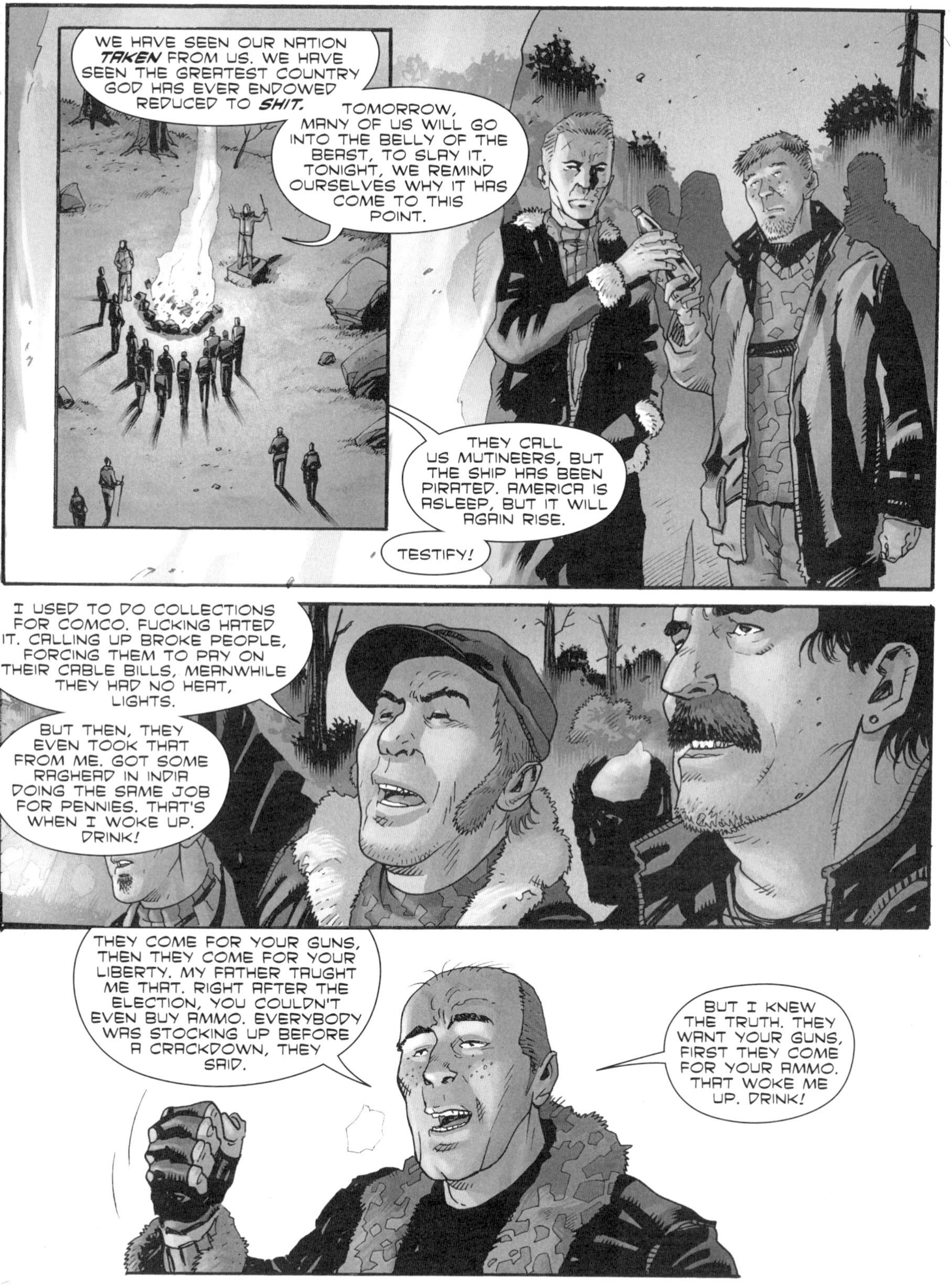
WE HAVE SEEN OUR NATION *TAKEN* FROM US. WE HAVE SEEN THE GREATEST COUNTRY GOD HAS EVER ENDOWED REDUCED TO *SHIT.*
TOMORROW, MANY OF US WILL GO INTO THE BELLY OF THE BEAST, TO SLAY IT. TONIGHT, WE REMIND OURSELVES WHY IT HAS COME TO THIS POINT.
THEY CALL US MUTINEERS, BUT THE SHIP HAS BEEN PIRATED. AMERICA IS ASLEEP, BUT IT WILL AGAIN RISE.
TESTIFY!
I USED TO DO COLLECTIONS FOR COMCO. FUCKING HATED IT. CALLING UP BROKE PEOPLE, FORCING THEM TO PAY ON THEIR CABLE BILLS, MEANWHILE THEY HAD NO HEAT, LIGHTS.
BUT THEN, THEY EVEN TOOK THAT FROM ME. GOT SOME RAGHEAD IN INDIA DOING THE SAME JOB FOR PENNIES. THAT'S WHEN I WOKE UP. DRINK!
THEY COME FOR YOUR GUNS, THEN THEY COME FOR YOUR LIBERTY. MY FATHER TAUGHT ME THAT. RIGHT AFTER THE ELECTION, YOU COULDN'T EVEN BUY AMMO. EVERYBODY WAS STOCKING UP BEFORE A CRACKDOWN, THEY SAID.
BUT I KNEW THE TRUTH. THEY WANT YOUR GUNS, FIRST THEY COME FOR YOUR AMMO. THAT WOKE ME UP. DRINK!

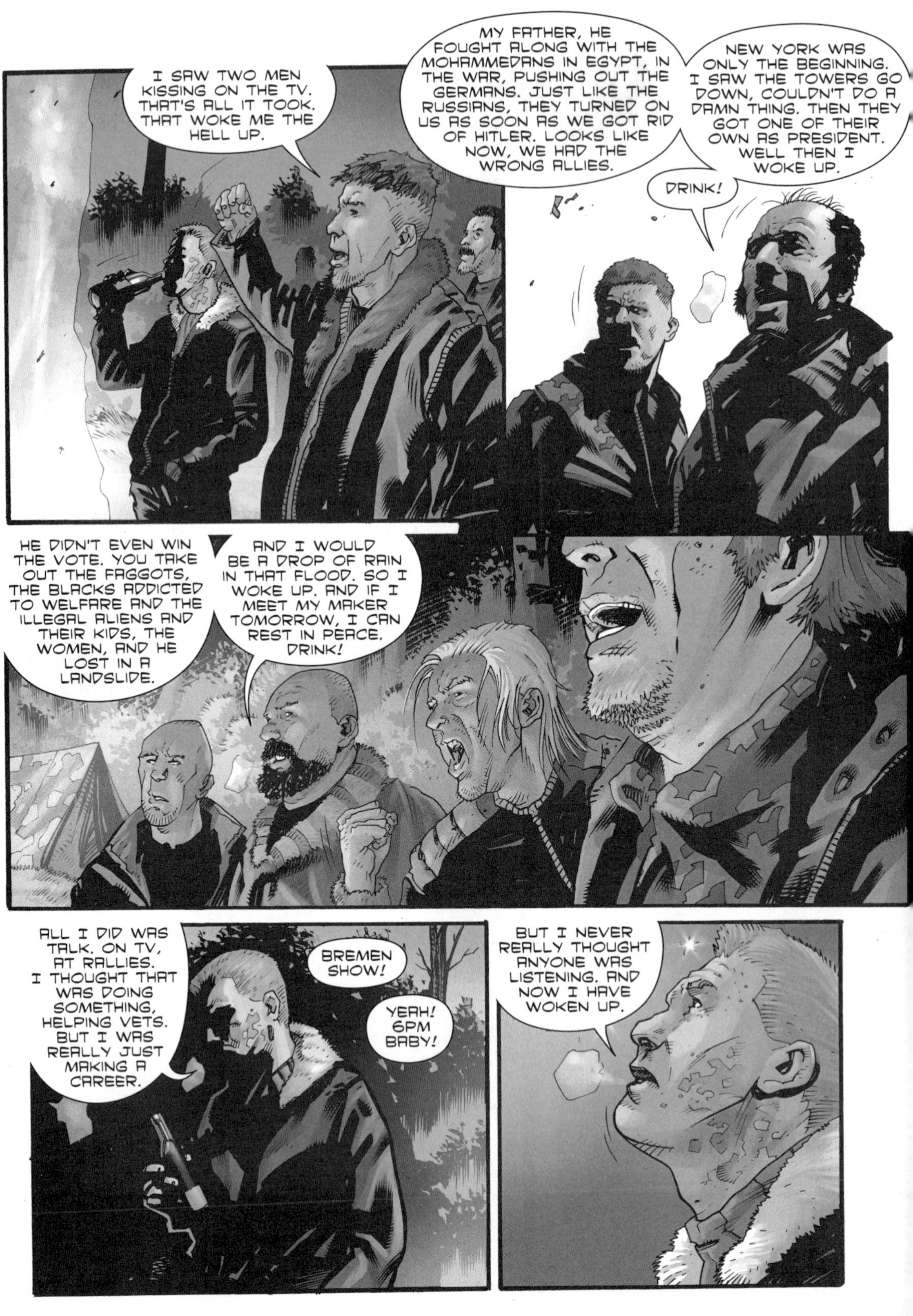
I SAW TWO MEN KISSING ON THE TV. THAT'S ALL IT TOOK. THAT WOKE ME THE HELL UP.
MY FATHER, HE FOUGHT ALONG WITH THE MOHAMMEDANS IN EGYPT, IN THE WAR, PUSHING OUT THE GERMANS. JUST LIKE THE RUSSIANS, THEY TURNED ON US AS SOON AS WE GOT RID OF HITLER. LOOKS LIKE NOW, WE HAD THE WRONG ALLIES.
NEW YORK WAS ONLY THE BEGINNING. I SAW THE TOWERS GO DOWN, COULDN'T DO A DAMN THING. THEN THEY GOT ONE OF THEIR OWN AS PRESIDENT. WELL THEN I WOKE UP.
DRINK!
HE DIDN'T EVEN WIN THE VOTE. YOU TAKE OUT THE FAGGOTS, THE BLACKS ADDICTED TO WELFARE AND THE ILLEGAL ALIENS AND THEIR KIDS, THE WOMEN, AND HE LOST IN A LANDSLIDE.
AND I WOULD BE A DROP OF RAIN IN THAT FLOOD. SO I WOKE UP. AND IF I MEET MY MAKER TOMORROW, I CAN REST IN PEACE. DRINK!
ALL I DID WAS TALK. ON TV, AT RALLIES. I THOUGHT THAT WAS DOING SOMETHING, HELPING VETS. BUT I WAS REALLY JUST MAKING A CAREER.
BREMEN SHOW!
YEAH! 6PM BABY!
BUT I NEVER REALLY THOUGHT ANYONE WAS LISTENING. AND NOW I HAVE WOKEN UP.

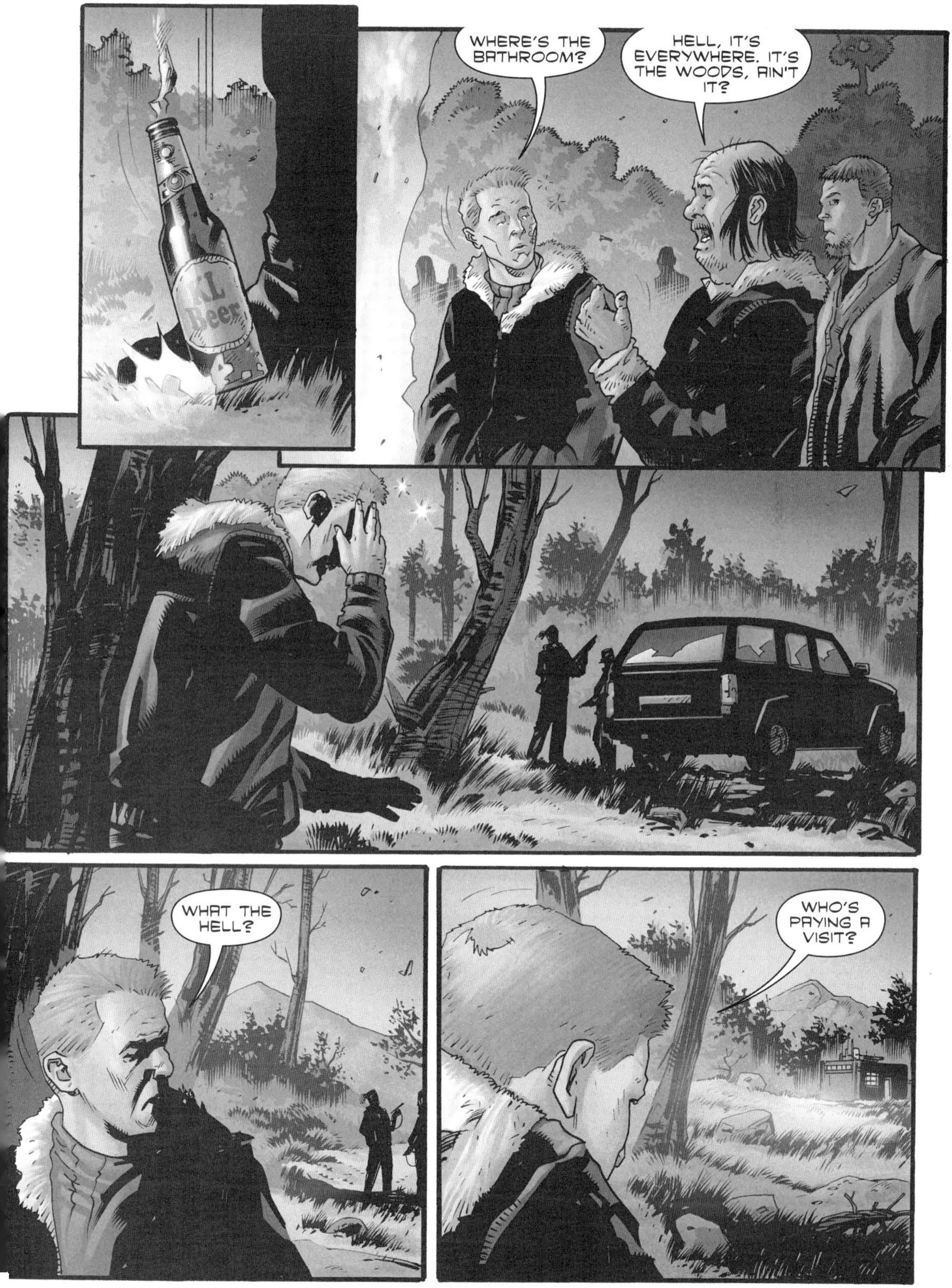
XL Beer
WHERE'S THE BATHROOM?
HELL, IT'S EVERYWHERE. IT'S THE WOODS, AIN'T IT?
WHAT THE HELL?
WHO'S PAYING A VISIT?

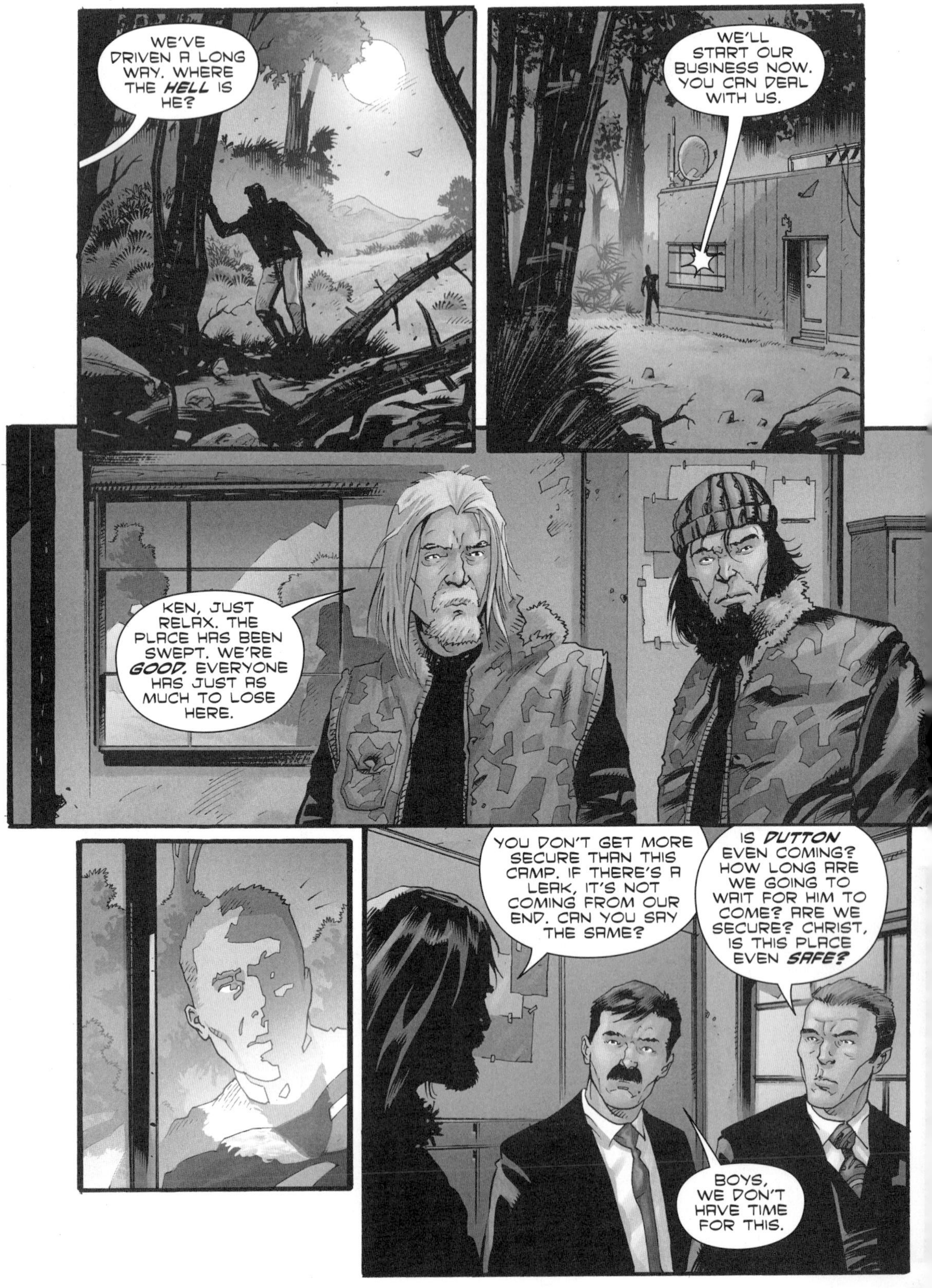
WE'VE DRIVEN A LONG WAY. WHERE THE *HELL* IS HE?
WE'LL START OUR BUSINESS NOW. YOU CAN DEAL WITH US.
KEN, JUST RELAX. THE PLACE HAS BEEN SWEPT. WE'RE *GOOD.* EVERYONE HAS JUST AS MUCH TO LOSE HERE.
YOU DON'T GET MORE SECURE THAN THIS CAMP. IF THERE'S A LEAK, IT'S NOT COMING FROM OUR END. CAN YOU SAY THE SAME?
IS *DUTTON* EVEN COMING? HOW LONG ARE WE GOING TO WAIT FOR HIM TO COME? ARE WE SECURE? CHRIST, IS THIS PLACE EVEN *SAFE?*
BOYS, WE DON'T HAVE TIME FOR THIS.

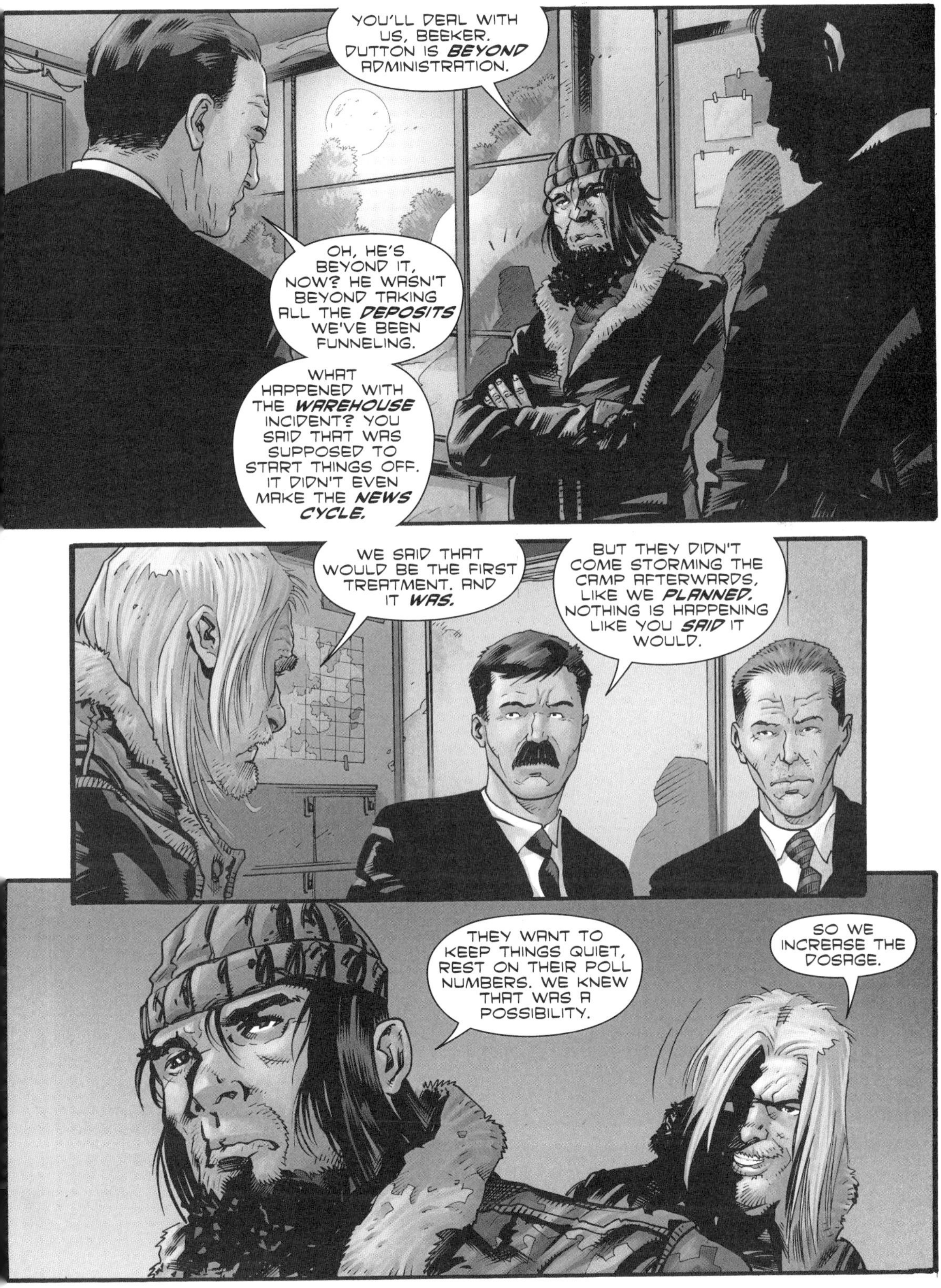
YOU'LL DEAL WITH US, BEEKER. DUTTON IS BEYOND ADMINISTRATION.
OH, HE'S BEYOND IT, NOW? HE WASN'T BEYOND TAKING ALL THE DEPOSITS WE'VE BEEN FUNNELING.
WHAT HAPPENED WITH THE WAREHOUSE INCIDENT? YOU SAID THAT WAS SUPPOSED TO START THINGS OFF. IT DIDN'T EVEN MAKE THE NEWS CYCLE.
WE SAID THAT WOULD BE THE FIRST TREATMENT. AND IT WAS.
BUT THEY DIDN'T COME STORMING THE CAMP AFTERWARDS, LIKE WE PLANNED. NOTHING IS HAPPENING LIKE YOU SAID IT WOULD.
THEY WANT TO KEEP THINGS QUIET, REST ON THEIR POLL NUMBERS. WE KNEW THAT WAS A POSSIBILITY.
SO WE INCREASE THE DOSAGE.

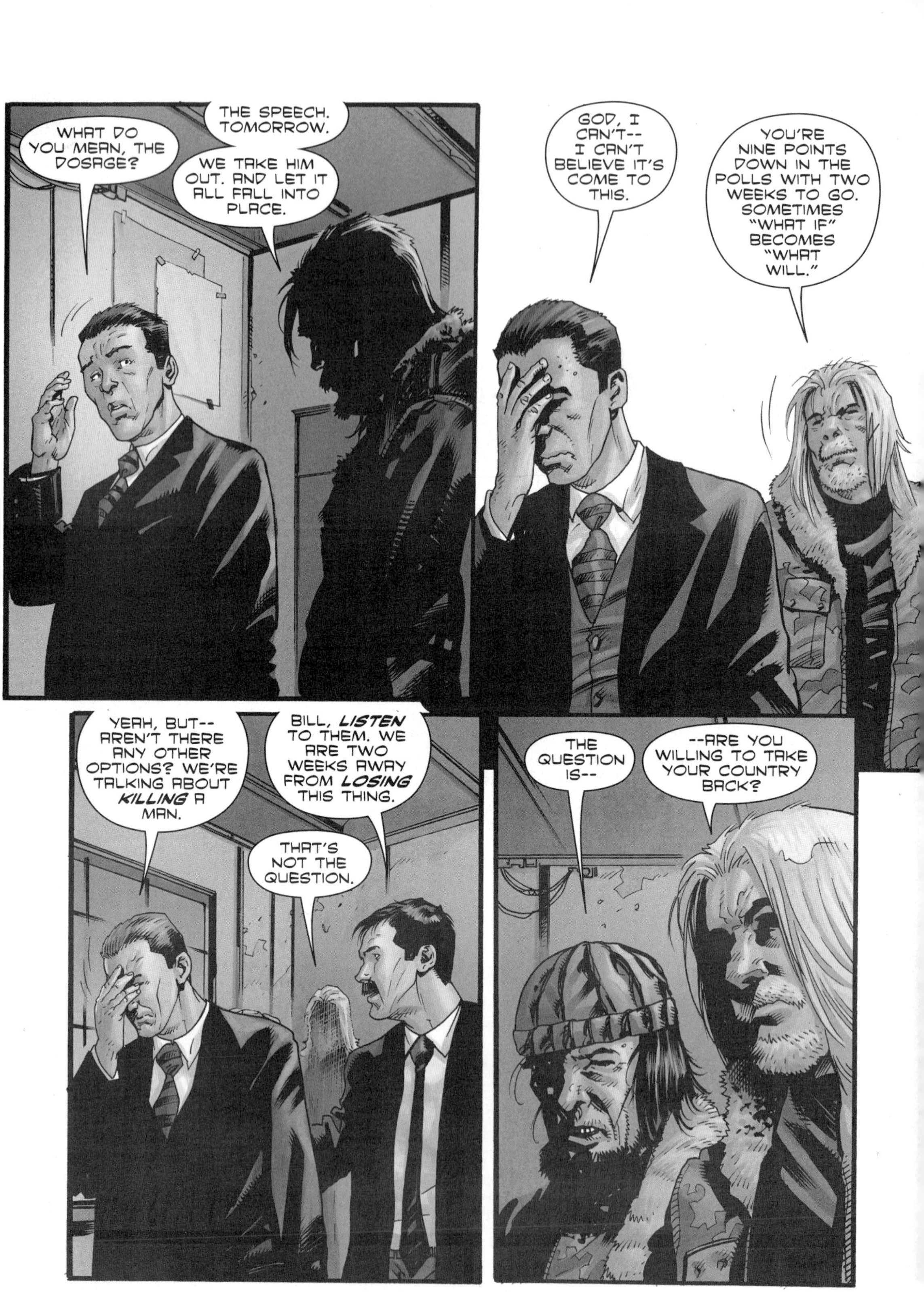
WHAT DO YOU MEAN, THE DOSAGE?
THE SPEECH. TOMORROW.
WE TAKE HIM OUT. AND LET IT ALL FALL INTO PLACE.
GOD, I CAN'T-- I CAN'T BELIEVE IT'S COME TO THIS.
YOU'RE NINE POINTS DOWN IN THE POLLS WITH TWO WEEKS TO GO. SOMETIMES "WHAT IF" BECOMES "WHAT WILL."
YEAH, BUT-- AREN'T THERE ANY OTHER OPTIONS? WE'RE TALKING ABOUT KILLING A MAN.
BILL, LISTEN TO THEM. WE ARE TWO WEEKS AWAY FROM LOSING THIS THING.
THAT'S NOT THE QUESTION.
THE QUESTION IS--
--ARE YOU WILLING TO TAKE YOUR COUNTRY BACK?

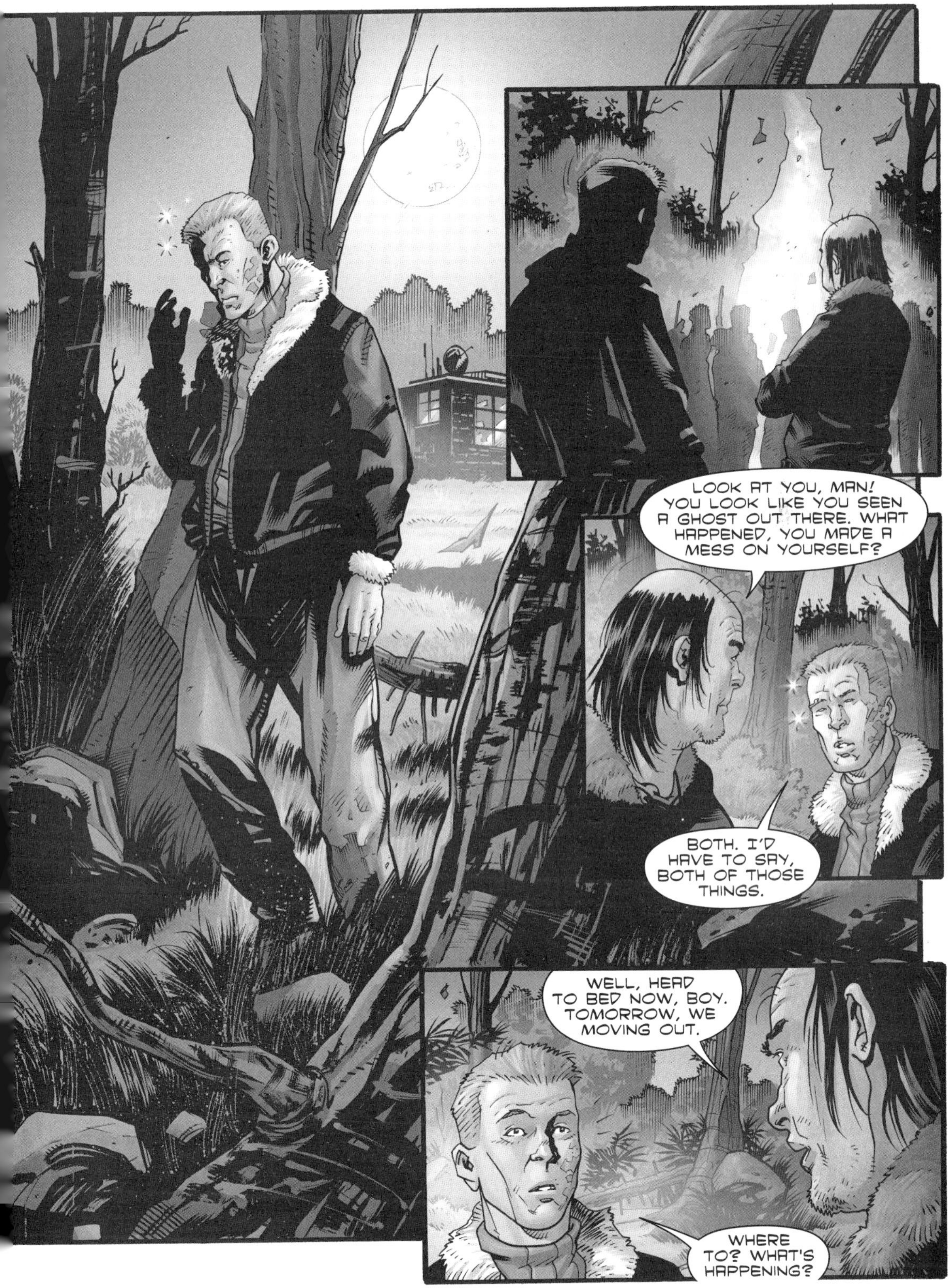
LOOK AT YOU, MAN! YOU LOOK LIKE YOU SEEN A GHOST OUT THERE. WHAT HAPPENED, YOU MADE A MESS ON YOURSELF?
BOTH. I'D HAVE TO SAY, BOTH OF THOSE THINGS.
WELL, HEAD TO BED NOW, BOY. TOMORROW, WE MOVING OUT.
WHERE TO? WHAT'S HAPPENING?

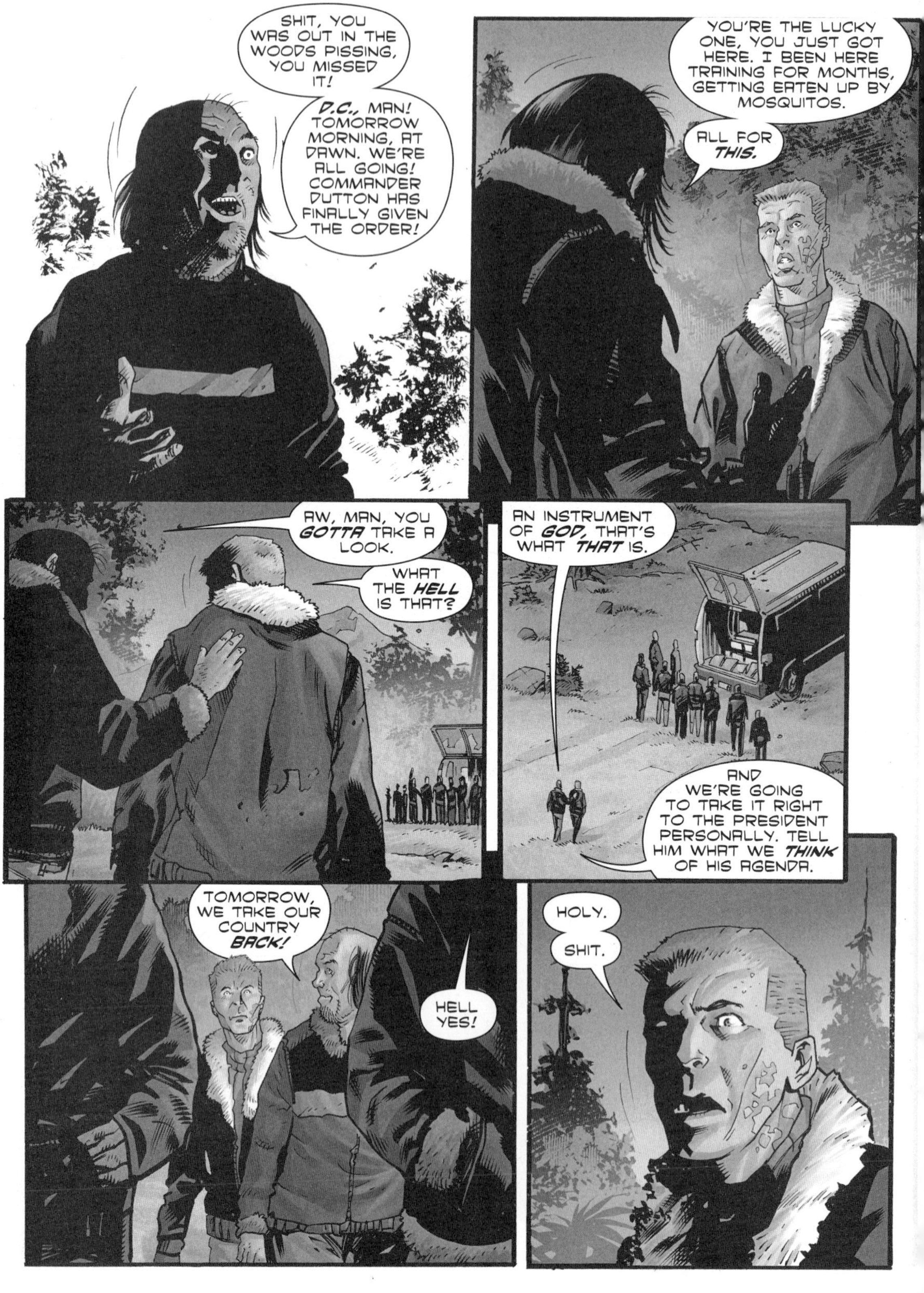
SHIT, YOU WAS OUT IN THE WOODS PISSING, YOU MISSED IT!
D.C., MAN! TOMORROW MORNING, AT DAWN. WE'RE ALL GOING! COMMANDER DUTTON HAS FINALLY GIVEN THE ORDER!
YOU'RE THE LUCKY ONE, YOU JUST GOT HERE. I BEEN HERE TRAINING FOR MONTHS, GETTING EATEN UP BY MOSQUITOS.
ALL FOR THIS.
AW, MAN, YOU GOTTA TAKE A LOOK.
WHAT THE HELL IS THAT?
AN INSTRUMENT OF GOD, THAT'S WHAT THAT IS.
AND WE'RE GOING TO TAKE IT RIGHT TO THE PRESIDENT PERSONALLY. TELL HIM WHAT WE THINK OF HIS AGENDA.
TOMORROW, WE TAKE OUR COUNTRY BACK!
HELL YES!
HOLY.
SHIT.

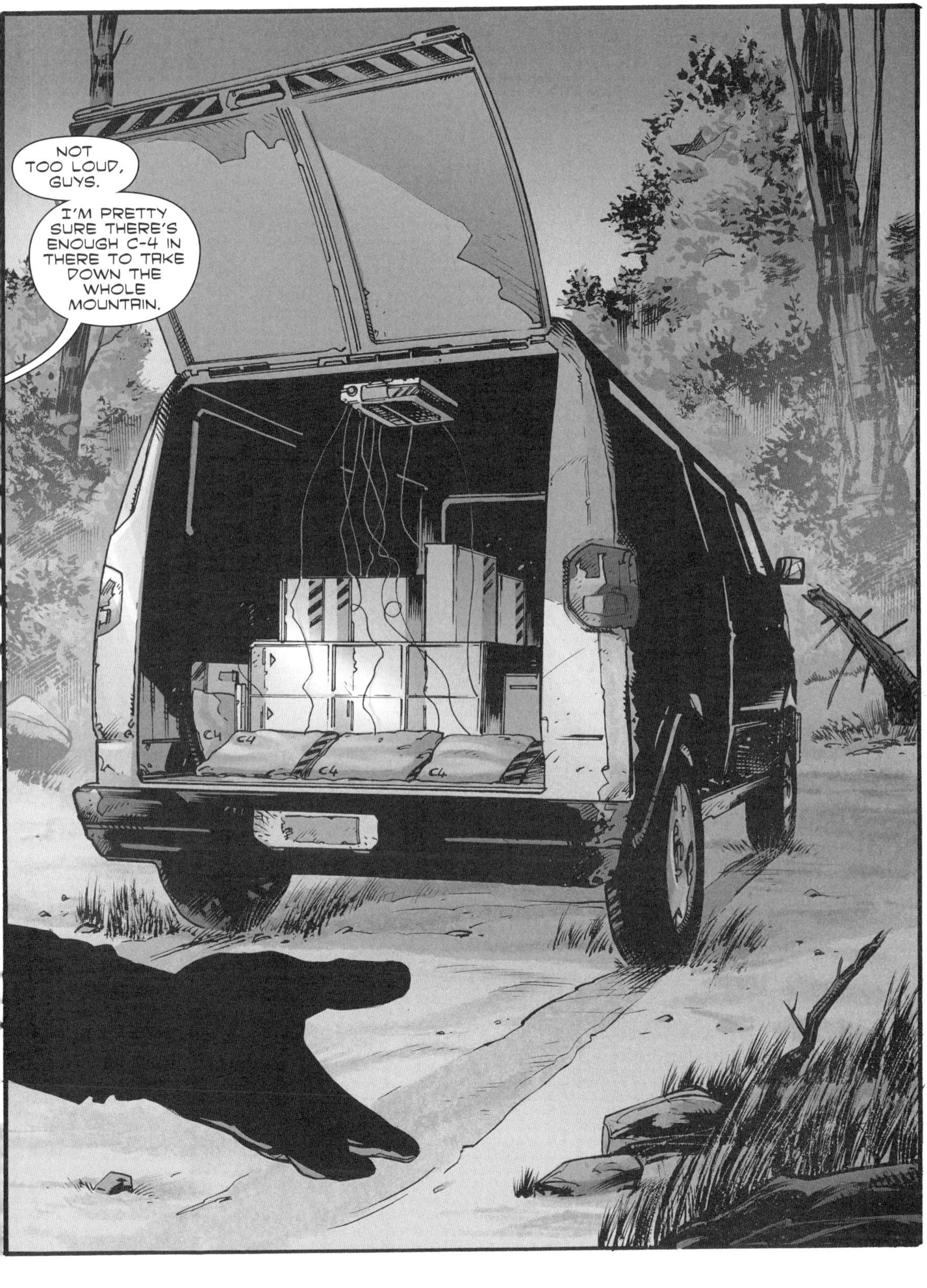
NOT TOO LOUD, GUYS.
I'M PRETTY SURE THERE'S ENOUGH C-4 IN THERE TO TAKE DOWN THE WHOLE MOUNTAIN.
C4
C4
C4
C4

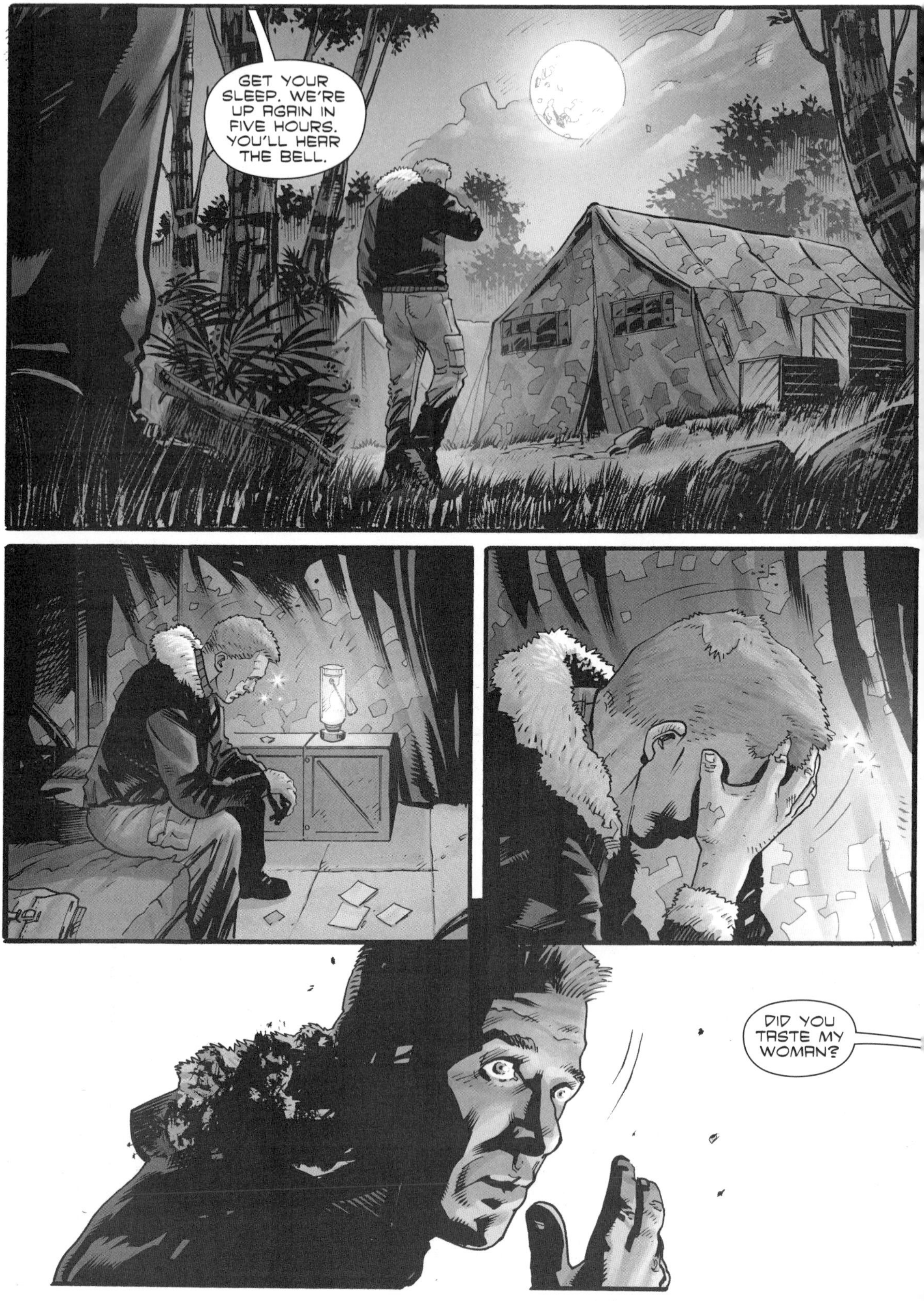
GET YOUR SLEEP. WE'RE UP AGAIN IN FIVE HOURS. YOU'LL HEAR THE BELL.
DID YOU TASTE MY WOMAN?

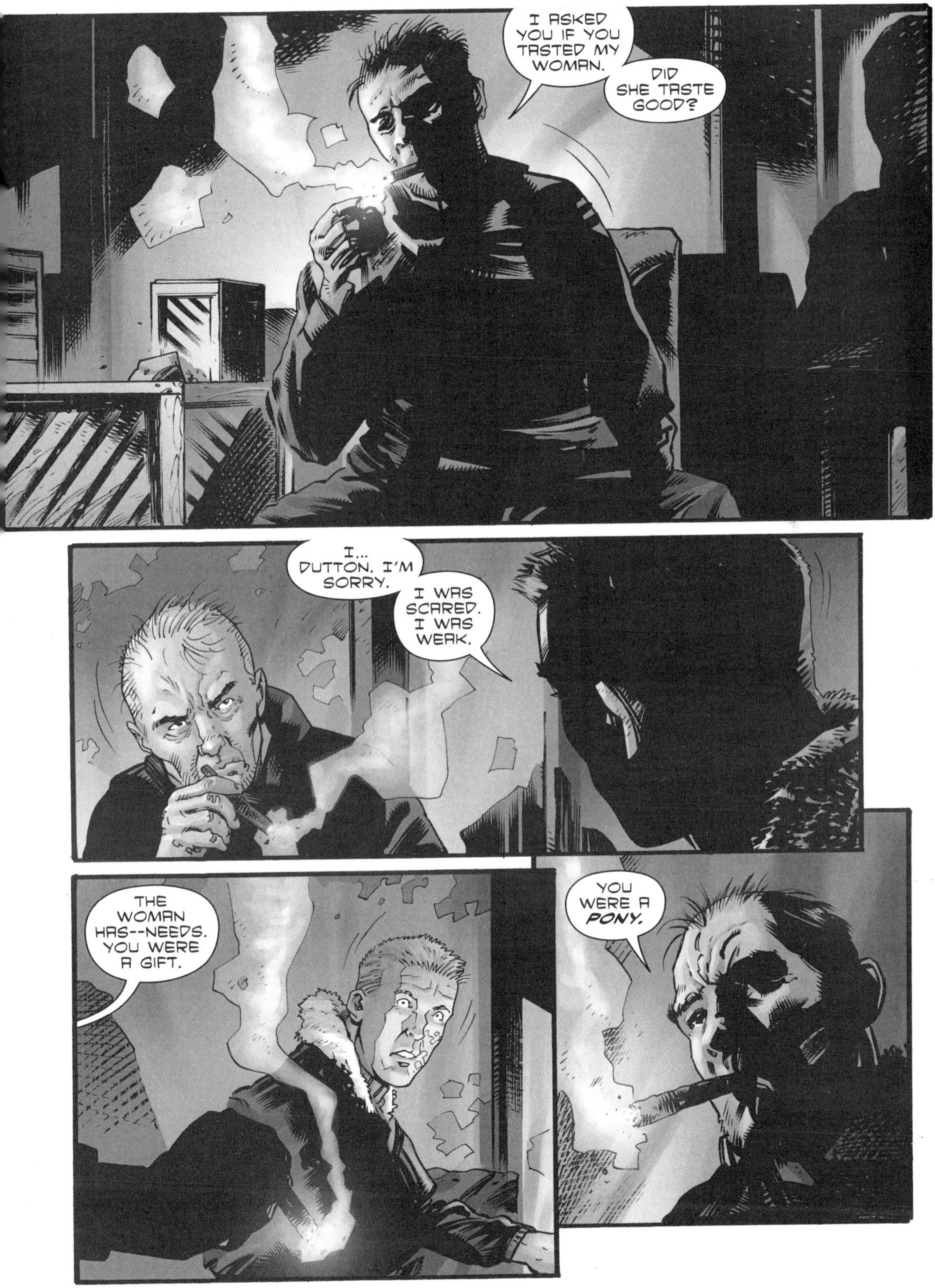
I ASKED YOU IF YOU TASTED MY WOMAN.
DID SHE TASTE GOOD?
I... DUTTON. I'M SORRY.
I WAS SCARED. I WAS WEAK.
THE WOMAN HAS--NEEDS. YOU WERE A GIFT.
YOU WERE A *PONY.*

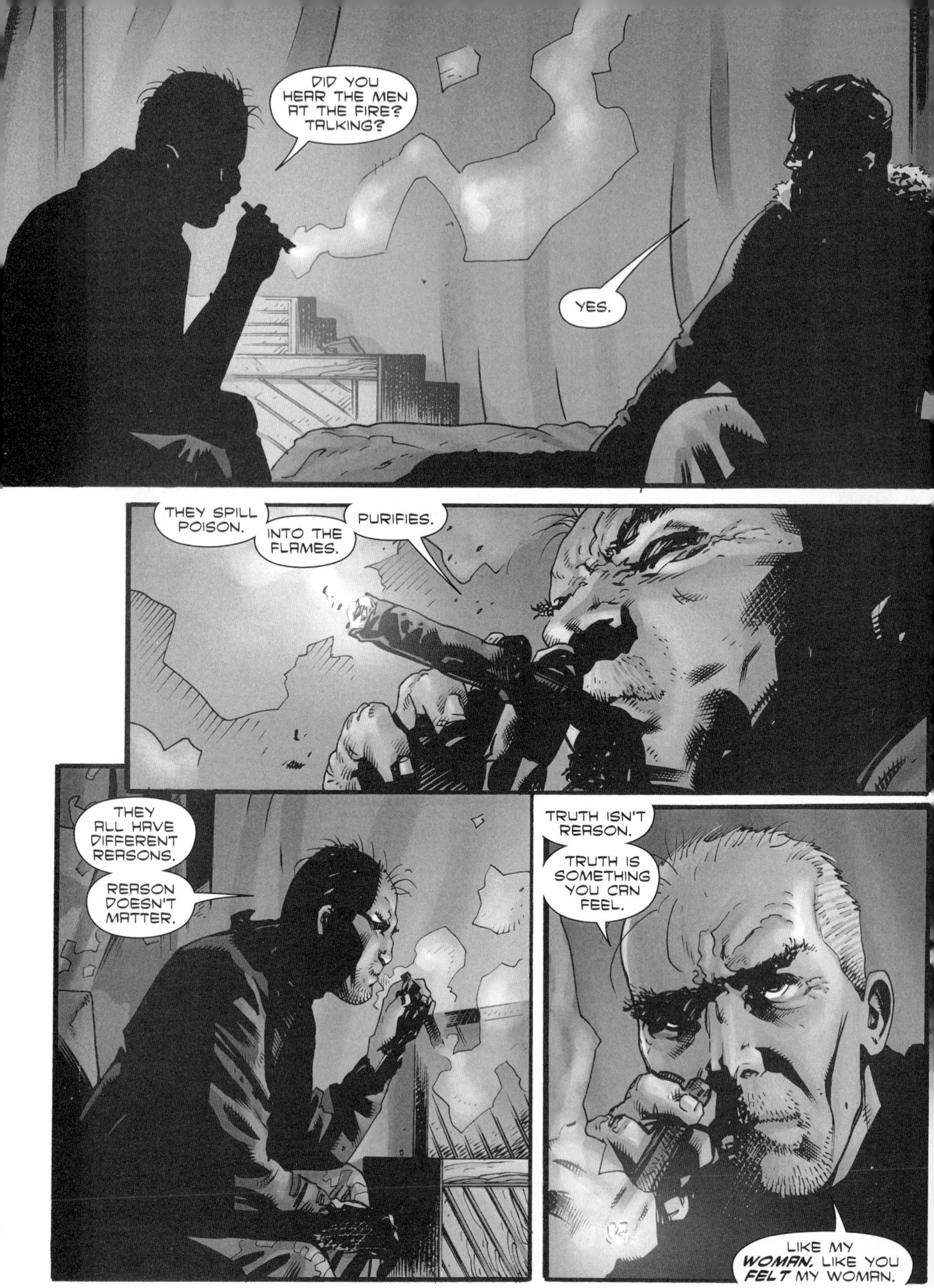
DID YOU HEAR THE MEN AT THE FIRE? TALKING?
YES.
THEY SPILL POISON.
INTO THE FLAMES.
PURIFIES.
THEY ALL HAVE DIFFERENT REASONS.
REASON DOESN'T MATTER.
TRUTH ISN'T REASON.
TRUTH IS SOMETHING YOU CAN FEEL.
LIKE MY WOMAN. LIKE YOU FELT MY WOMAN.

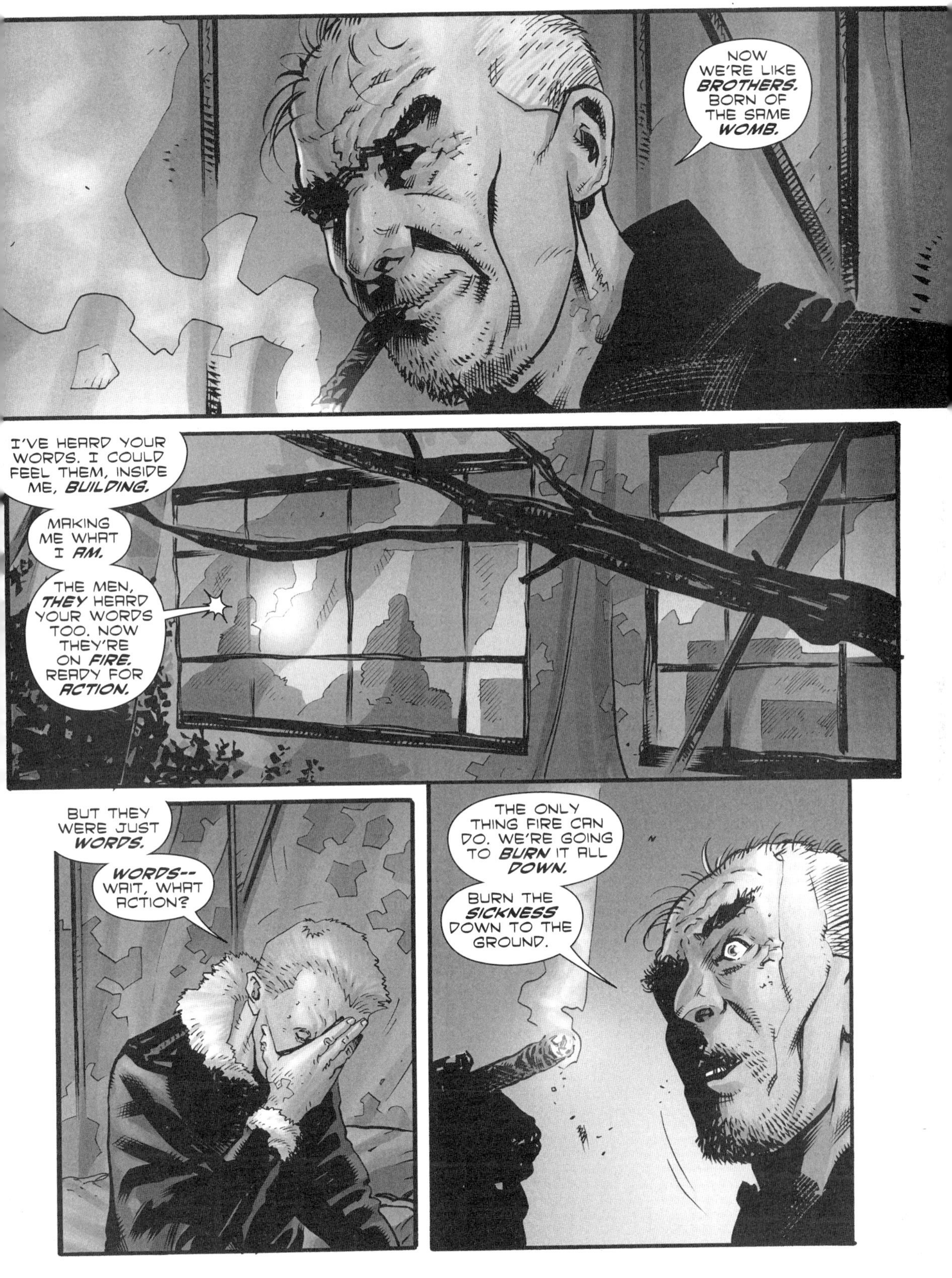
NOW WE'RE LIKE BROTHERS. BORN OF THE SAME WOMB.
I'VE HEARD YOUR WORDS. I COULD FEEL THEM, INSIDE ME, BUILDING.
MAKING ME WHAT I AM.
THE MEN, THEY HEARD YOUR WORDS TOO. NOW THEY'RE ON FIRE. READY FOR ACTION.
BUT THEY WERE JUST WORDS.
WORDS-- WAIT, WHAT ACTION?
THE ONLY THING FIRE CAN DO. WE'RE GOING TO BURN IT ALL DOWN.
BURN THE SICKNESS DOWN TO THE GROUND.

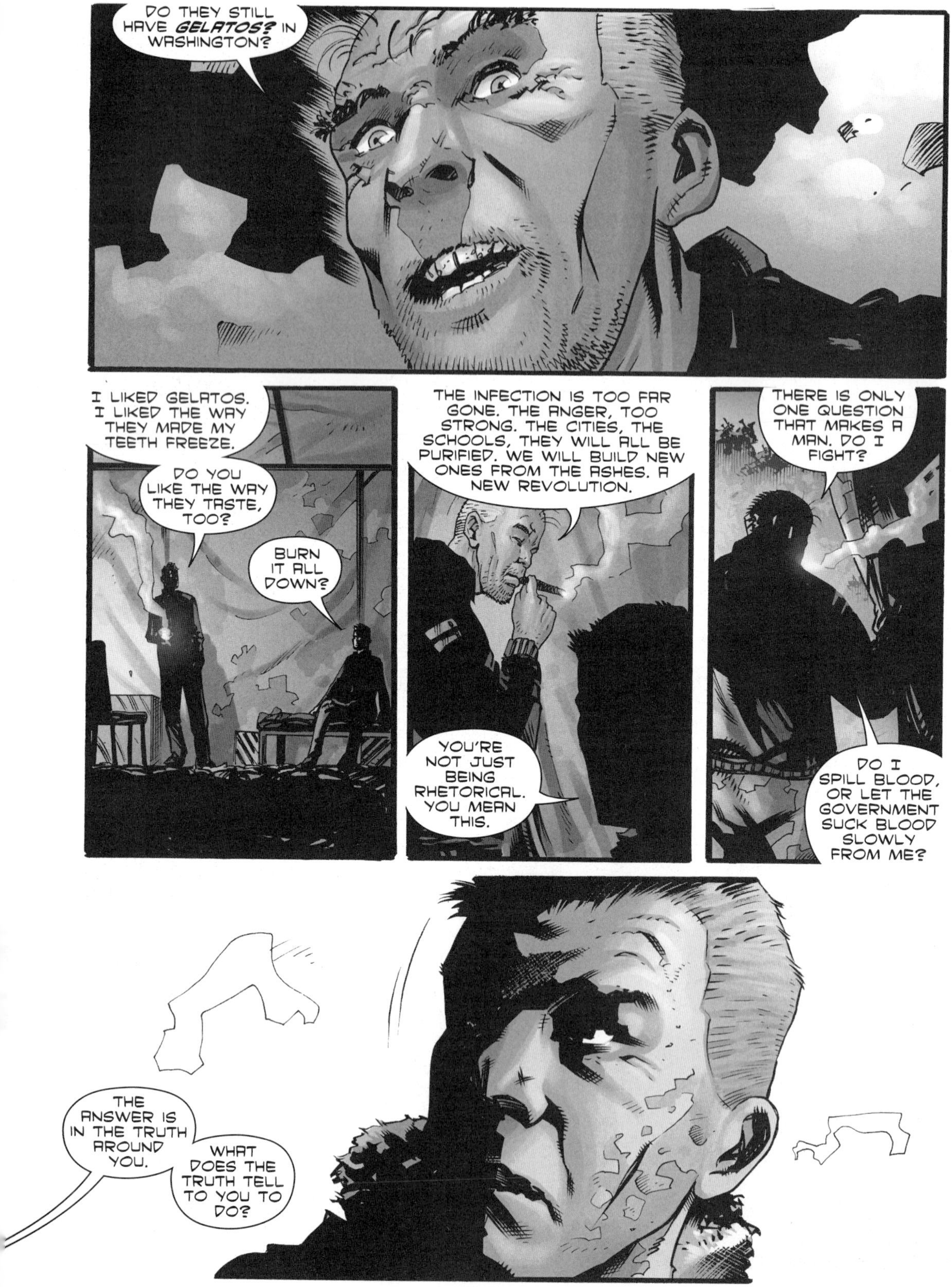
DO THEY STILL HAVE *GELATOS?* IN WASHINGTON?
I LIKED GELATOS. I LIKED THE WAY THEY MADE MY TEETH FREEZE.
DO YOU LIKE THE WAY THEY TASTE, TOO?
BURN IT ALL DOWN?
THE INFECTION IS TOO FAR GONE. THE ANGER, TOO STRONG. THE CITIES, THE SCHOOLS, THEY WILL ALL BE PURIFIED. WE WILL BUILD NEW ONES FROM THE ASHES. A NEW REVOLUTION.
YOU'RE NOT JUST BEING RHETORICAL. YOU MEAN THIS.
THERE IS ONLY ONE QUESTION THAT MAKES A MAN. DO I FIGHT?
DO I SPILL BLOOD, OR LET THE GOVERNMENT SUCK BLOOD SLOWLY FROM ME?
THE ANSWER IS IN THE TRUTH AROUND YOU.
WHAT DOES THE TRUTH TELL TO YOU TO DO?

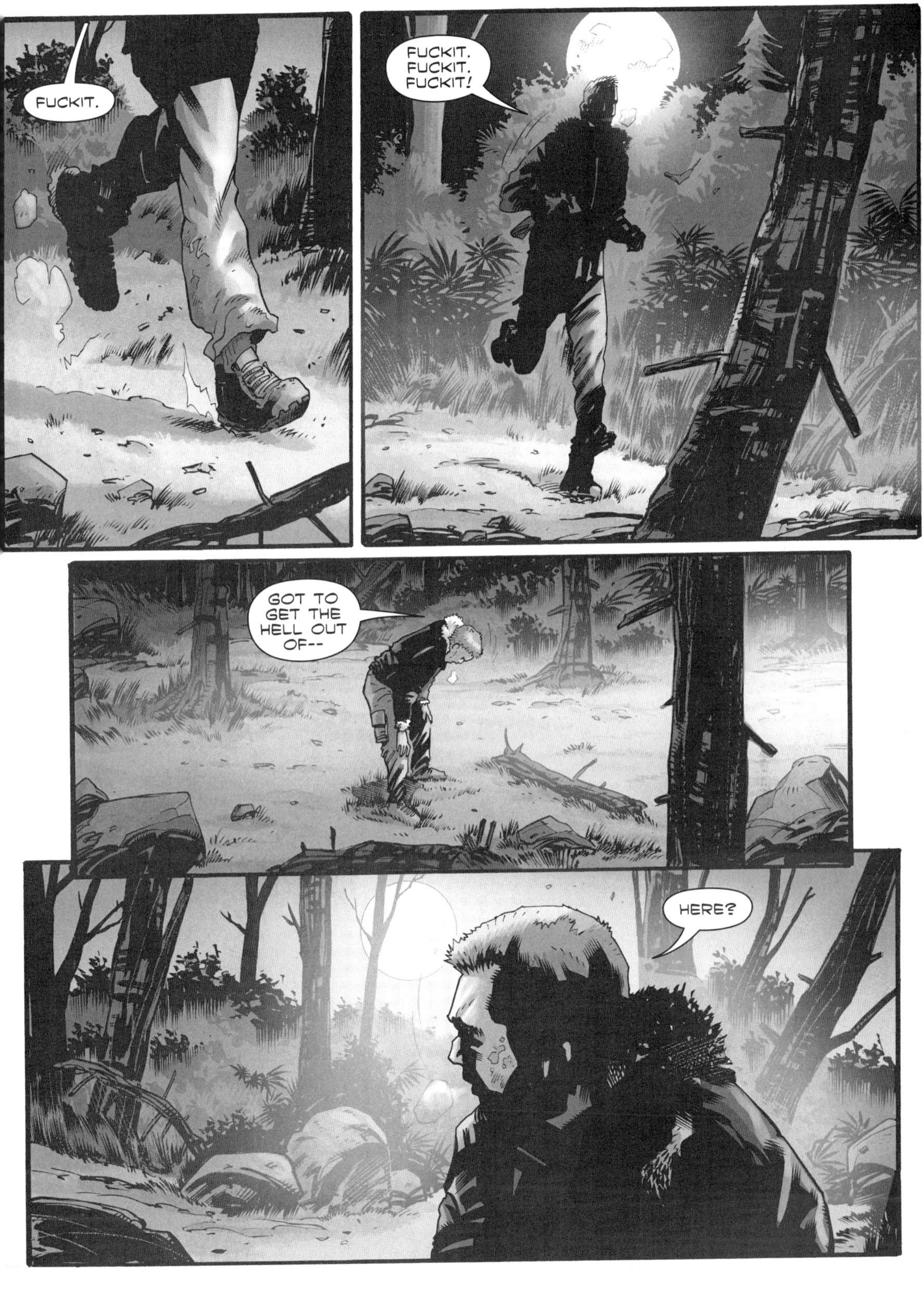
FUCKIT.
FUCKIT. FUCKIT. FUCKIT!
GOT TO GET THE HELL OUT OF--
HERE?

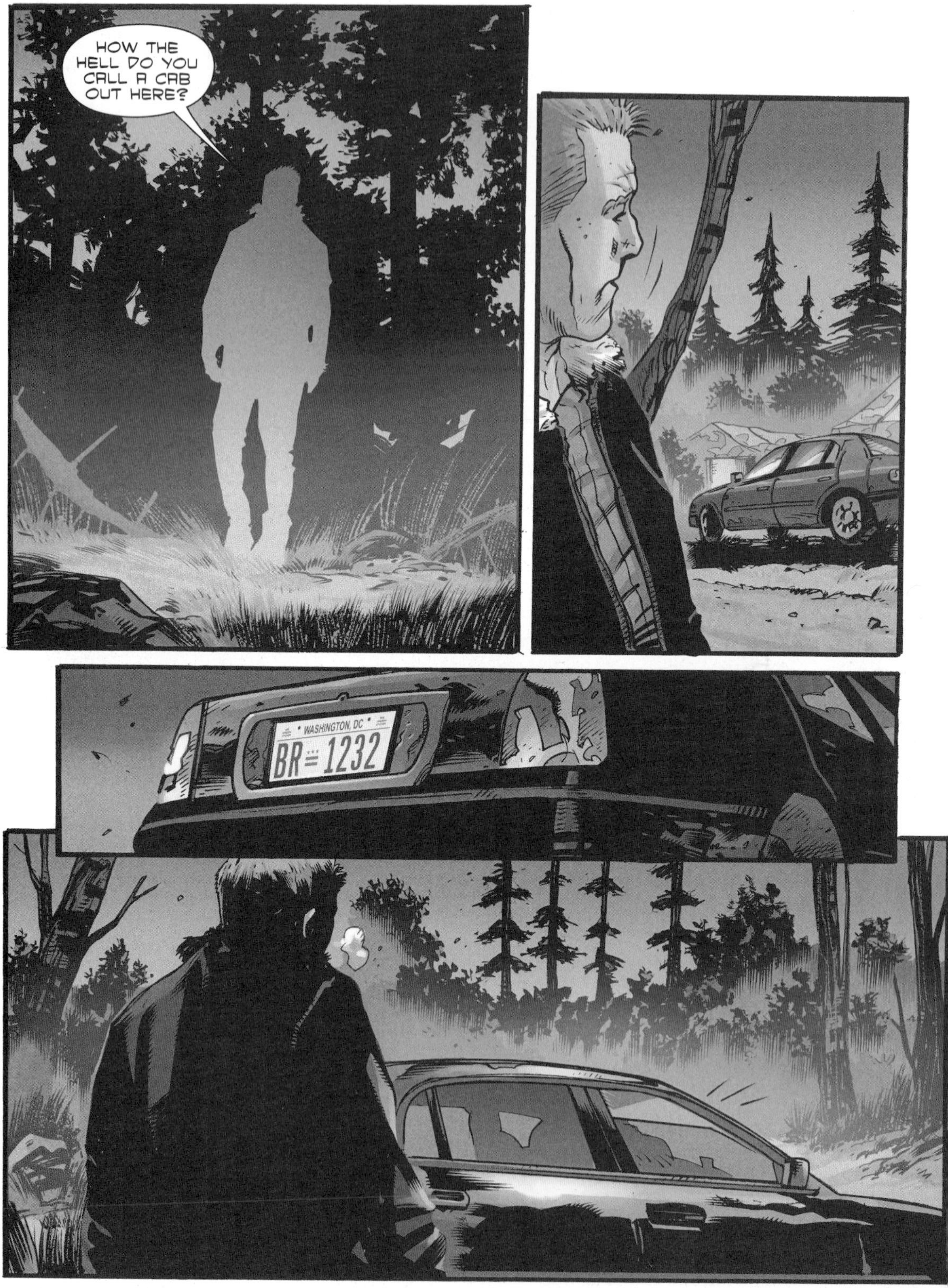
HOW THE HELL DO YOU CALL A CAB OUT HERE?
WASHINGTON, DC
BR 1232

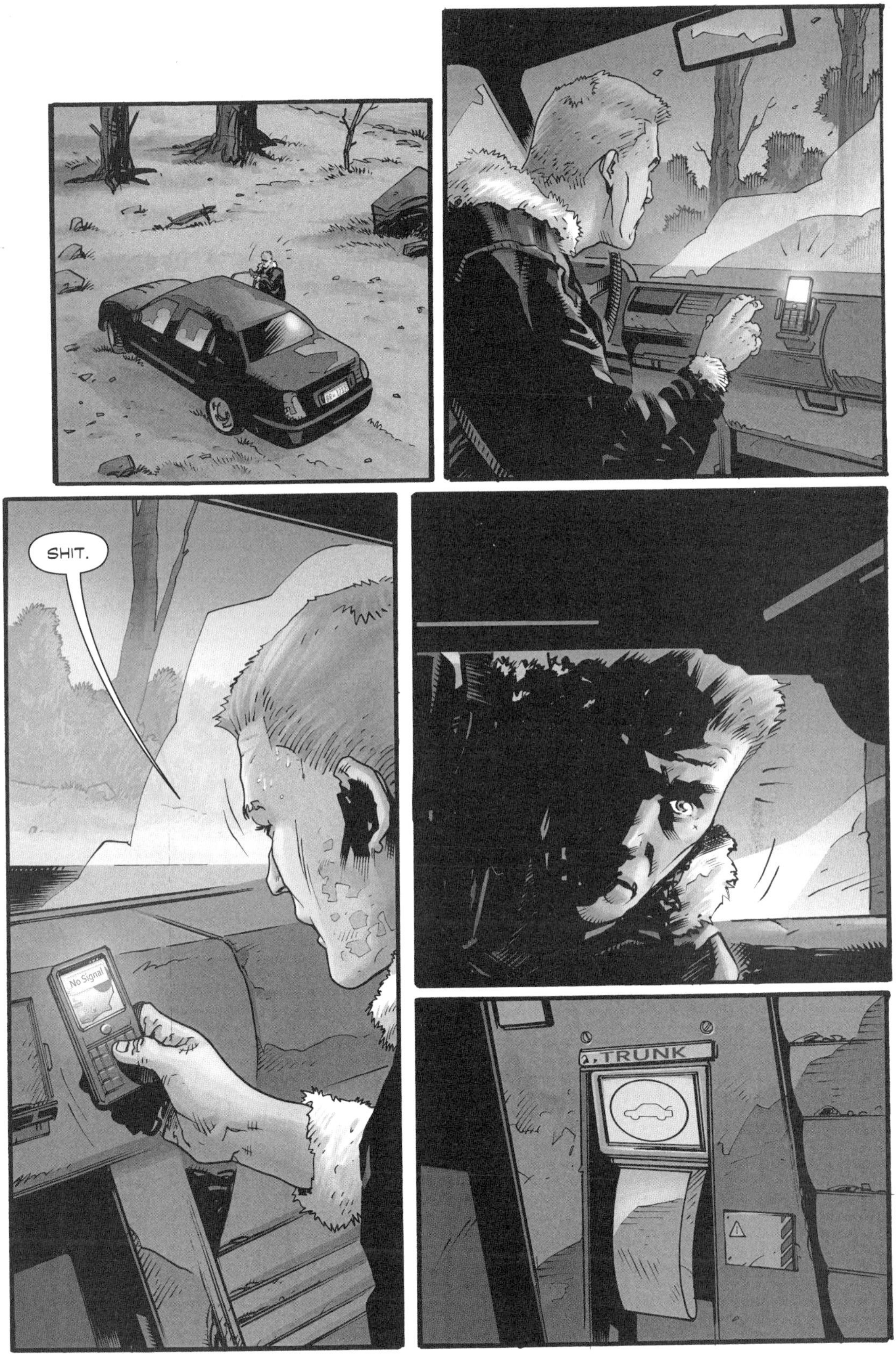
SHIT.
No Signal
TRUNK

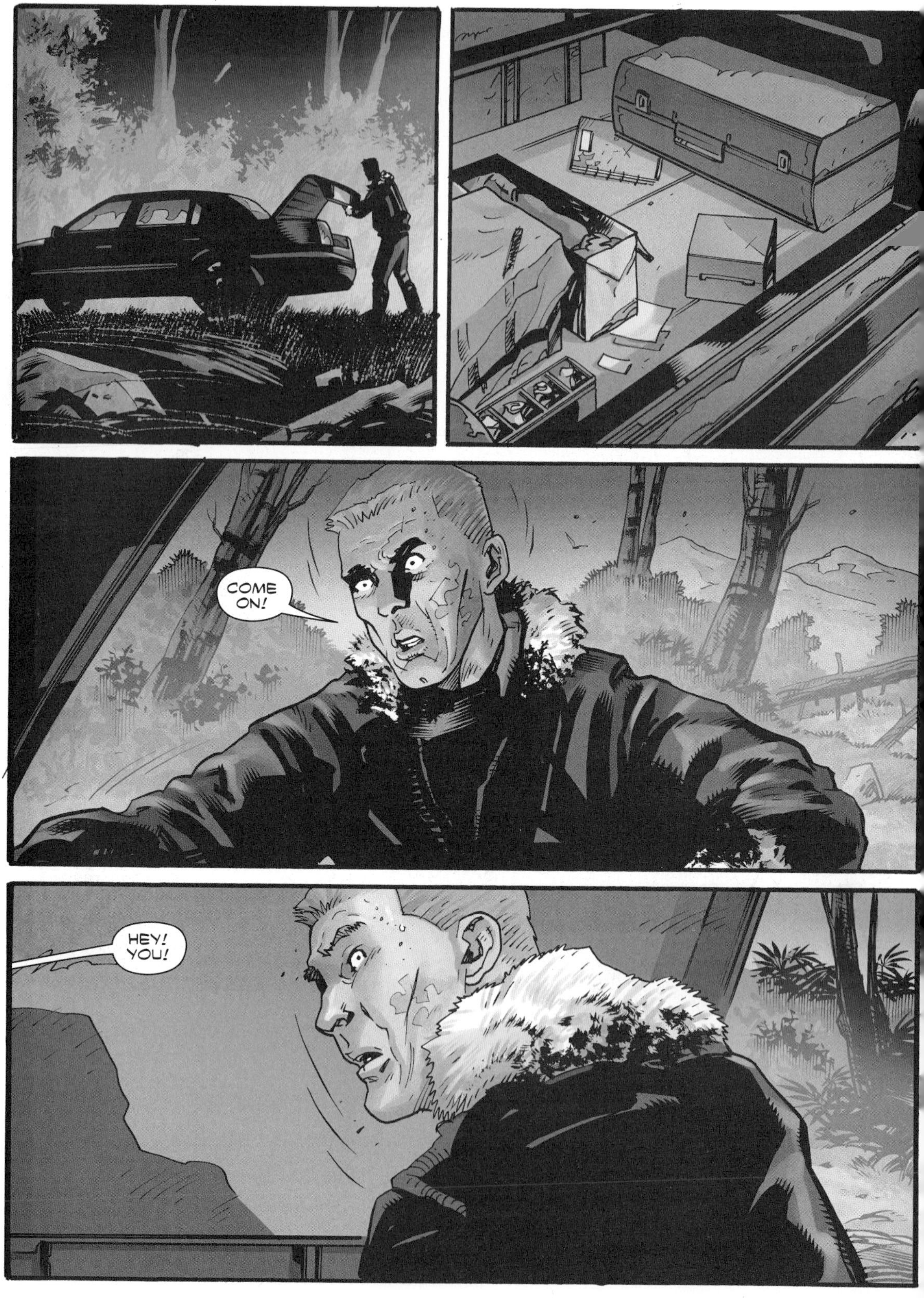
COME ON!
HEY! YOU!

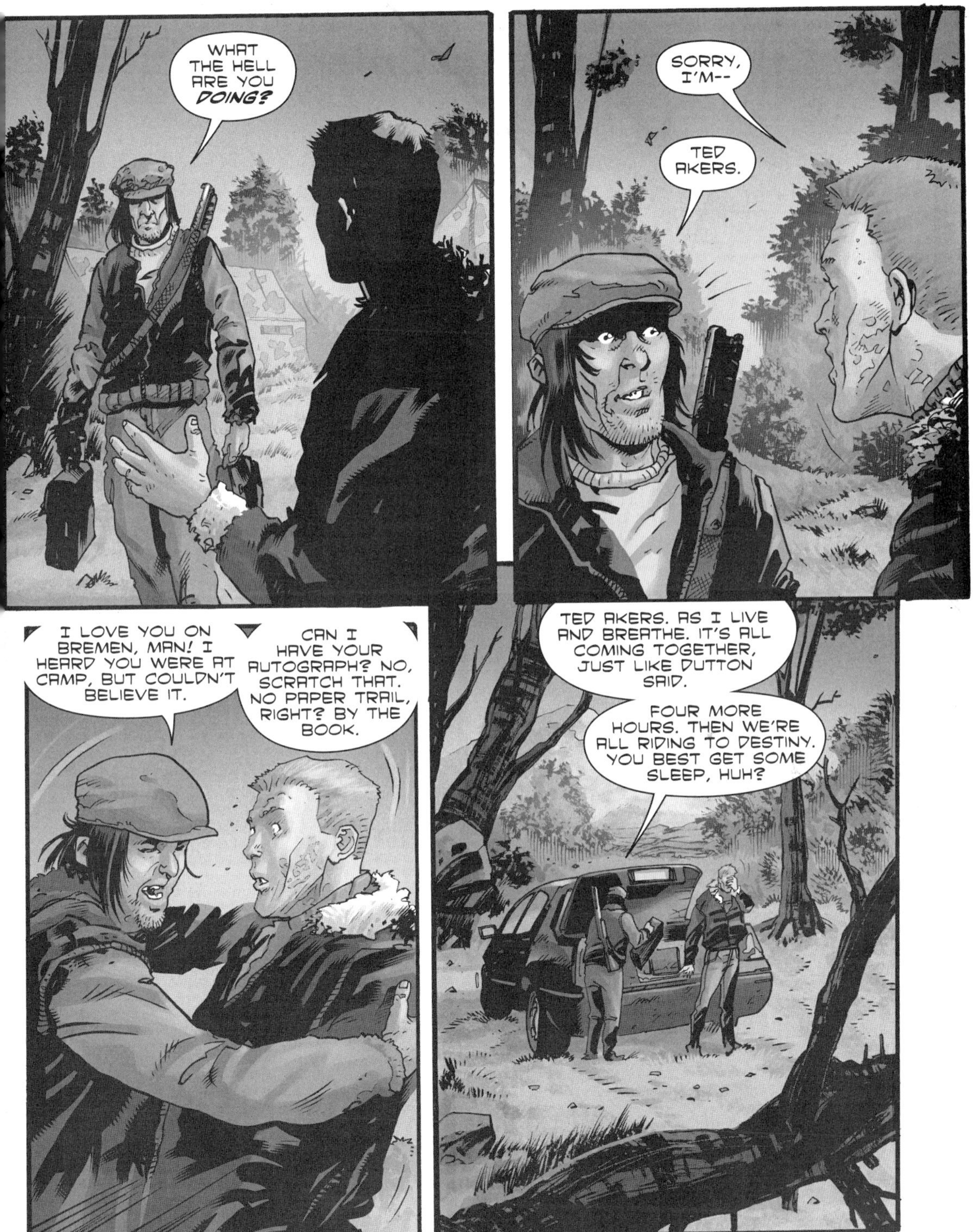
WHAT THE HELL ARE YOU DOING?
SORRY, I'M--
TED AKERS.
I LOVE YOU ON BREMEN, MAN! I HEARD YOU WERE AT CAMP, BUT COULDN'T BELIEVE IT.
CAN I HAVE YOUR AUTOGRAPH? NO, SCRATCH THAT. NO PAPER TRAIL, RIGHT? BY THE BOOK.
TED AKERS. AS I LIVE AND BREATHE. IT'S ALL COMING TOGETHER, JUST LIKE DUTTON SAID.
FOUR MORE HOURS. THEN WE'RE ALL RIDING TO DESTINY. YOU BEST GET SOME SLEEP, HUH?

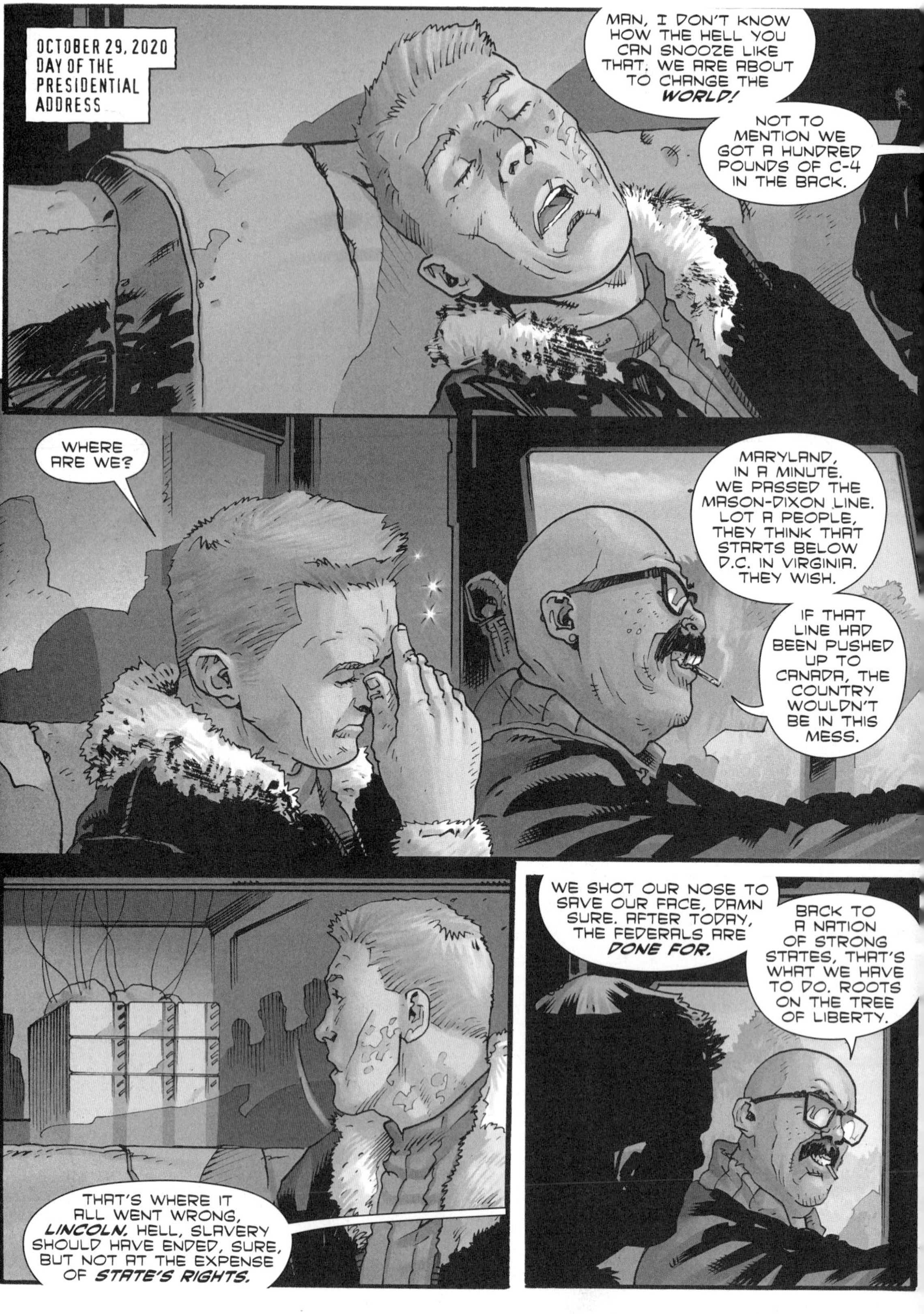
OCTOBER 29, 2020 DAY OF THE PRESIDENTIAL ADDRESS
MAN, I DON'T KNOW HOW THE HELL YOU CAN SNOOZE LIKE THAT. WE ARE ABOUT TO CHANGE THE WORLD!
NOT TO MENTION WE GOT A HUNDRED POUNDS OF C-4 IN THE BACK.
WHERE ARE WE?
MARYLAND, IN A MINUTE. WE PASSED THE MASON-DIXON LINE. LOT A PEOPLE, THEY THINK THAT STARTS BELOW D.C. IN VIRGINIA. THEY WISH.
IF THAT LINE HAD BEEN PUSHED UP TO CANADA, THE COUNTRY WOULDN'T BE IN THIS MESS.
THAT'S WHERE IT ALL WENT WRONG, LINCOLN. HELL, SLAVERY SHOULD HAVE ENDED, SURE, BUT NOT AT THE EXPENSE OF STATE'S RIGHTS.
WE SHOT OUR NOSE TO SAVE OUR FACE, DAMN SURE. AFTER TODAY, THE FEDERALS ARE DONE FOR.
BACK TO A NATION OF STRONG STATES, THAT'S WHAT WE HAVE TO DO. ROOTS ON THE TREE OF LIBERTY.

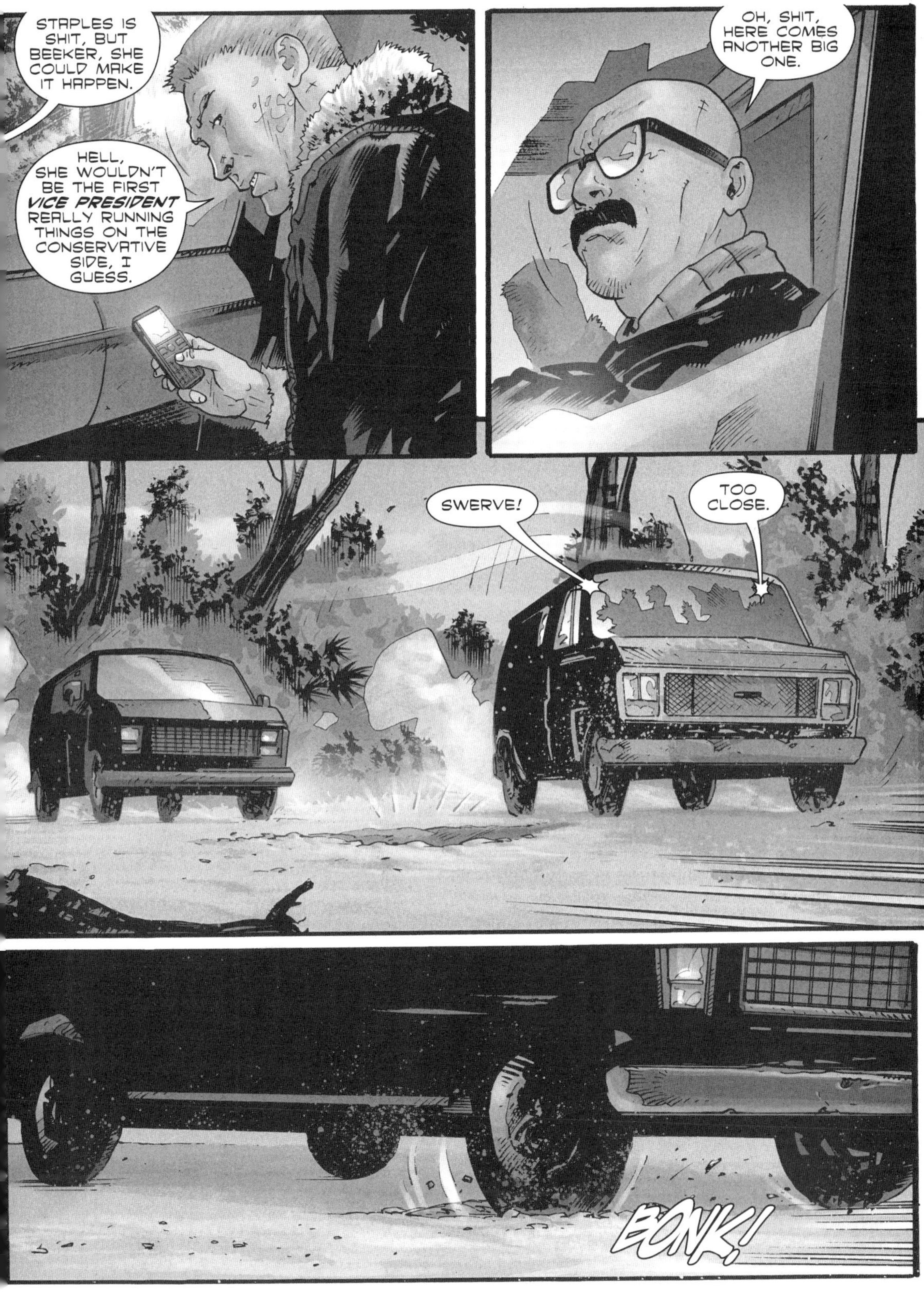
STAPLES IS SHIT, BUT BEEKER, SHE COULD MAKE IT HAPPEN.
HELL, SHE WOULDN'T BE THE FIRST *VICE PRESIDENT* REALLY RUNNING THINGS ON THE CONSERVATIVE SIDE, I GUESS.
OH, SHIT, HERE COMES ANOTHER BIG ONE.
SWERVE!
TOO CLOSE.
BONK!

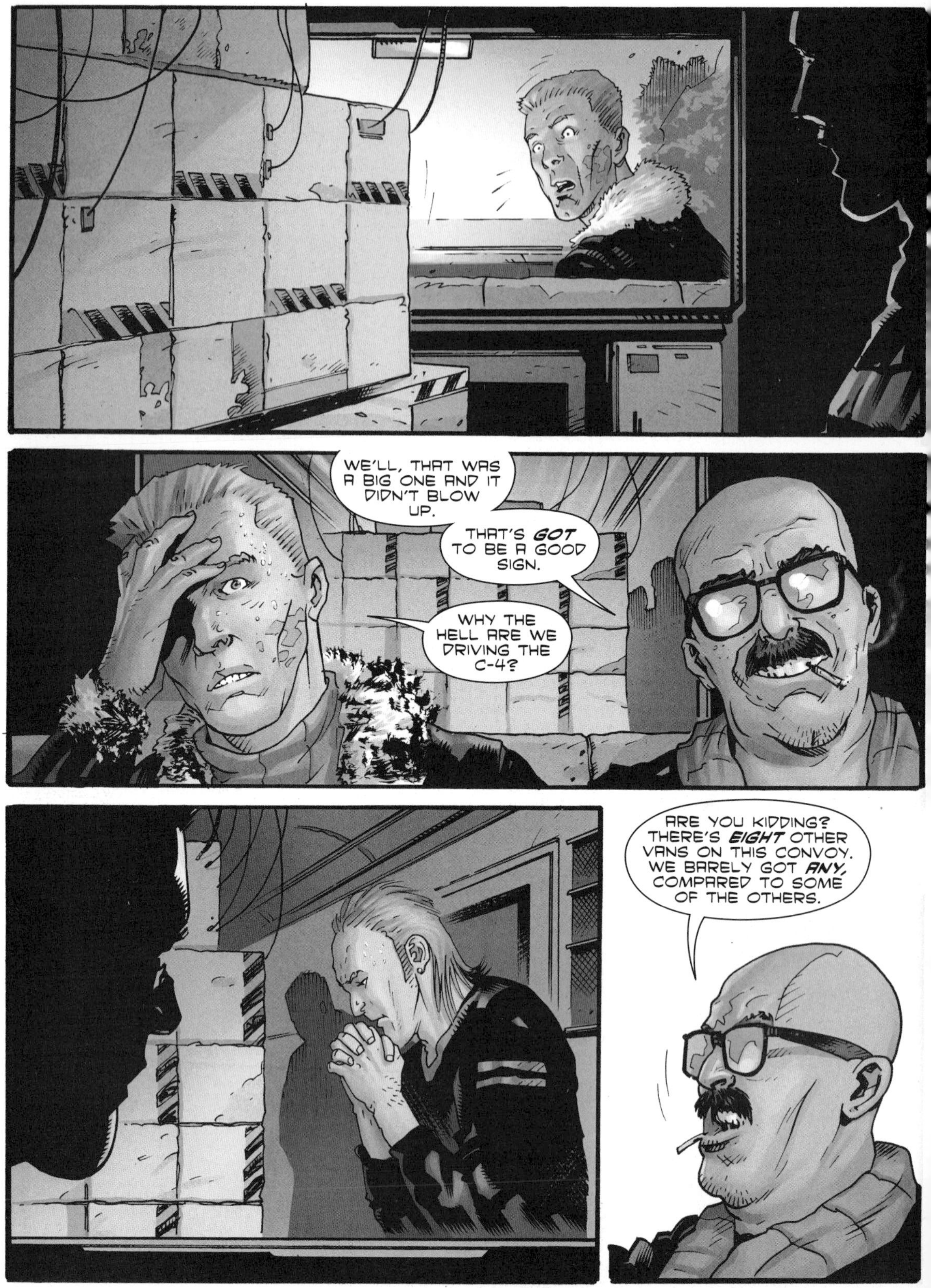
WE'LL, THAT WAS A BIG ONE AND IT DIDN'T BLOW UP.
THAT'S GOT TO BE A GOOD SIGN.
WHY THE HELL ARE WE DRIVING THE C-4?
ARE YOU KIDDING? THERE'S EIGHT OTHER VANS ON THIS CONVOY. WE BARELY GOT ANY, COMPARED TO SOME OF THE OTHERS.

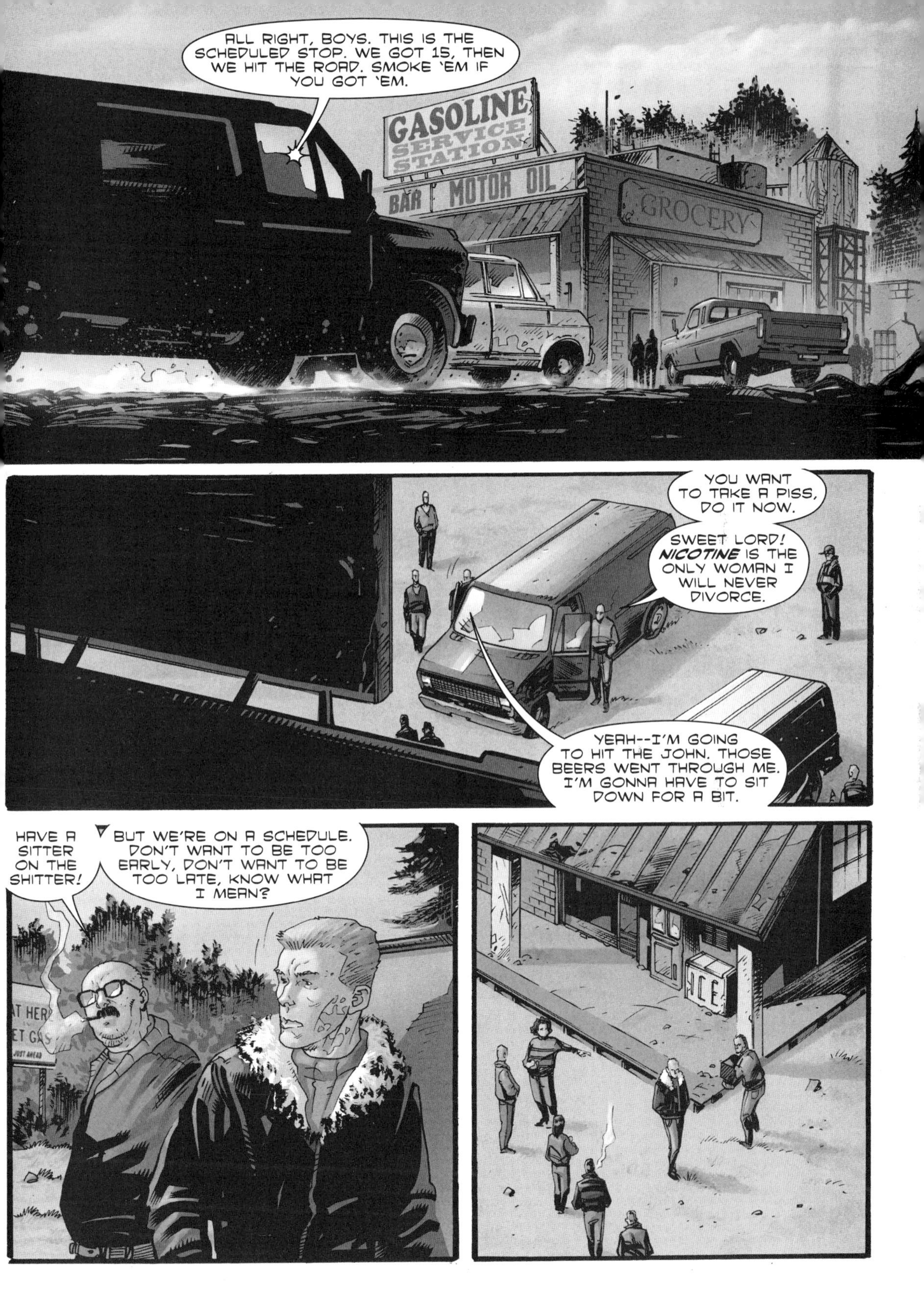
ALL RIGHT, BOYS. THIS IS THE SCHEDULED STOP. WE GOT 15, THEN WE HIT THE ROAD. SMOKE 'EM IF YOU GOT 'EM.
GASOLINE SERVICE STATION
BAR
MOTOR OIL
GROCERY
YOU WANT TO TAKE A PISS, DO IT NOW.
SWEET LORD! ***NICOTINE*** IS THE ONLY WOMAN I WILL NEVER DIVORCE.
YEAH--I'M GOING TO HIT THE JOHN. THOSE BEERS WENT THROUGH ME. I'M GONNA HAVE TO SIT DOWN FOR A BIT.
HAVE A SITTER ON THE SHITTER!
BUT WE'RE ON A SCHEDULE. DON'T WANT TO BE TOO EARLY, DON'T WANT TO BE TOO LATE, KNOW WHAT I MEAN?
ICE

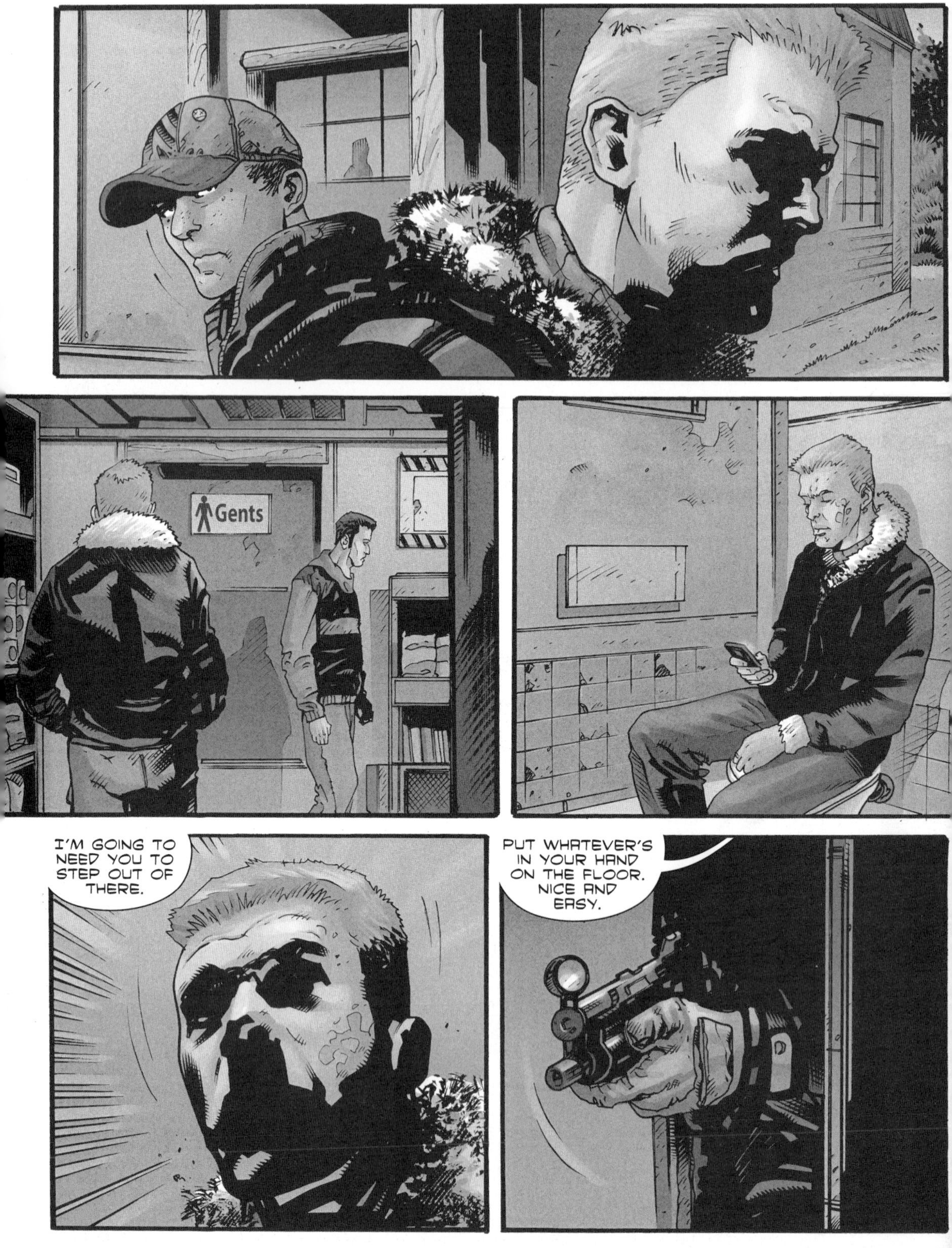
Gents
I'M GOING TO NEED YOU TO STEP OUT OF THERE.
PUT WHATEVER'S IN YOUR HAND ON THE FLOOR. NICE AND EASY.

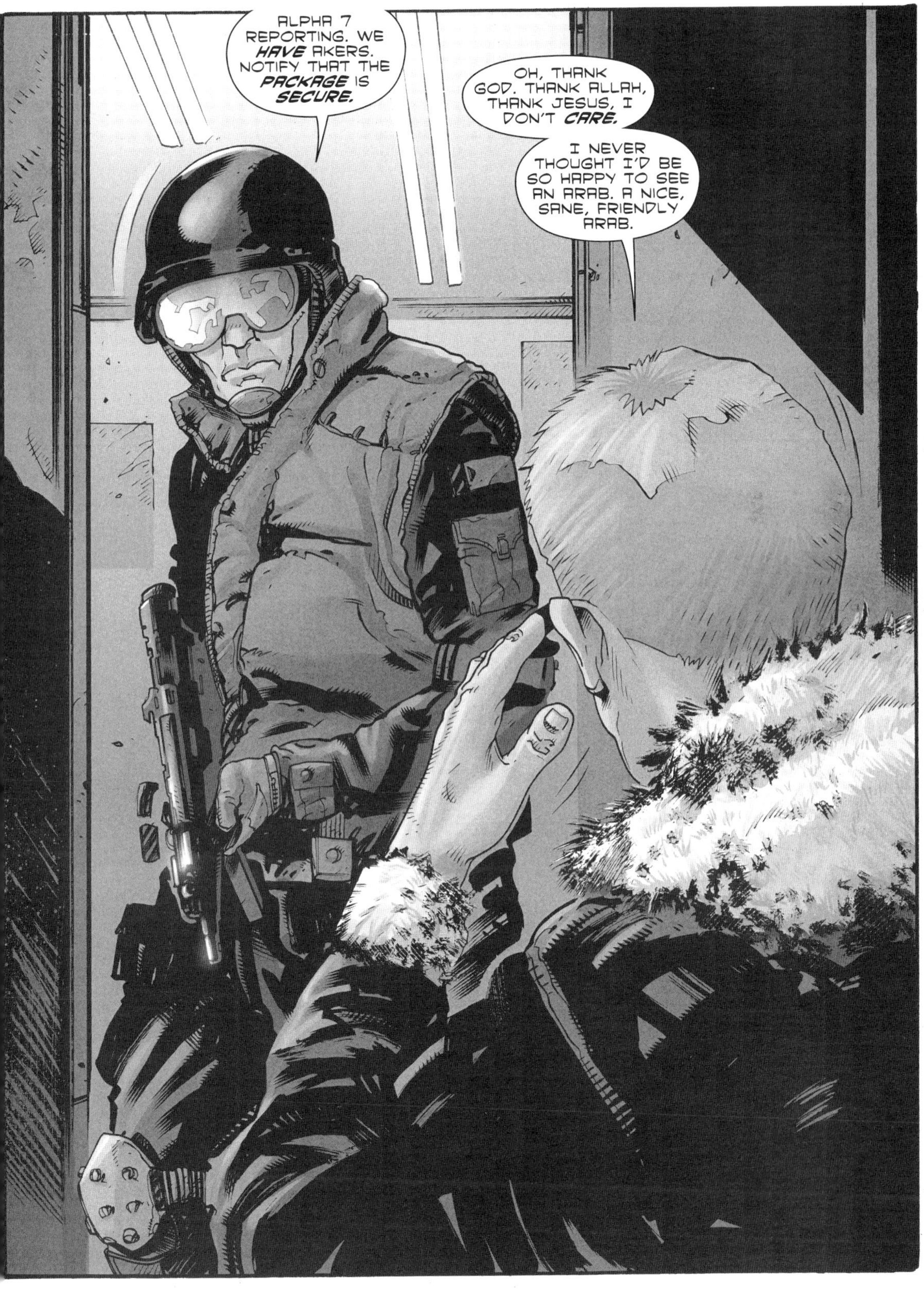
ALPHA 7 REPORTING. WE *HAVE* AKERS. NOTIFY THAT THE *PACKAGE* IS *SECURE.*
OH, THANK GOD. THANK ALLAH, THANK JESUS, I DON'T *CARE.*
I NEVER THOUGHT I'D BE SO HAPPY TO SEE AN ARAB. A NICE, SANE, FRIENDLY ARAB.

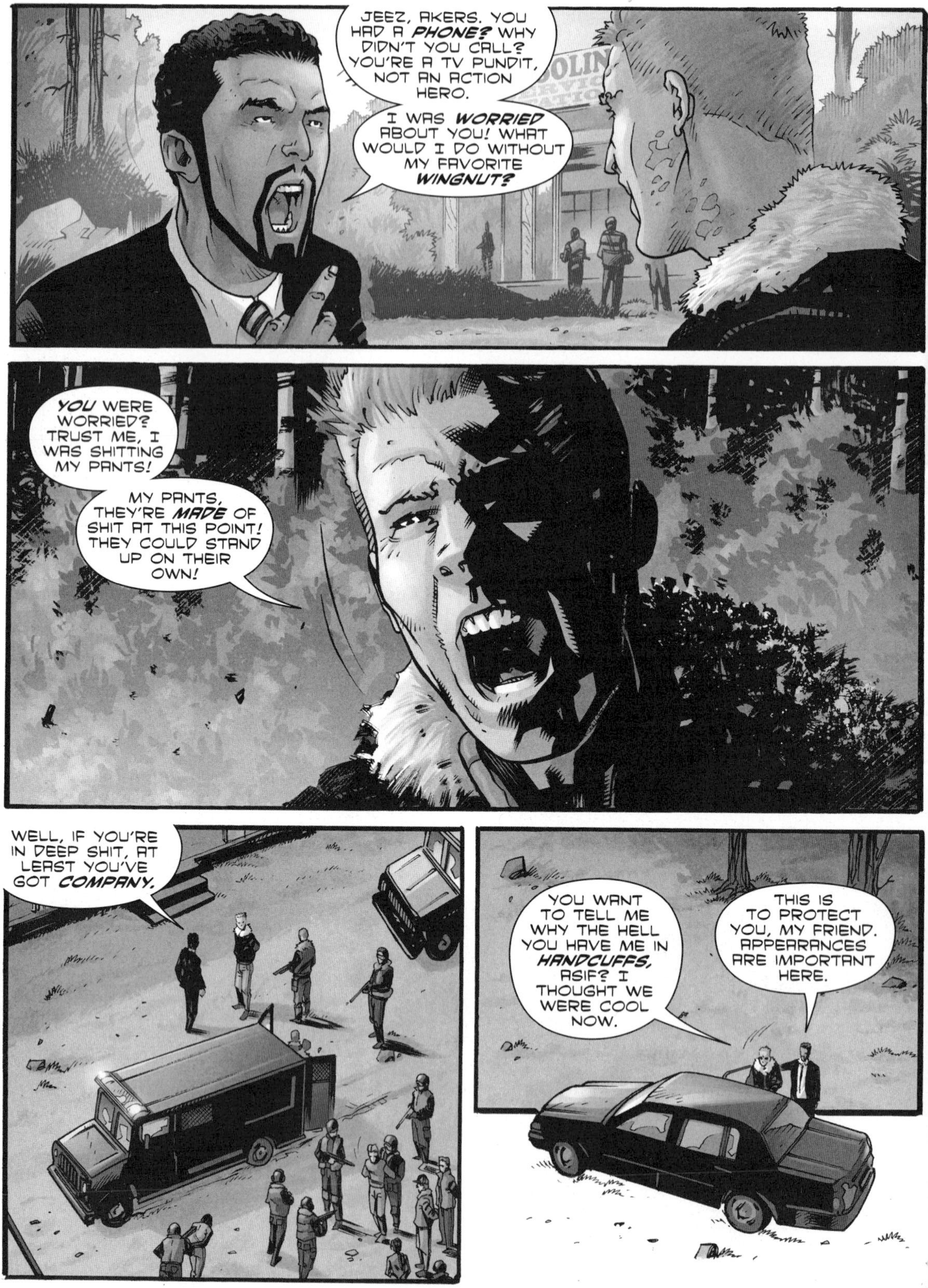

JEEZ, AKERS. YOU HAD A *PHONE?* WHY DIDN'T YOU CALL? YOU'RE A TV PUNDIT, NOT AN ACTION HERO.
I WAS *WORRIED* ABOUT YOU! WHAT WOULD I DO WITHOUT MY FAVORITE *WINGNUT?*
YOU WERE WORRIED? TRUST ME, I WAS SHITTING MY PANTS!
MY PANTS, THEY'RE *MADE* OF SHIT AT THIS POINT! THEY COULD STAND UP ON THEIR OWN!
WELL, IF YOU'RE IN DEEP SHIT, AT LEAST YOU'VE GOT *COMPANY.*
YOU WANT TO TELL ME WHY THE HELL YOU HAVE ME IN *HANDCUFFS,* ASIF? I THOUGHT WE WERE COOL NOW.
THIS IS TO PROTECT YOU, MY FRIEND. APPEARANCES ARE IMPORTANT HERE.

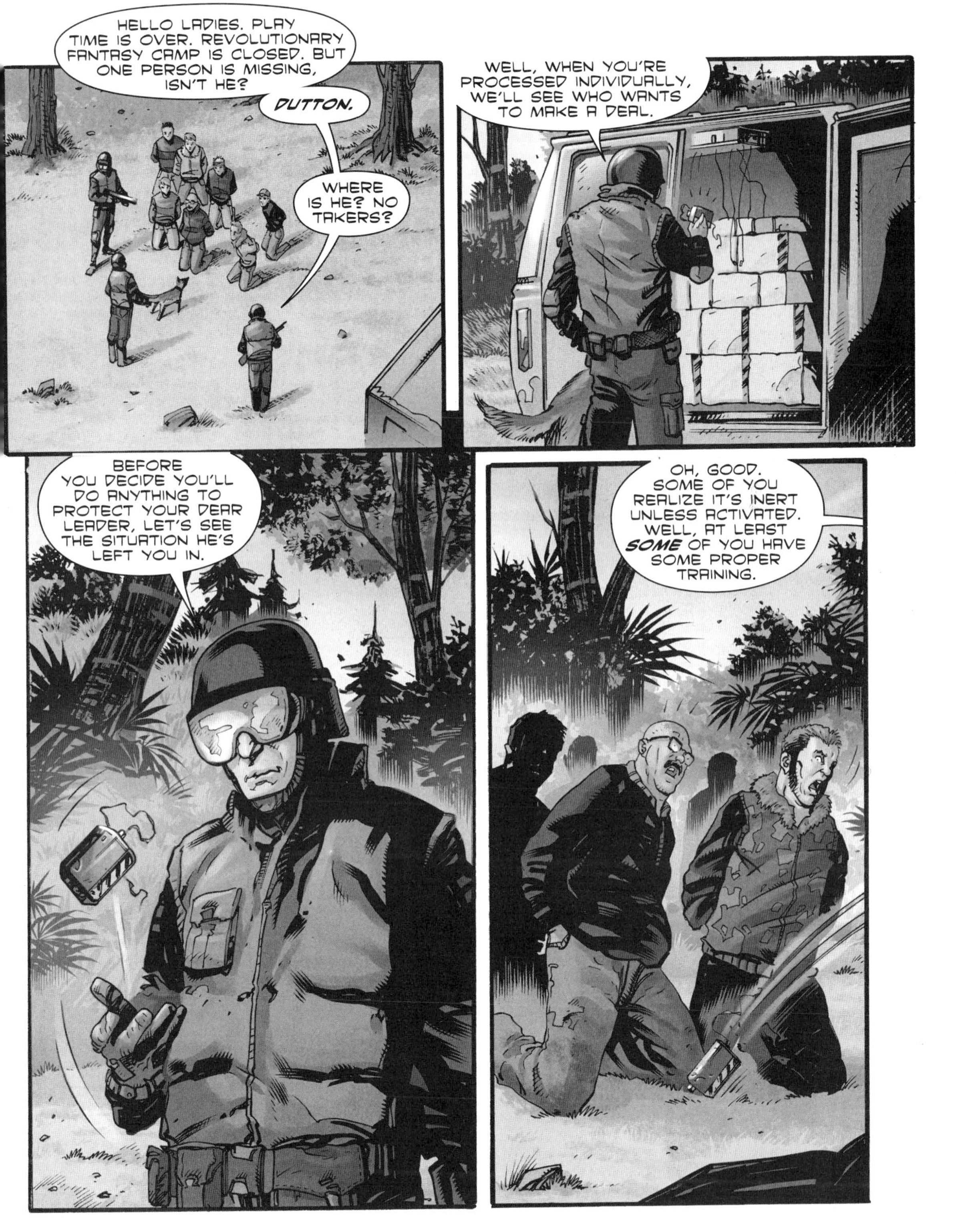
HELLO LADIES. PLAY TIME IS OVER. REVOLUTIONARY FANTASY CAMP IS CLOSED. BUT ONE PERSON IS MISSING, ISN'T HE?
DUTTON.
WHERE IS HE? NO TAKERS?
WELL, WHEN YOU'RE PROCESSED INDIVIDUALLY, WE'LL SEE WHO WANTS TO MAKE A DEAL.
BEFORE YOU DECIDE YOU'LL DO ANYTHING TO PROTECT YOUR DEAR LEADER, LET'S SEE THE SITUATION HE'S LEFT YOU IN.
OH, GOOD. SOME OF YOU REALIZE IT'S INERT UNLESS ACTIVATED. WELL, AT LEAST SOME OF YOU HAVE SOME PROPER TRAINING.

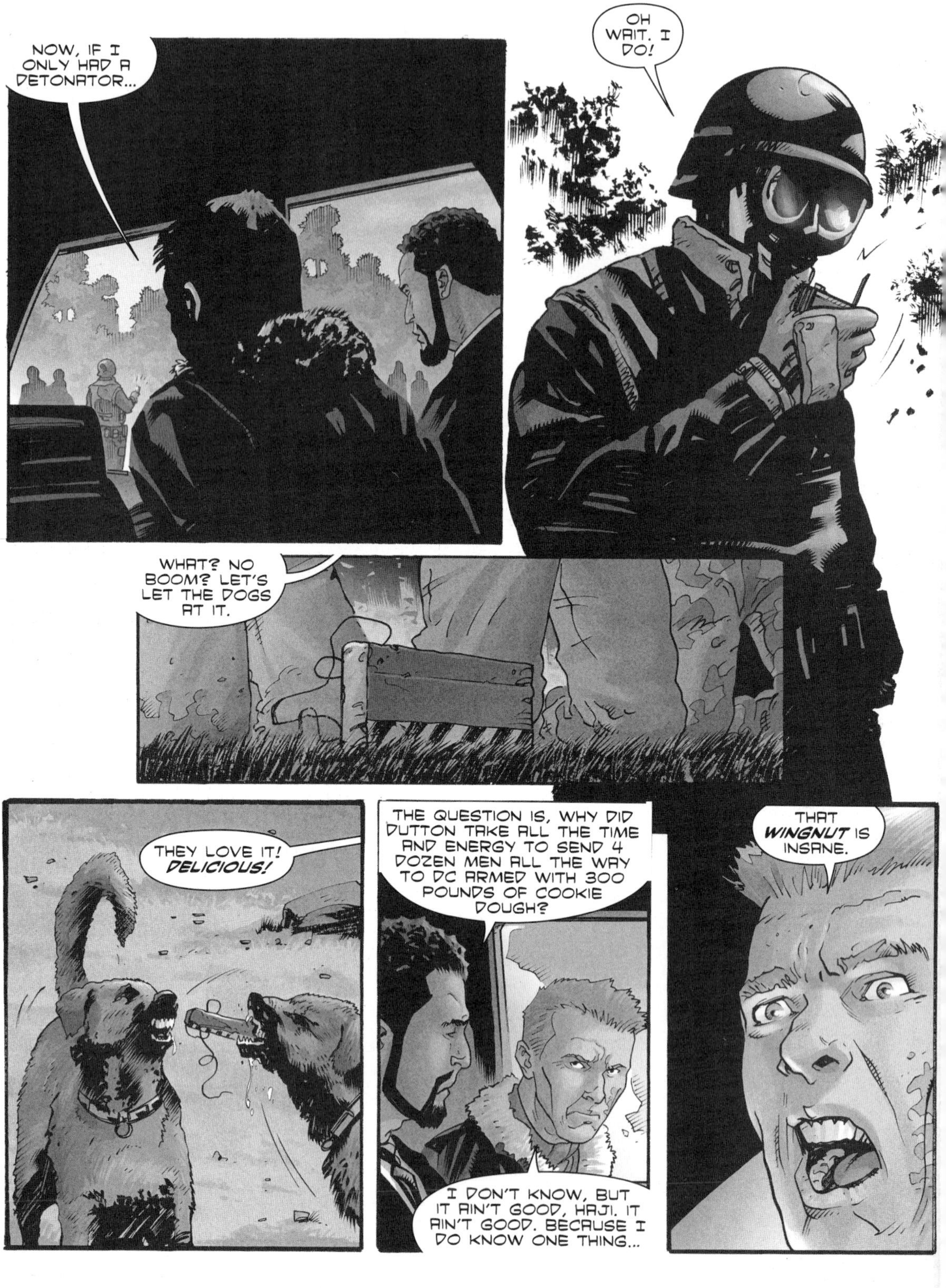
NOW, IF I ONLY HAD A DETONATOR...
OH WAIT. I DO!
WHAT? NO BOOM? LET'S LET THE DOGS AT IT.
THEY LOVE IT! ***DELICIOUS!***
THE QUESTION IS, WHY DID DUTTON TAKE ALL THE TIME AND ENERGY TO SEND 4 DOZEN MEN ALL THE WAY TO DC ARMED WITH 300 POUNDS OF COOKIE DOUGH?
I DON'T KNOW, BUT IT AIN'T GOOD, HAJI. IT AIN'T GOOD. BECAUSE I DO KNOW ONE THING...
THAT ***WINGNUT*** IS INSANE.

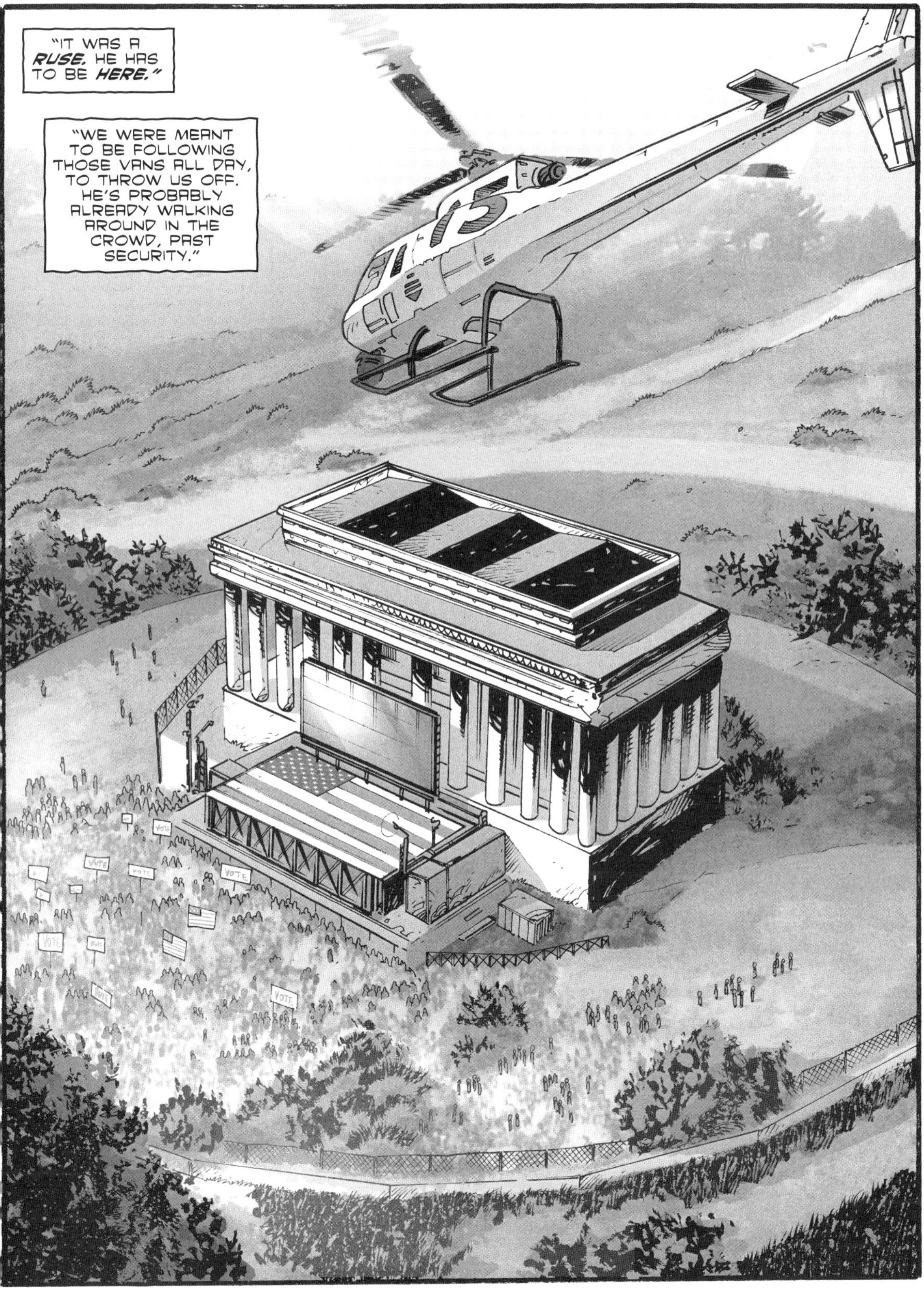
"IT WAS A RUSE. HE HAS TO BE HERE."
"WE WERE MEANT TO BE FOLLOWING THOSE VANS ALL DAY, TO THROW US OFF. HE'S PROBABLY ALREADY WALKING AROUND IN THE CROWD, PAST SECURITY."
VOTE

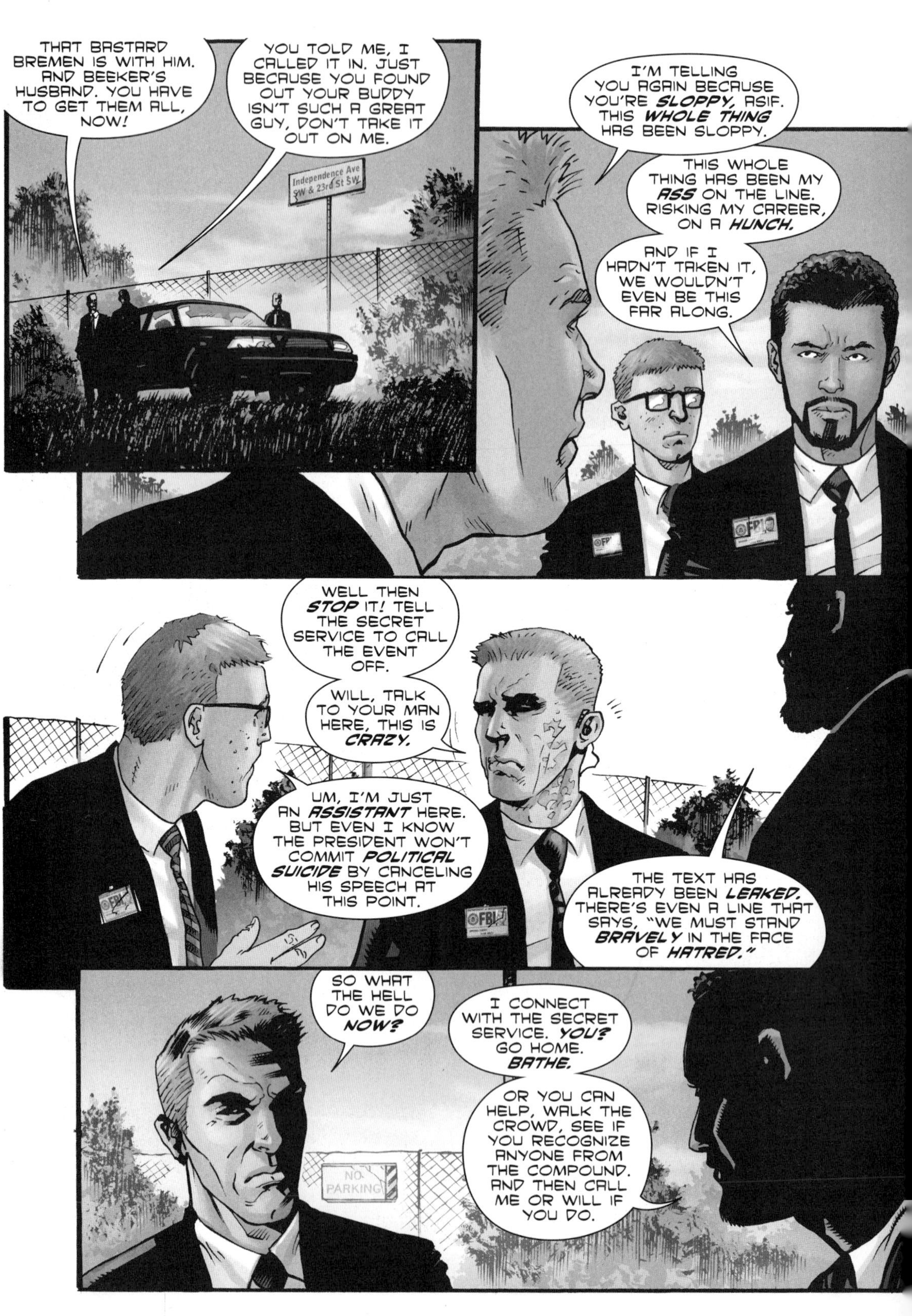
THAT BASTARD BREMEN IS WITH HIM. AND BEEKER'S HUSBAND. YOU HAVE TO GET THEM ALL, NOW!
YOU TOLD ME, I CALLED IT IN. JUST BECAUSE YOU FOUND OUT YOUR BUDDY ISN'T SUCH A GREAT GUY, DON'T TAKE IT OUT ON ME.
Independence Ave SW & 23rd St SW
I'M TELLING YOU AGAIN BECAUSE YOU'RE SLOPPY, ASIF. THIS WHOLE THING HAS BEEN SLOPPY.
THIS WHOLE THING HAS BEEN MY ASS ON THE LINE. RISKING MY CAREER, ON A HUNCH.
AND IF I HADN'T TAKEN IT, WE WOULDN'T EVEN BE THIS FAR ALONG.
FBI
WELL THEN STOP IT! TELL THE SECRET SERVICE TO CALL THE EVENT OFF.
WILL, TALK TO YOUR MAN HERE, THIS IS CRAZY.
UM, I'M JUST AN ASSISTANT HERE. BUT EVEN I KNOW THE PRESIDENT WON'T COMMIT POLITICAL SUICIDE BY CANCELING HIS SPEECH AT THIS POINT.
THE TEXT HAS ALREADY BEEN LEAKED. THERE'S EVEN A LINE THAT SAYS, "WE MUST STAND BRAVELY IN THE FACE OF HATRED."
FBI
SO WHAT THE HELL DO WE DO NOW?
I CONNECT WITH THE SECRET SERVICE. YOU? GO HOME. BATHE.
OR YOU CAN HELP, WALK THE CROWD, SEE IF YOU RECOGNIZE ANYONE FROM THE COMPOUND. AND THEN CALL ME OR WILL IF YOU DO.
NO PARKING

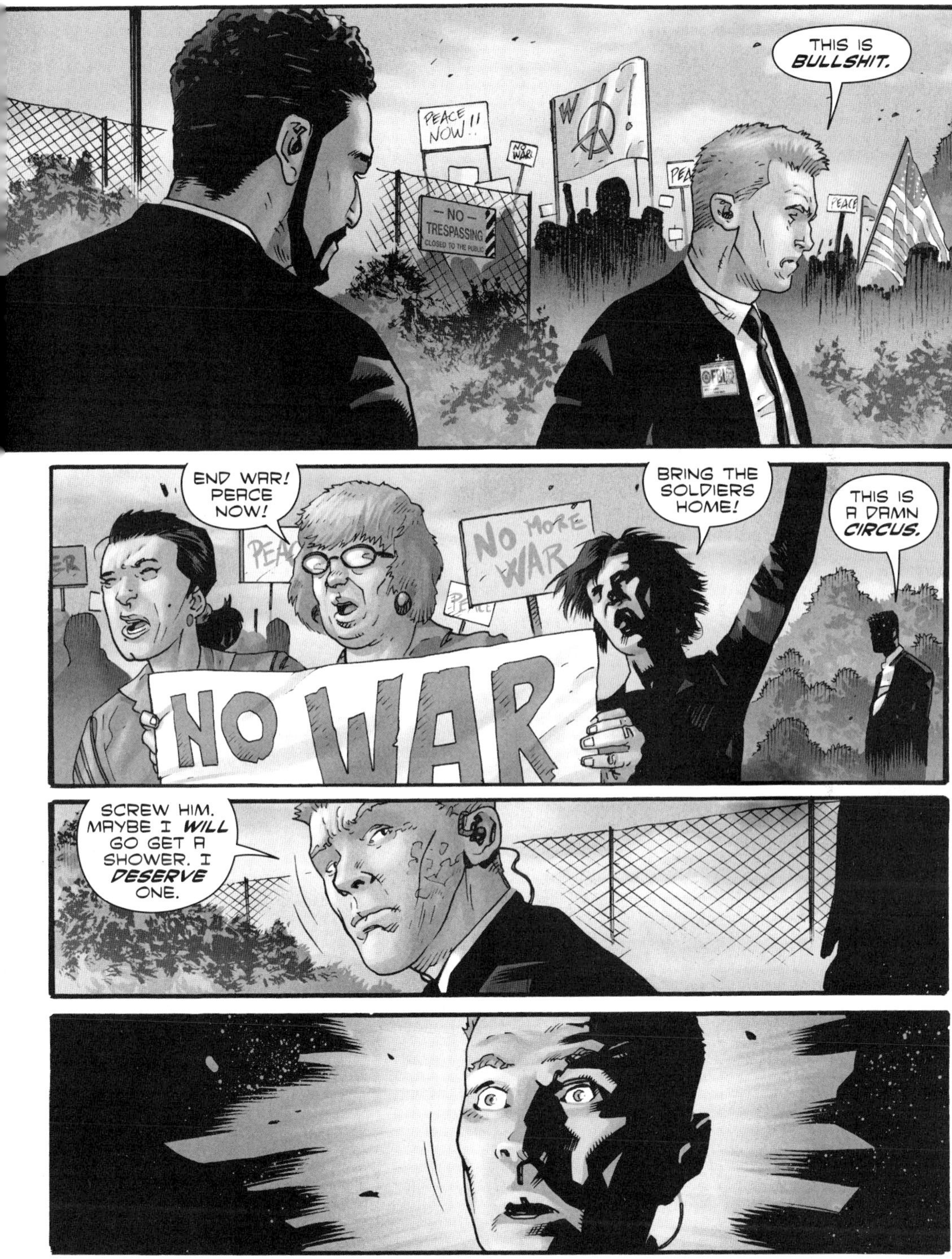
THIS IS BULLSHIT.
PEACE NOW!!
NO WAR
NO TRESPASSING CLOSED TO THE PUBLIC
END WAR! PEACE NOW!
NO MORE WAR
BRING THE SOLDIERS HOME!
THIS IS A DAMN CIRCUS.
NO WAR
SCREW HIM. MAYBE I WILL GO GET A SHOWER. I DESERVE ONE.

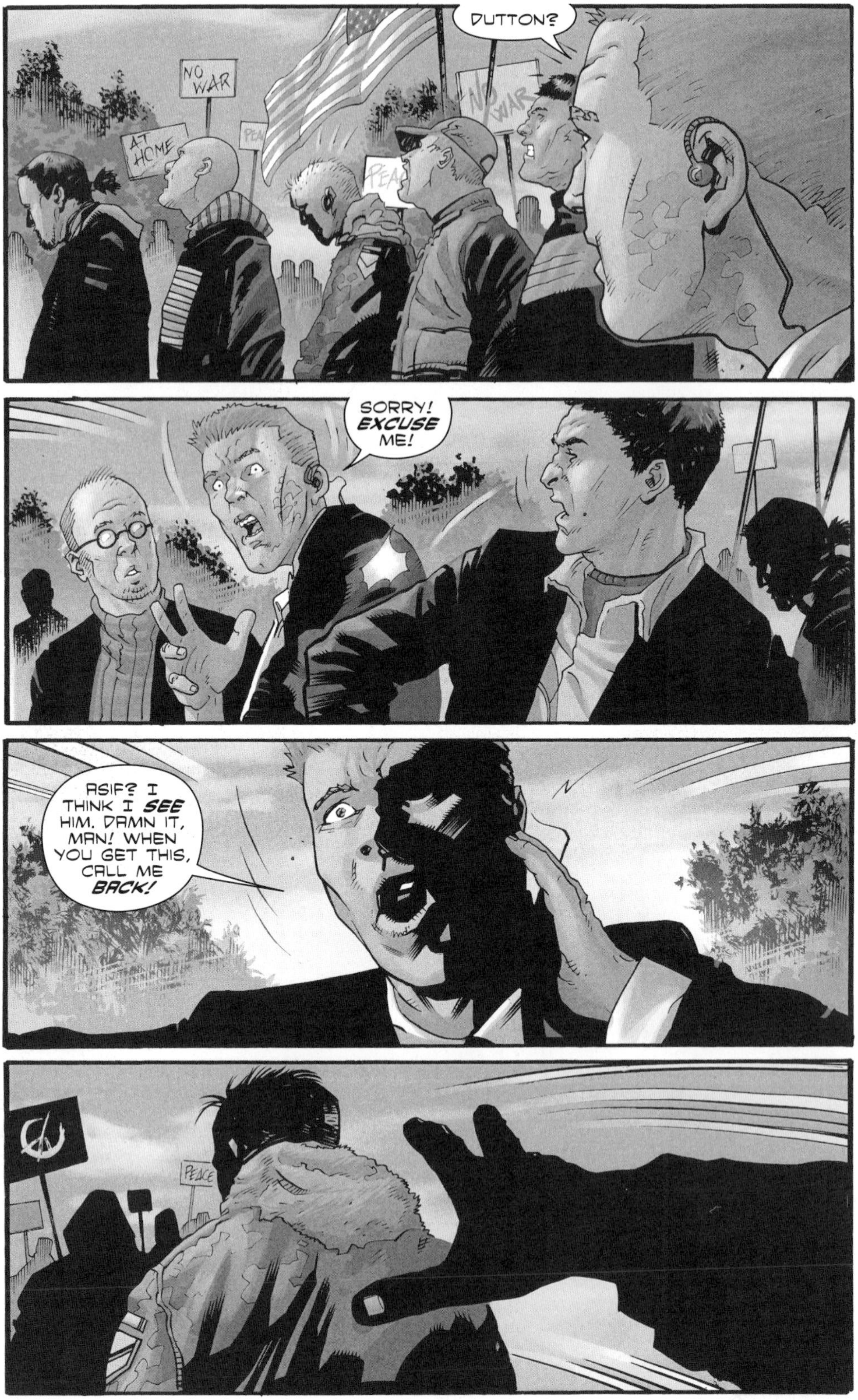
DUTTON?
NO WAR
AT HOME
NO WAR
SORRY! EXCUSE ME!
ASIF? I THINK I SEE HIM. DAMN IT, MAN! WHEN YOU GET THIS, CALL ME BACK!
PEACE

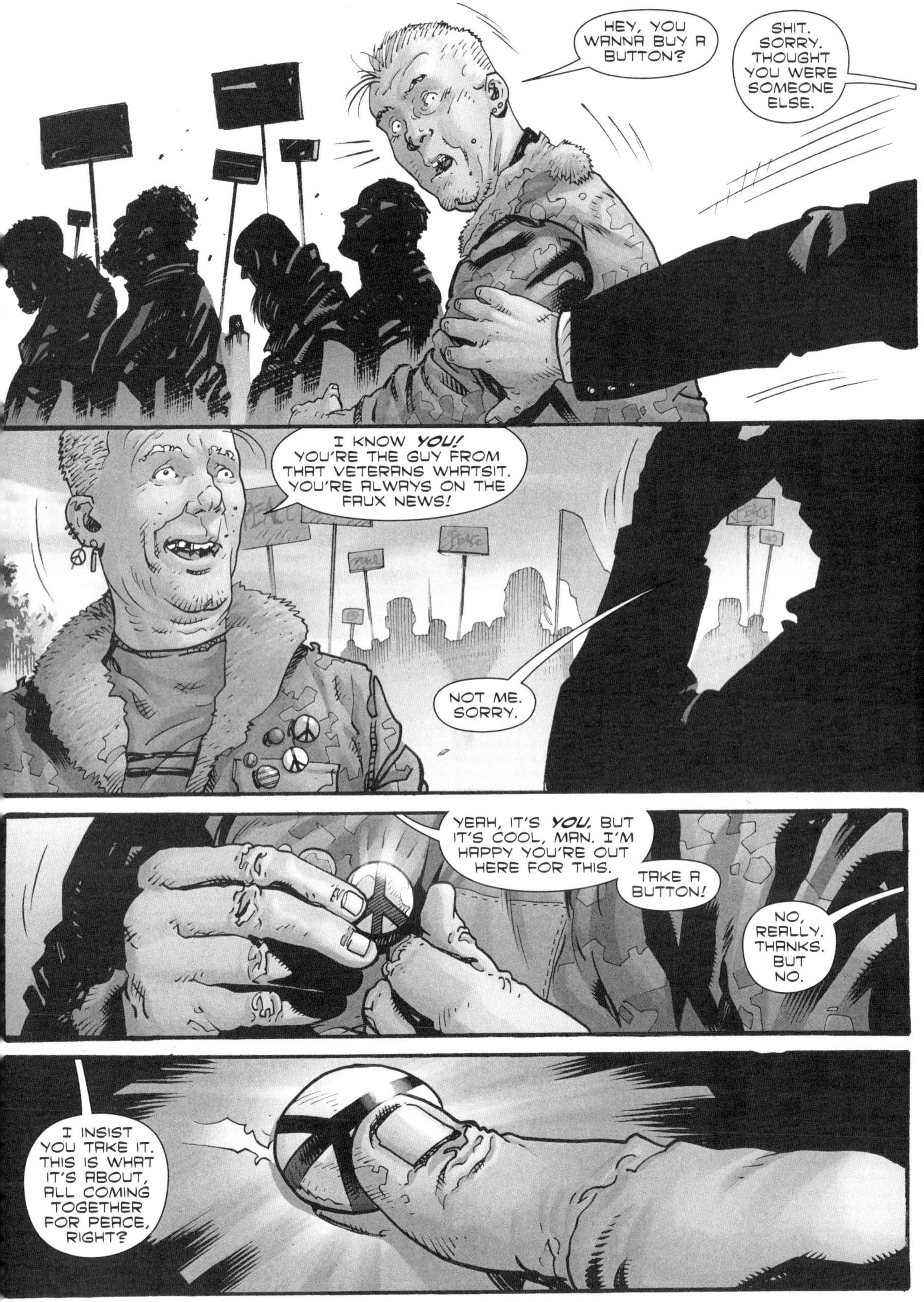
HEY, YOU WANNA BUY A BUTTON?
SHIT. SORRY. THOUGHT YOU WERE SOMEONE ELSE.
I KNOW YOU! YOU'RE THE GUY FROM THAT VETERANS WHATSIT. YOU'RE ALWAYS ON THE FAUX NEWS!
NOT ME. SORRY.
YEAH, IT'S YOU. BUT IT'S COOL, MAN. I'M HAPPY YOU'RE OUT HERE FOR THIS.
TAKE A BUTTON!
NO, REALLY. THANKS. BUT NO.
I INSIST YOU TAKE IT. THIS IS WHAT IT'S ABOUT, ALL COMING TOGETHER FOR PEACE, RIGHT?

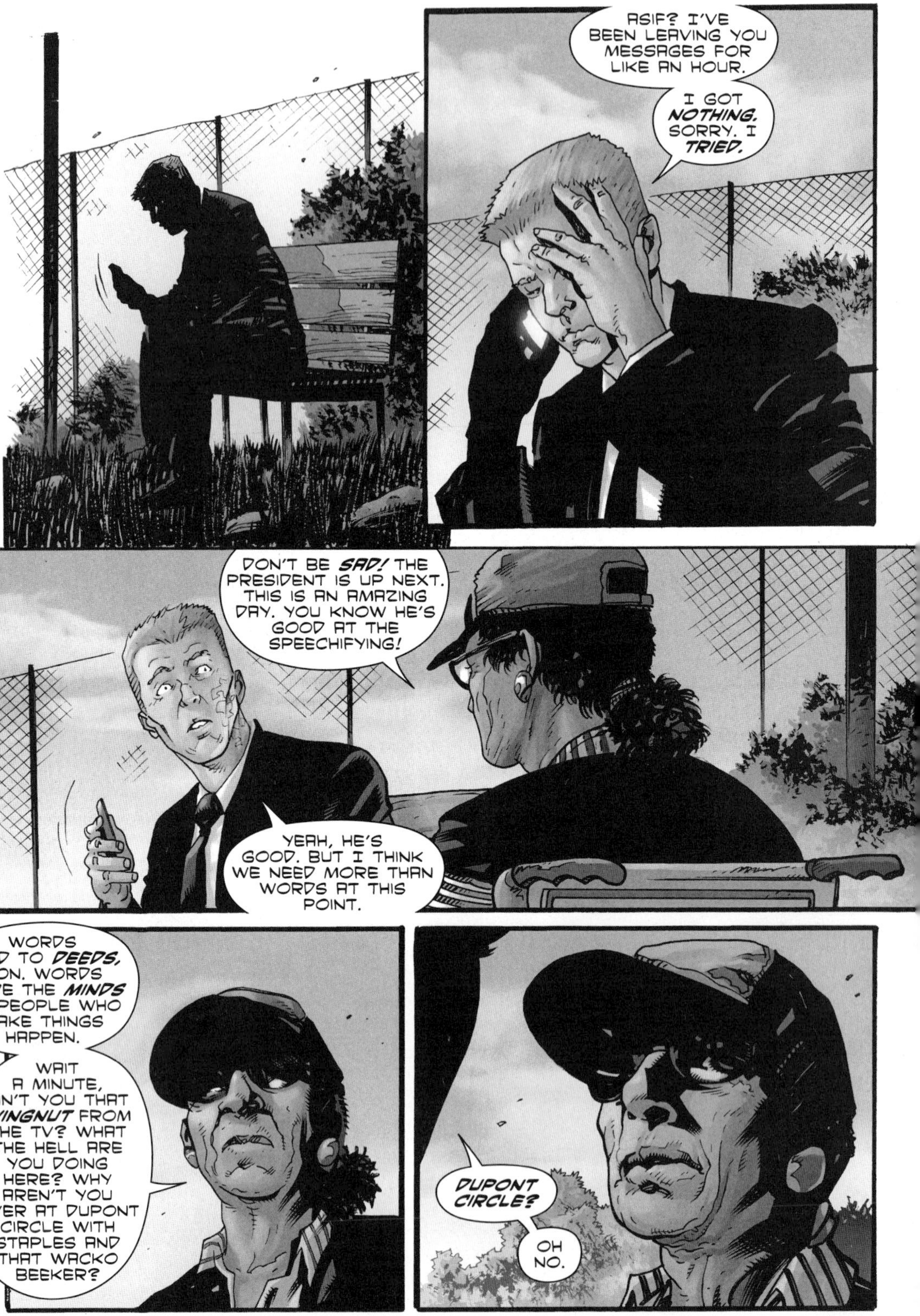
ASIF? I'VE BEEN LEAVING YOU MESSAGES FOR LIKE AN HOUR.
I GOT **NOTHING.** SORRY. I **TRIED.**
DON'T BE **SAD!** THE PRESIDENT IS UP NEXT. THIS IS AN AMAZING DAY. YOU KNOW HE'S GOOD AT THE SPEECHIFYING!
YEAH, HE'S GOOD. BUT I THINK WE NEED MORE THAN WORDS AT THIS POINT.
WORDS LEAD TO **DEEDS,** SON. WORDS GUIDE THE **MINDS** OF PEOPLE WHO MAKE THINGS HAPPEN.
WAIT A MINUTE, AIN'T YOU THAT **WINGNUT** FROM THE TV? WHAT THE HELL ARE YOU DOING HERE? WHY AREN'T YOU OVER AT DUPONT CIRCLE WITH STAPLES AND THAT WACKO BEEKER?
DUPONT CIRCLE?
OH NO.

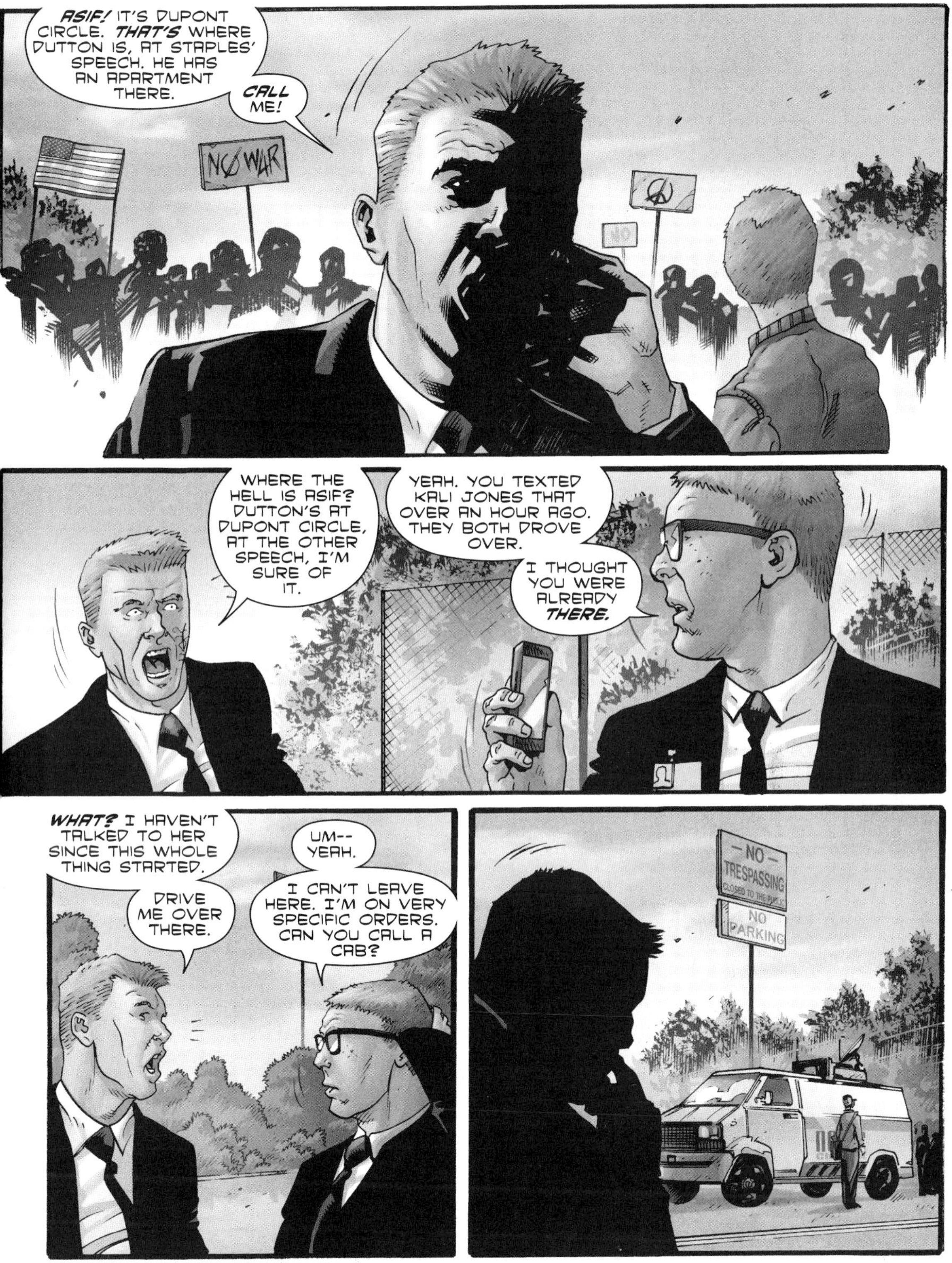
ASIF! IT'S DUPONT CIRCLE. THAT'S WHERE DUTTON IS, AT STAPLES' SPEECH. HE HAS AN APARTMENT THERE.
CALL ME!
NO WAR
NO
WHERE THE HELL IS ASIF? DUTTON'S AT DUPONT CIRCLE, AT THE OTHER SPEECH, I'M SURE OF IT.
YEAH. YOU TEXTED KALI JONES THAT OVER AN HOUR AGO. THEY BOTH DROVE OVER.
I THOUGHT YOU WERE ALREADY THERE.
WHAT? I HAVEN'T TALKED TO HER SINCE THIS WHOLE THING STARTED.
DRIVE ME OVER THERE.
UM-- YEAH.
I CAN'T LEAVE HERE. I'M ON VERY SPECIFIC ORDERS. CAN YOU CALL A CAB?
NO TRESPASSING
CLOSED TO THE PUBLIC
NO PARKING

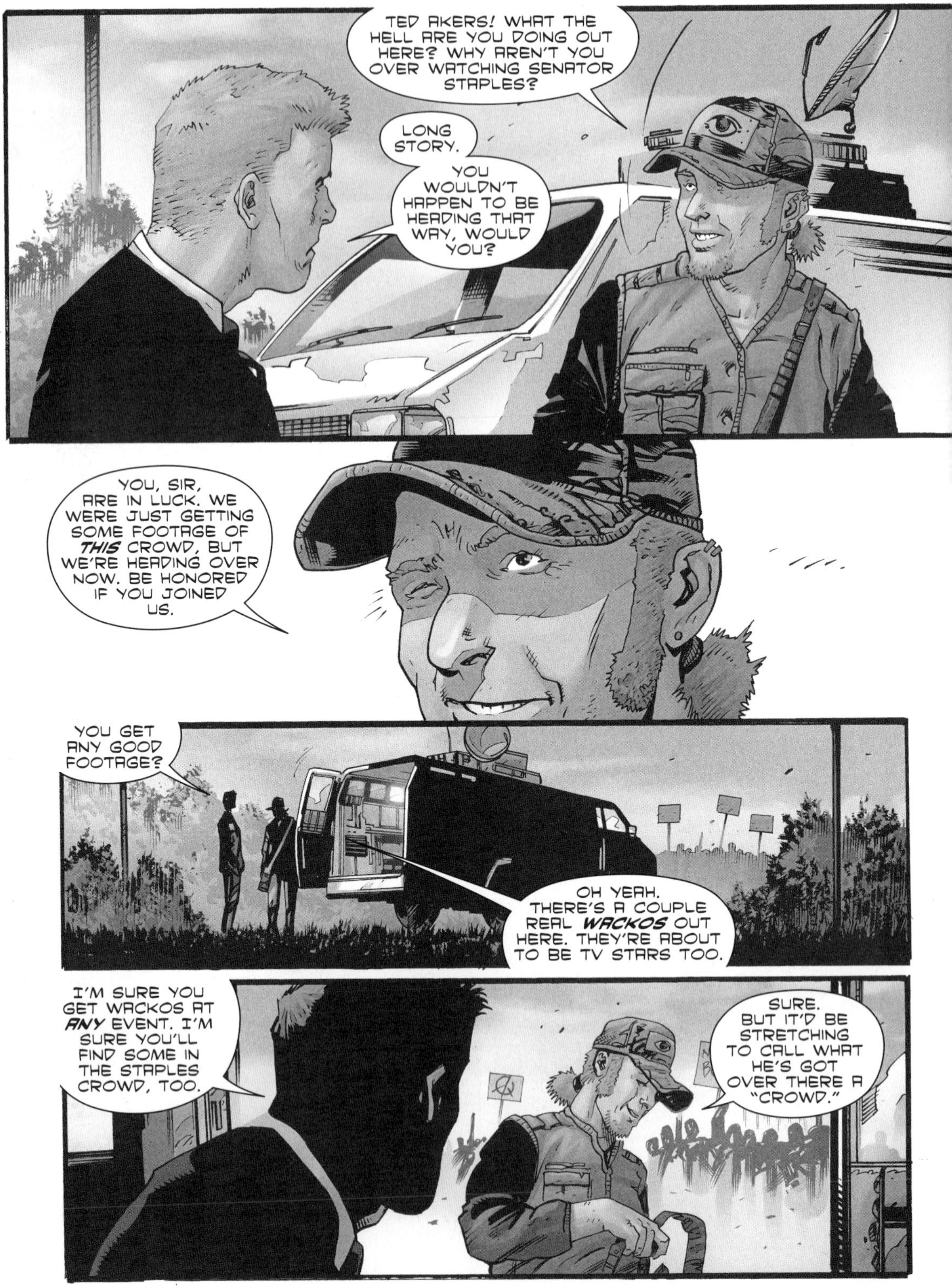
TED AKERS! WHAT THE HELL ARE YOU DOING OUT HERE? WHY AREN'T YOU OVER WATCHING SENATOR STAPLES?
LONG STORY.
YOU WOULDN'T HAPPEN TO BE HEADING THAT WAY, WOULD YOU?
YOU, SIR, ARE IN LUCK. WE WERE JUST GETTING SOME FOOTAGE OF THIS CROWD, BUT WE'RE HEADING OVER NOW. BE HONORED IF YOU JOINED US.
YOU GET ANY GOOD FOOTAGE?
OH YEAH. THERE'S A COUPLE REAL WACKOS OUT HERE. THEY'RE ABOUT TO BE TV STARS TOO.
I'M SURE YOU GET WACKOS AT ANY EVENT. I'M SURE YOU'LL FIND SOME IN THE STAPLES CROWD, TOO.
SURE. BUT IT'D BE STRETCHING TO CALL WHAT HE'S GOT OVER THERE A "CROWD."

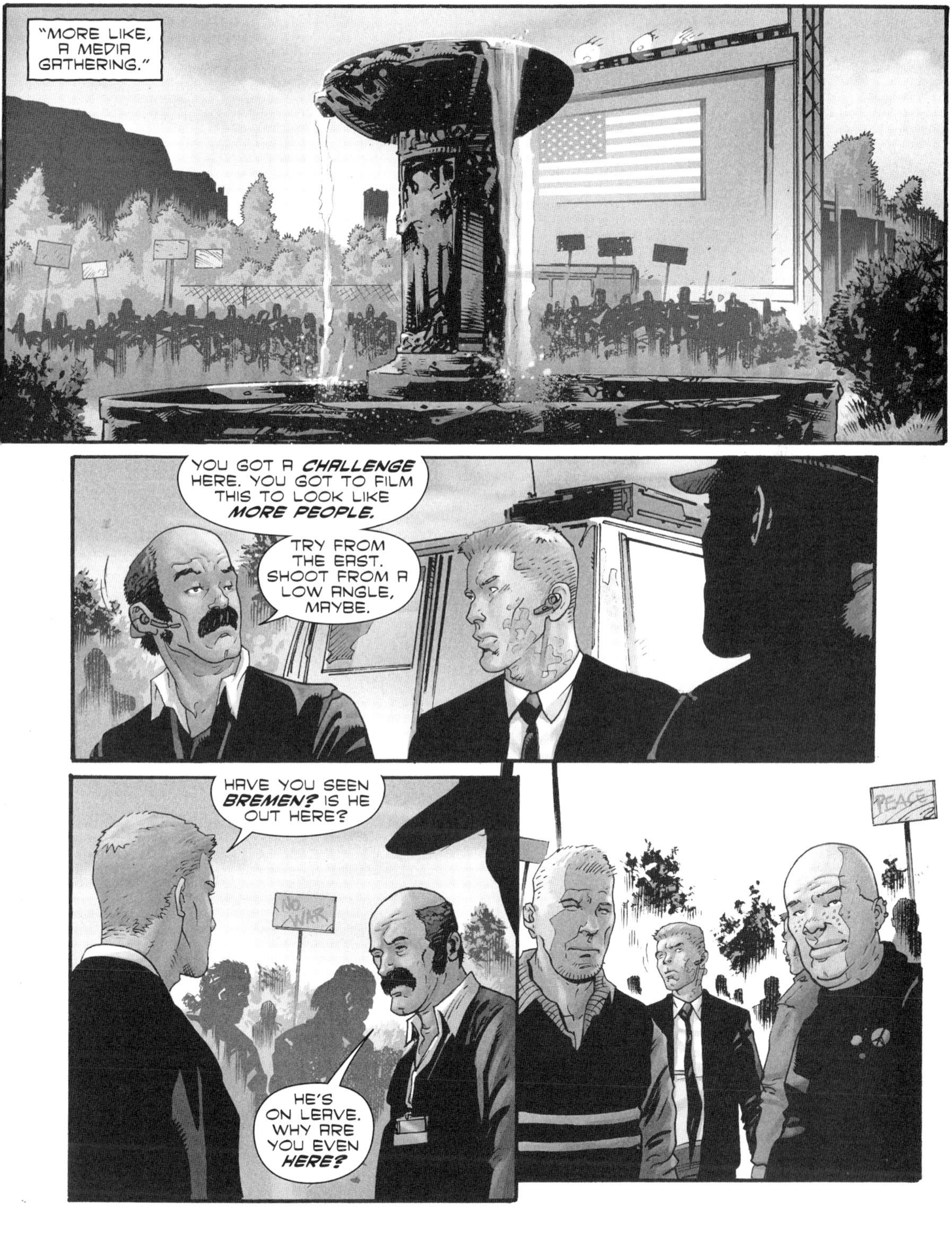
"MORE LIKE, A MEDIA GATHERING."
YOU GOT A CHALLENGE HERE. YOU GOT TO FILM THIS TO LOOK LIKE MORE PEOPLE.
TRY FROM THE EAST. SHOOT FROM A LOW ANGLE, MAYBE.
HAVE YOU SEEN BREMEN? IS HE OUT HERE?
NO WAR
HE'S ON LEAVE. WHY ARE YOU EVEN HERE?
PEACE

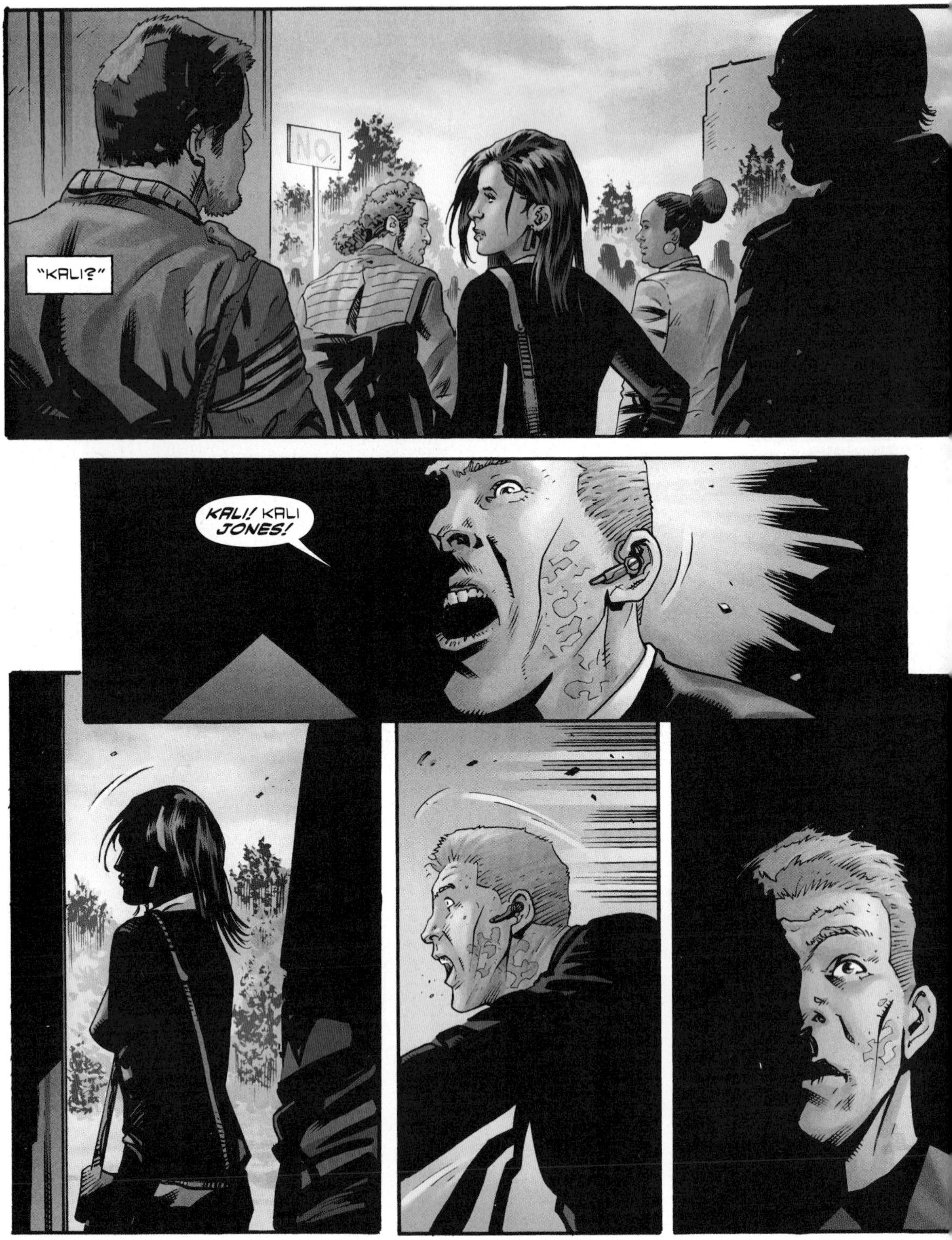
"KALI?"
NO
KALI! KALI JONES!

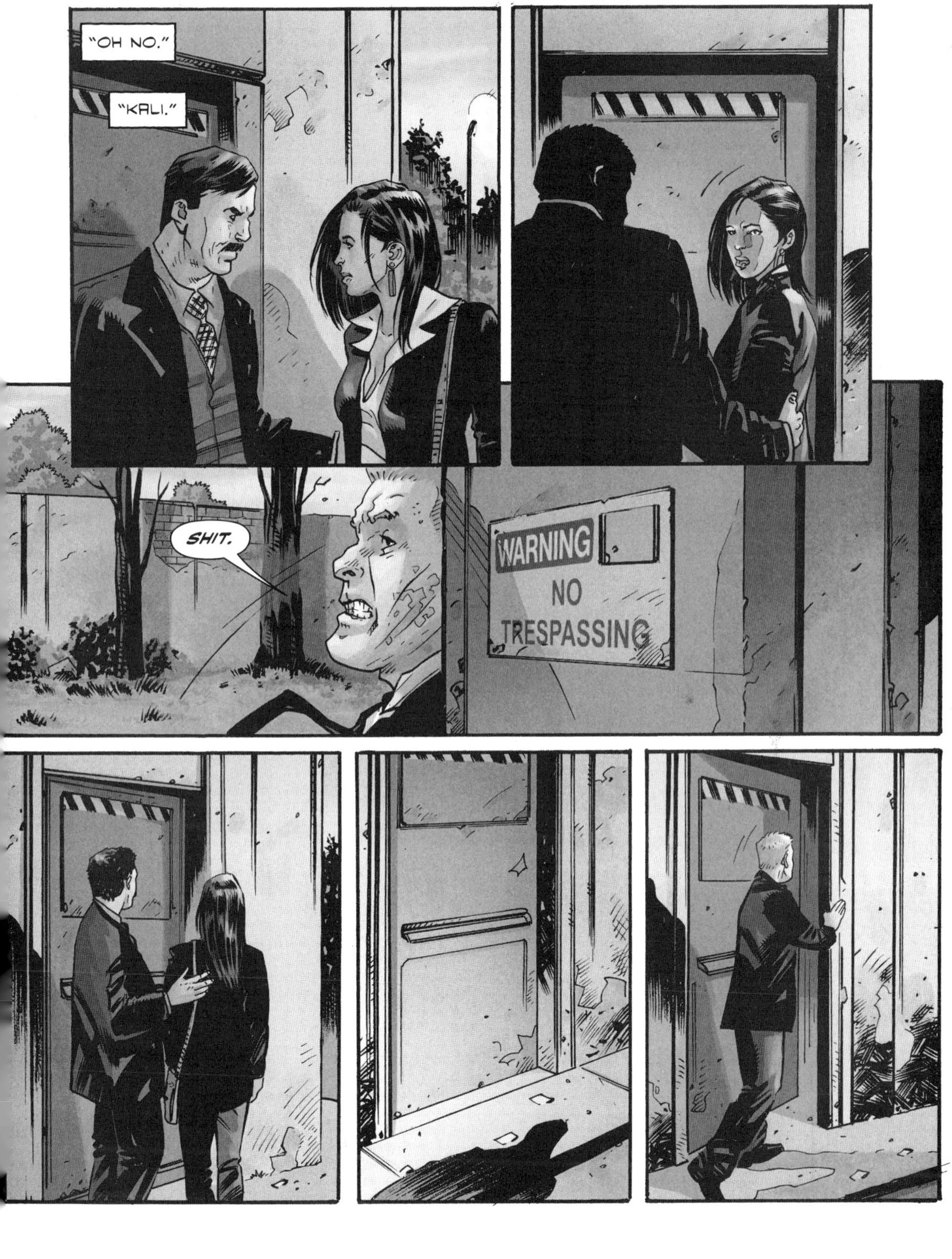
"OH NO."
"KALI."
SHIT.
WARNING
NO
TRESPASSING

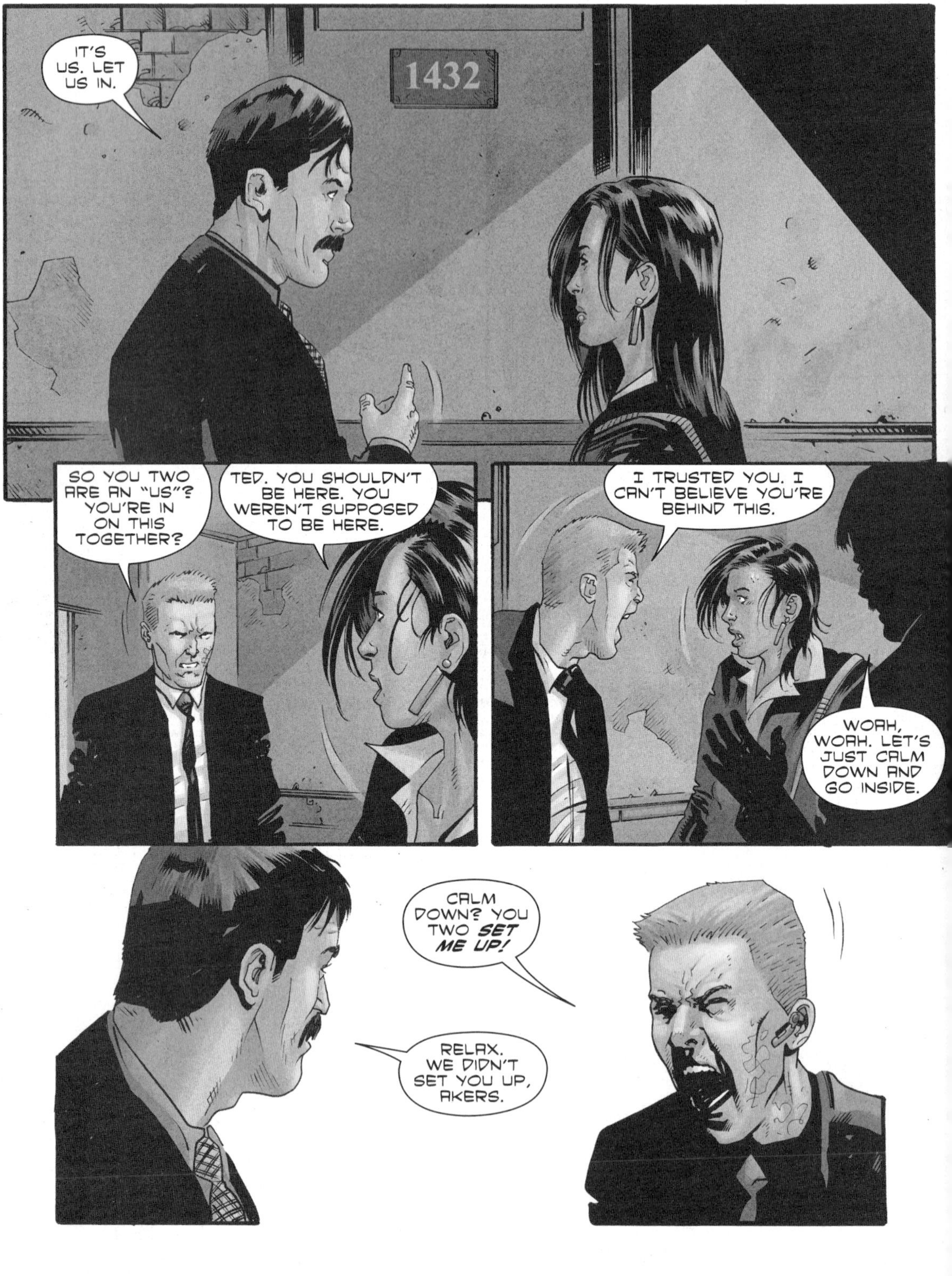
1432
IT'S US. LET US IN.
SO YOU TWO ARE AN "US"? YOU'RE IN ON THIS TOGETHER?
TED. YOU SHOULDN'T BE HERE. YOU WEREN'T SUPPOSED TO BE HERE.
I TRUSTED YOU. I CAN'T BELIEVE YOU'RE BEHIND THIS.
WOAH, WOAH. LET'S JUST CALM DOWN AND GO INSIDE.
CALM DOWN? YOU TWO *SET ME UP!*
RELAX. WE DIDN'T SET YOU UP, AKERS.

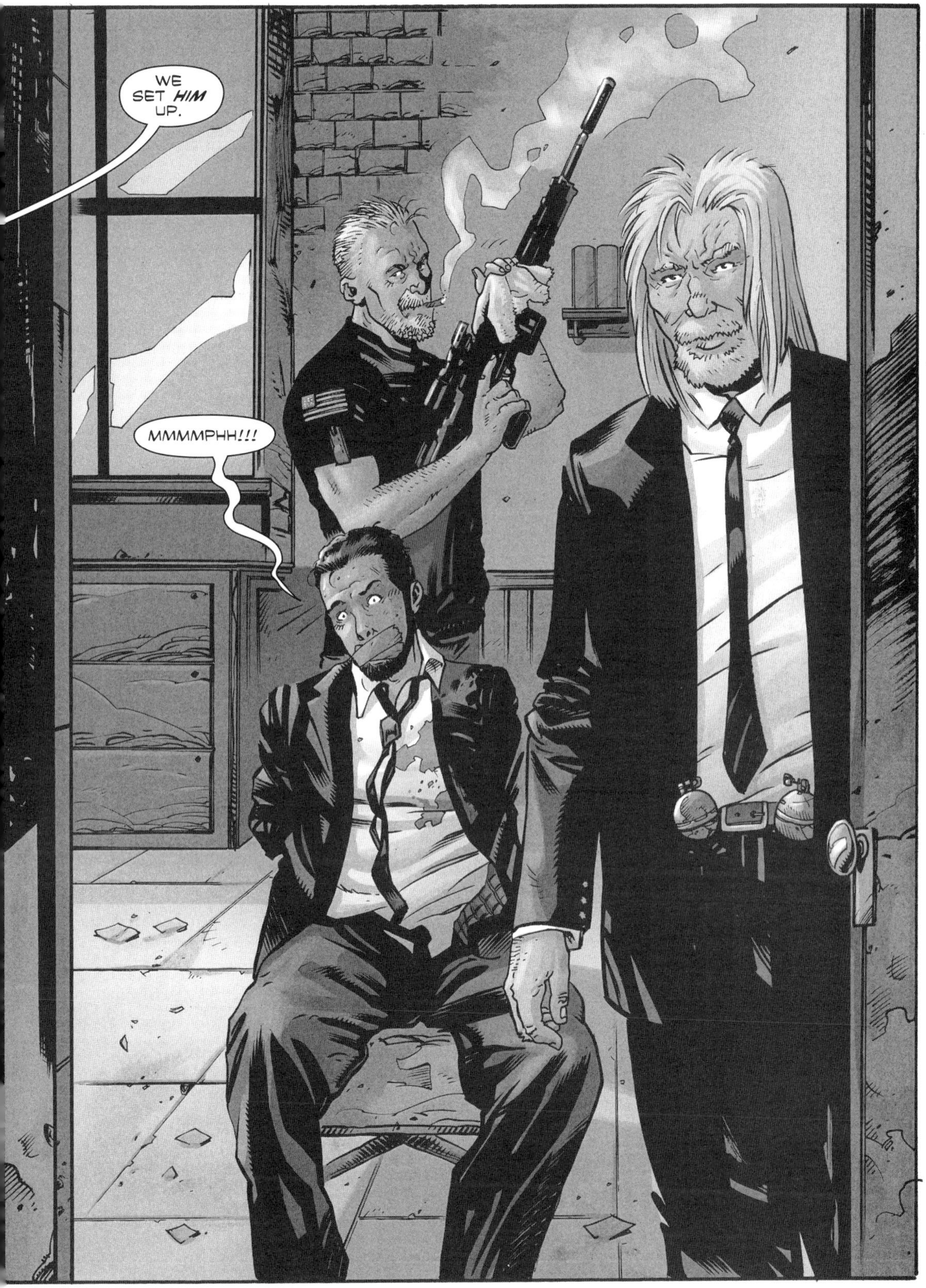
WE SET *HIM* UP.
MMMMPHH!!!

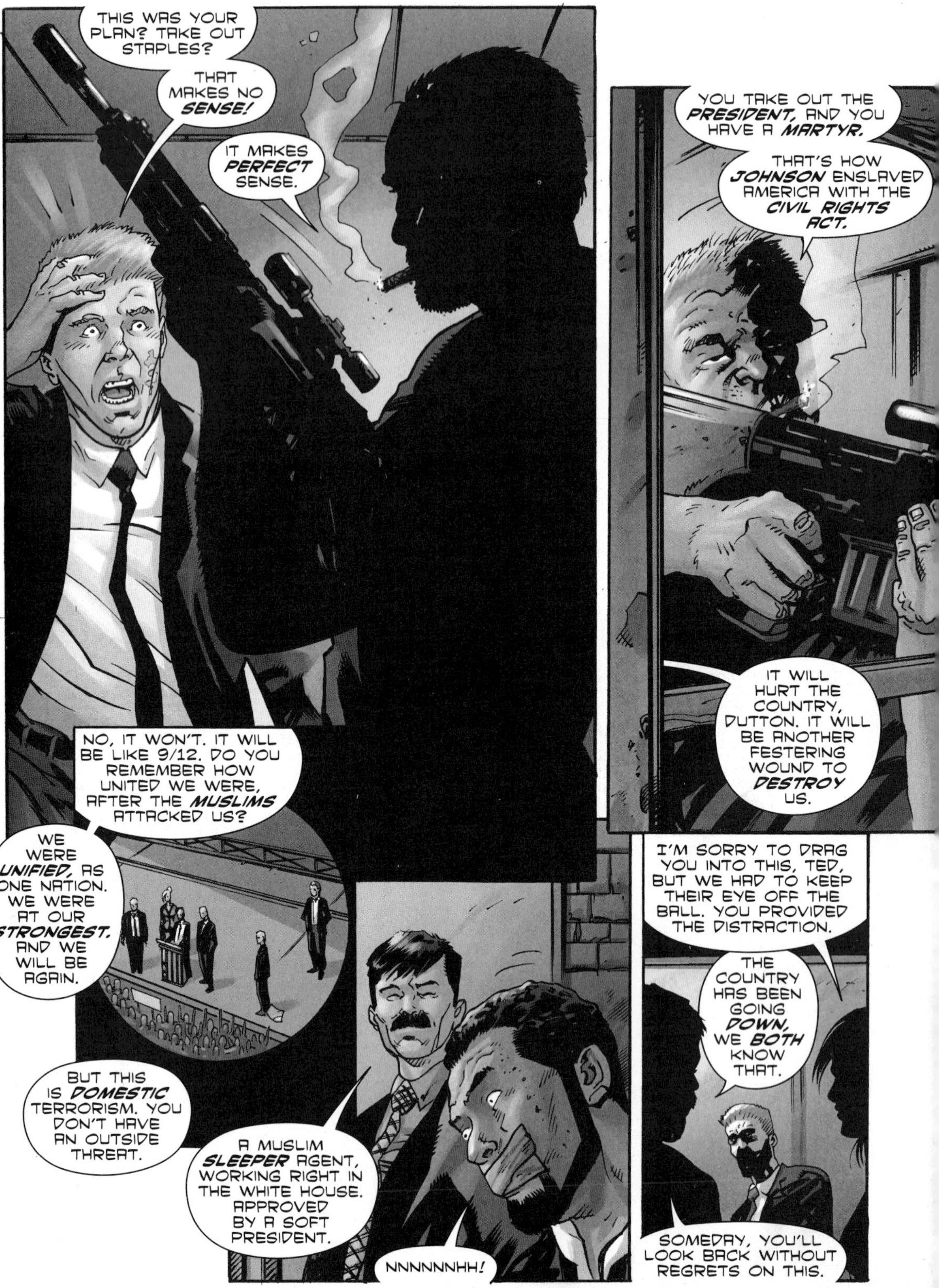

THIS WAS YOUR PLAN? TAKE OUT STAPLES?
THAT MAKES NO SENSE!
IT MAKES PERFECT SENSE.
YOU TAKE OUT THE PRESIDENT, AND YOU HAVE A MARTYR.
THAT'S HOW JOHNSON ENSLAVED AMERICA WITH THE CIVIL RIGHTS ACT.
IT WILL HURT THE COUNTRY, DUTTON. IT WILL BE ANOTHER FESTERING WOUND TO DESTROY US.
NO, IT WON'T. IT WILL BE LIKE 9/12. DO YOU REMEMBER HOW UNITED WE WERE, AFTER THE MUSLIMS ATTACKED US?
WE WERE UNIFIED, AS ONE NATION. WE WERE AT OUR STRONGEST. AND WE WILL BE AGAIN.
BUT THIS IS DOMESTIC TERRORISM. YOU DON'T HAVE AN OUTSIDE THREAT.
A MUSLIM SLEEPER AGENT, WORKING RIGHT IN THE WHITE HOUSE. APPROVED BY A SOFT PRESIDENT.
NNNNNNHH!
I'M SORRY TO DRAG YOU INTO THIS, TED, BUT WE HAD TO KEEP THEIR EYE OFF THE BALL. YOU PROVIDED THE DISTRACTION.
THE COUNTRY HAS BEEN GOING DOWN, WE BOTH KNOW THAT.
SOMEDAY, YOU'LL LOOK BACK WITHOUT REGRETS ON THIS.

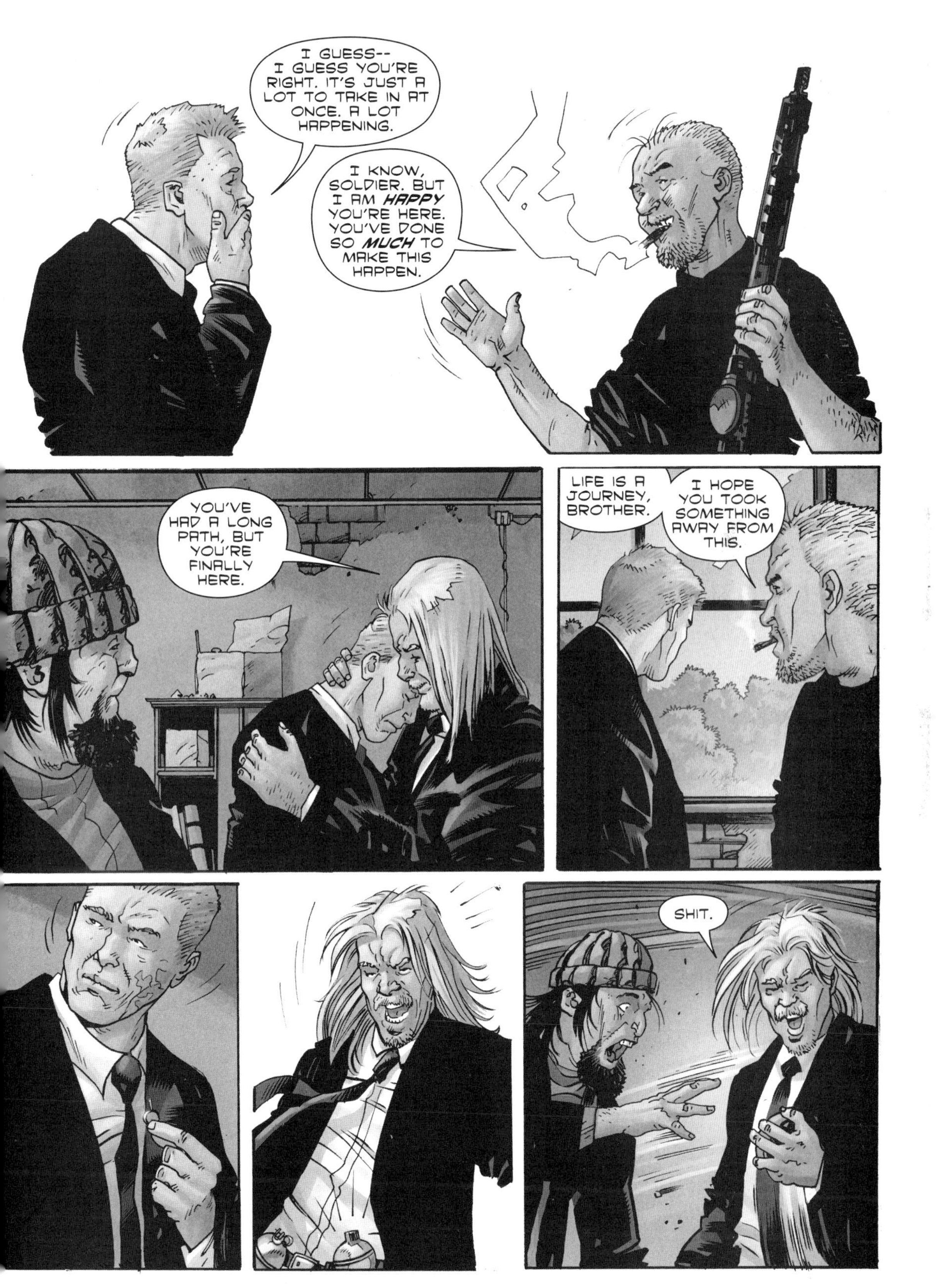
I GUESS--
I GUESS YOU'RE RIGHT. IT'S JUST A LOT TO TAKE IN AT ONCE. A LOT HAPPENING.
I KNOW, SOLDIER. BUT I AM HAPPY YOU'RE HERE. YOU'VE DONE SO MUCH TO MAKE THIS HAPPEN.
YOU'VE HAD A LONG PATH, BUT YOU'RE FINALLY HERE.
LIFE IS A JOURNEY, BROTHER.
I HOPE YOU TOOK SOMETHING AWAY FROM THIS.
SHIT.

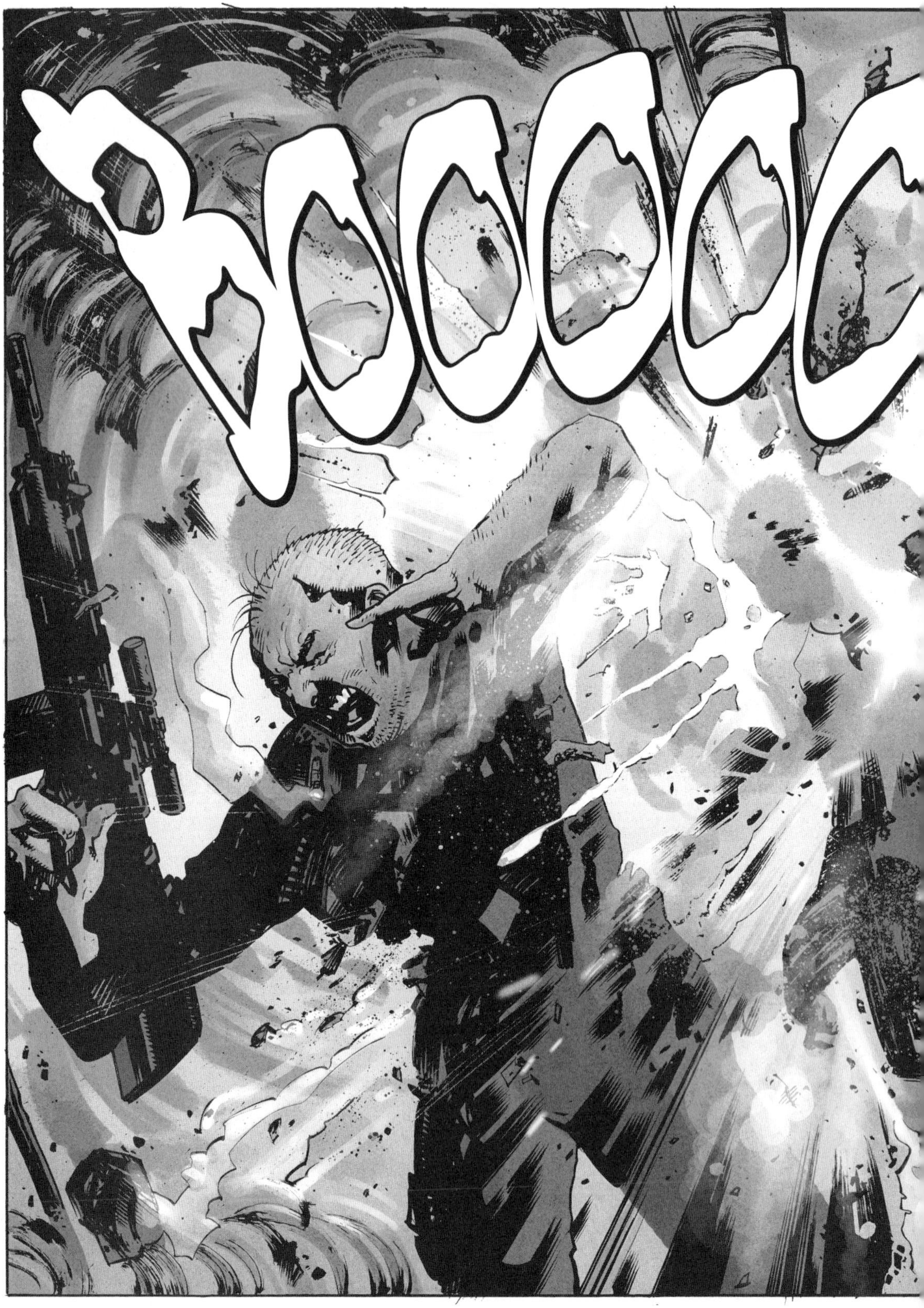
BOOOOOO

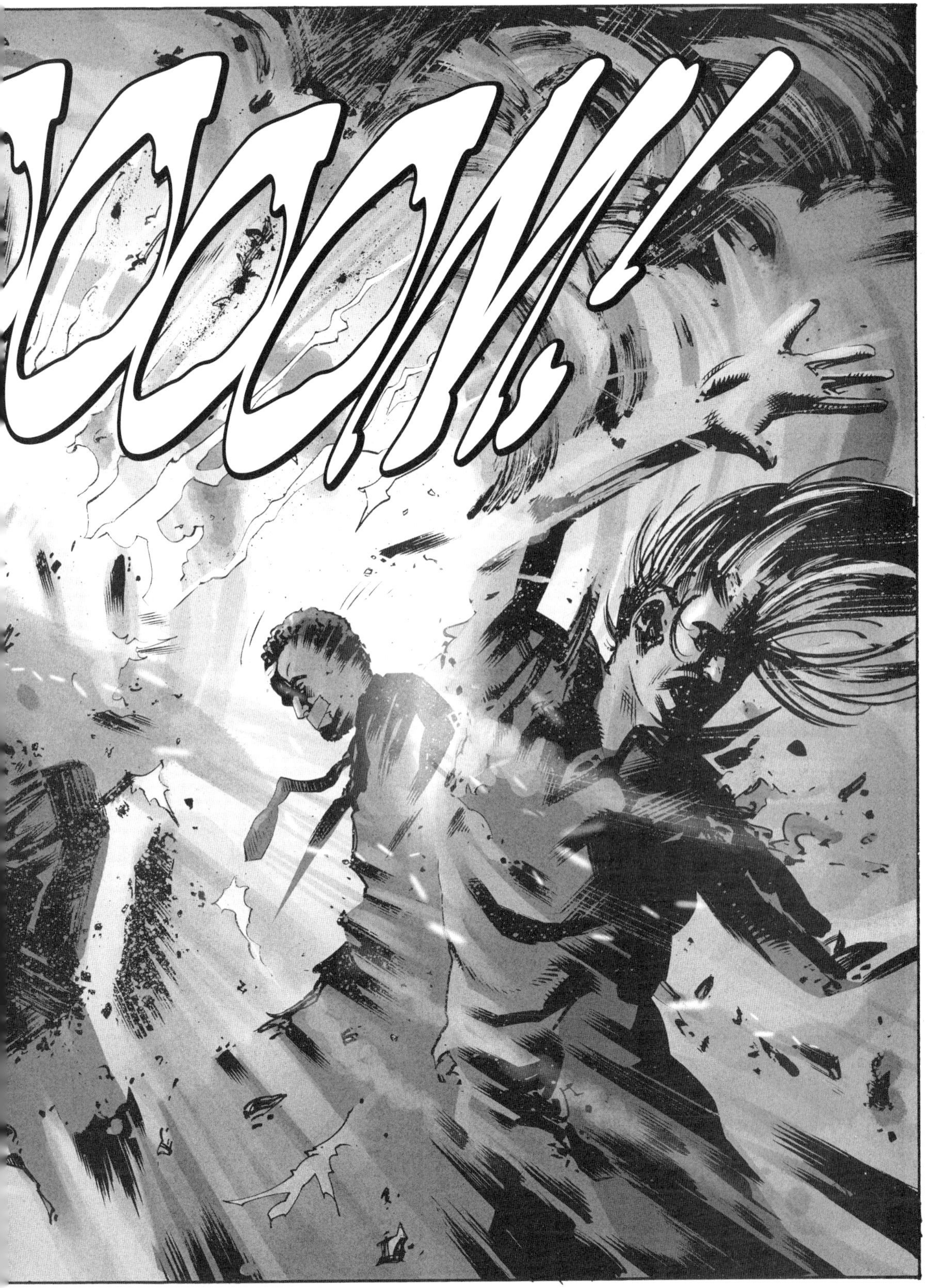
OOOM!

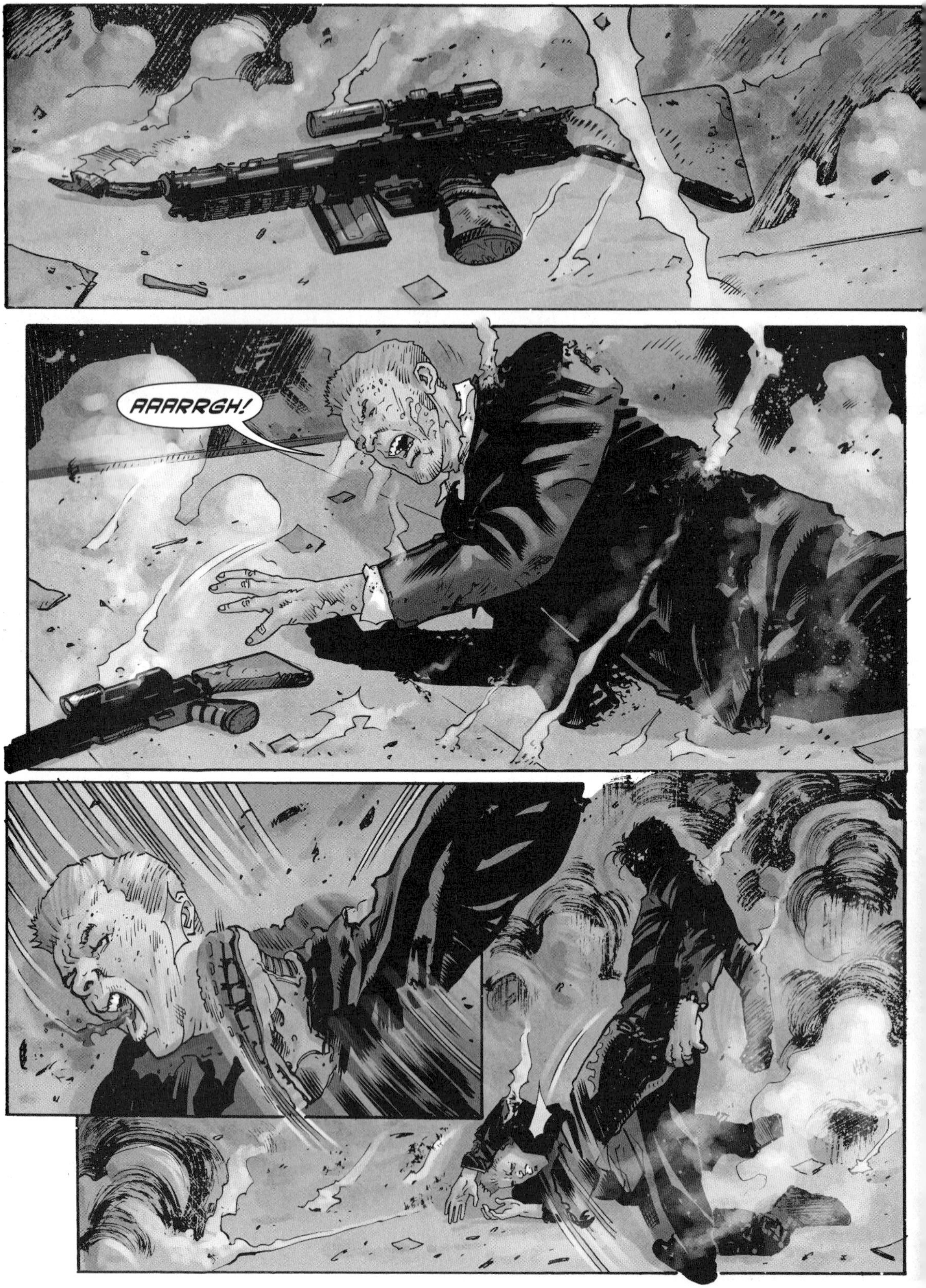
AAARRGH!

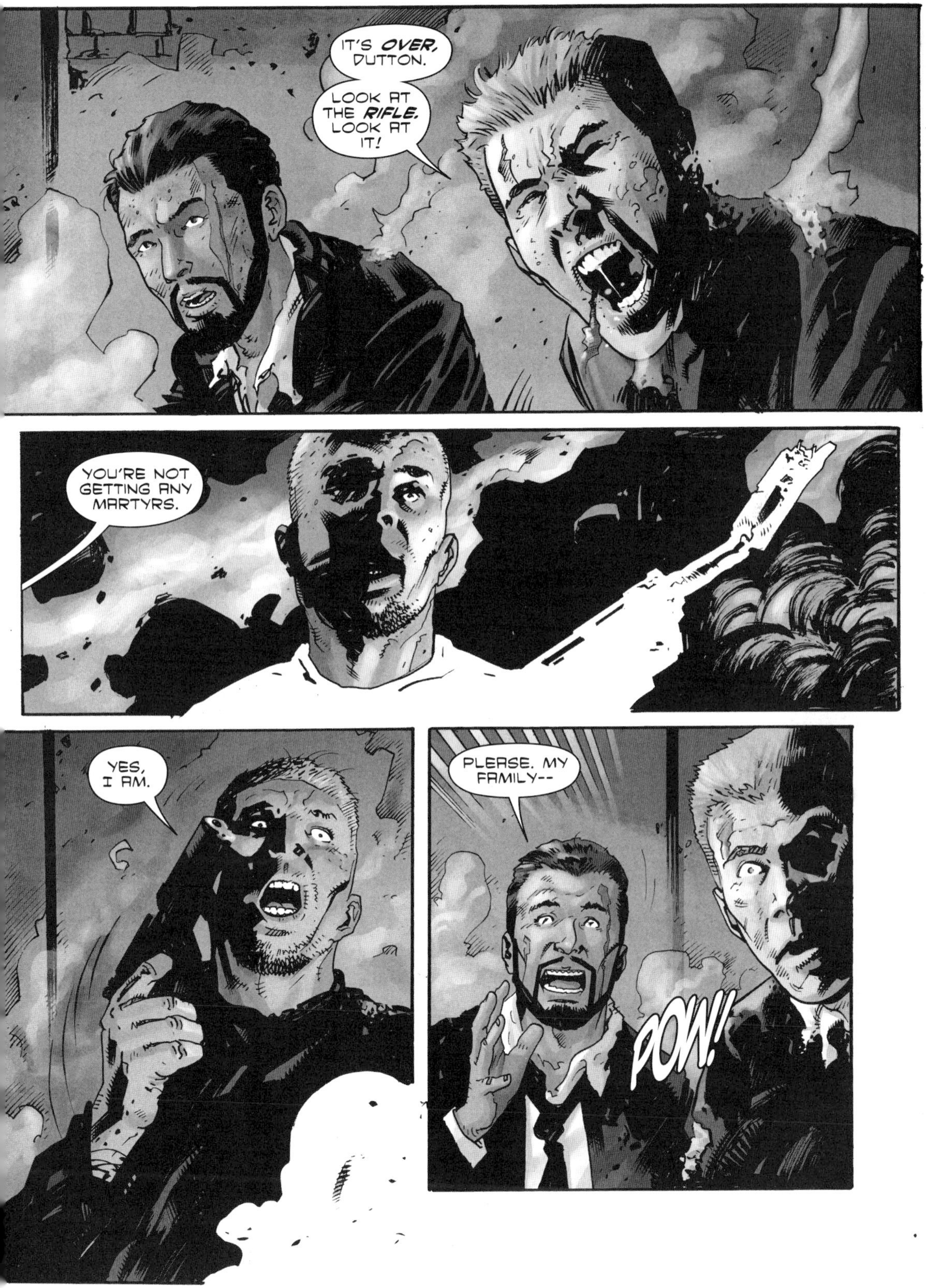
IT'S OVER, DUTTON.
LOOK AT THE RIFLE. LOOK AT IT!
YOU'RE NOT GETTING ANY MARTYRS.
YES, I AM.
PLEASE. MY FAMILY--
POW!

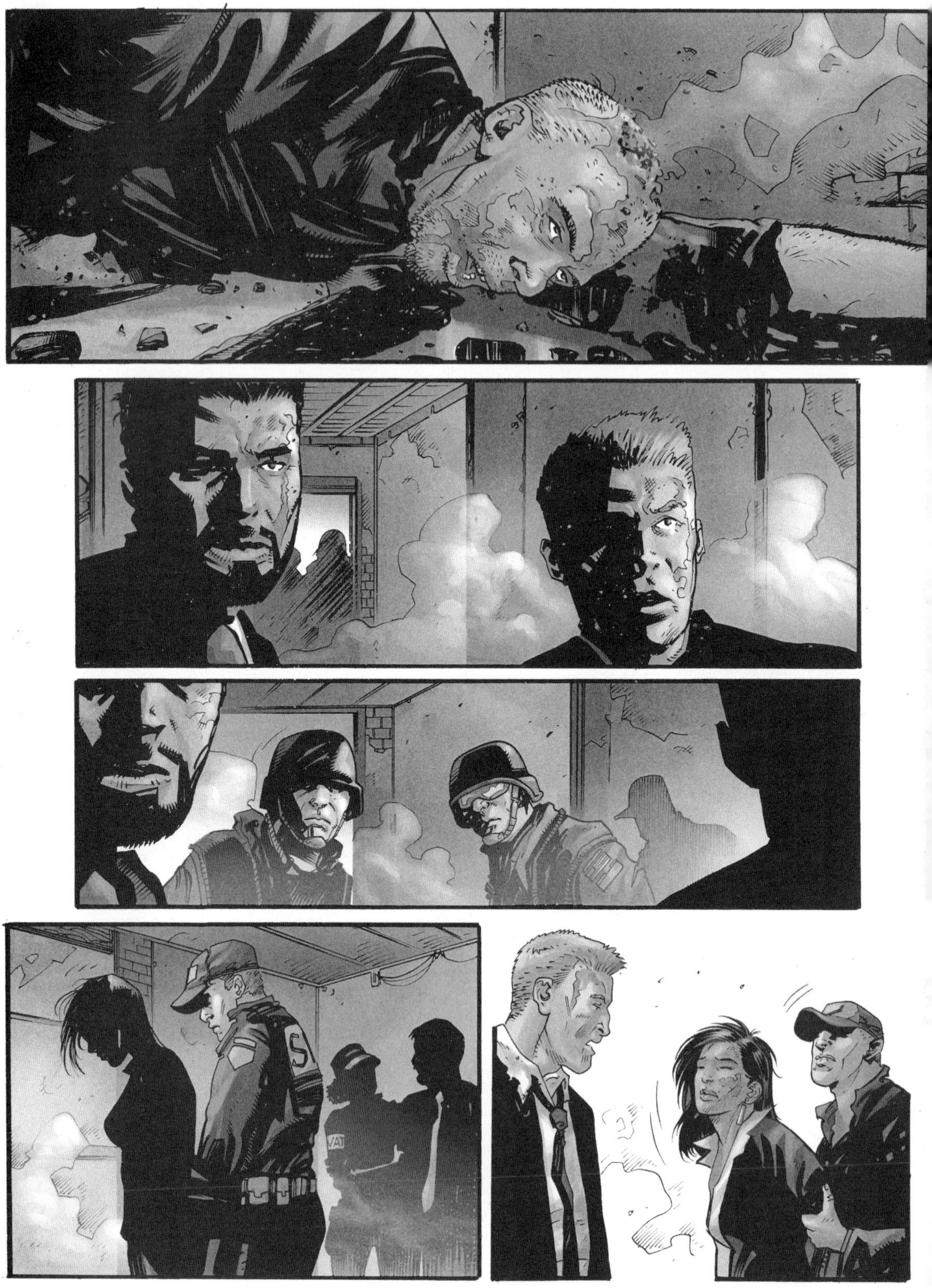

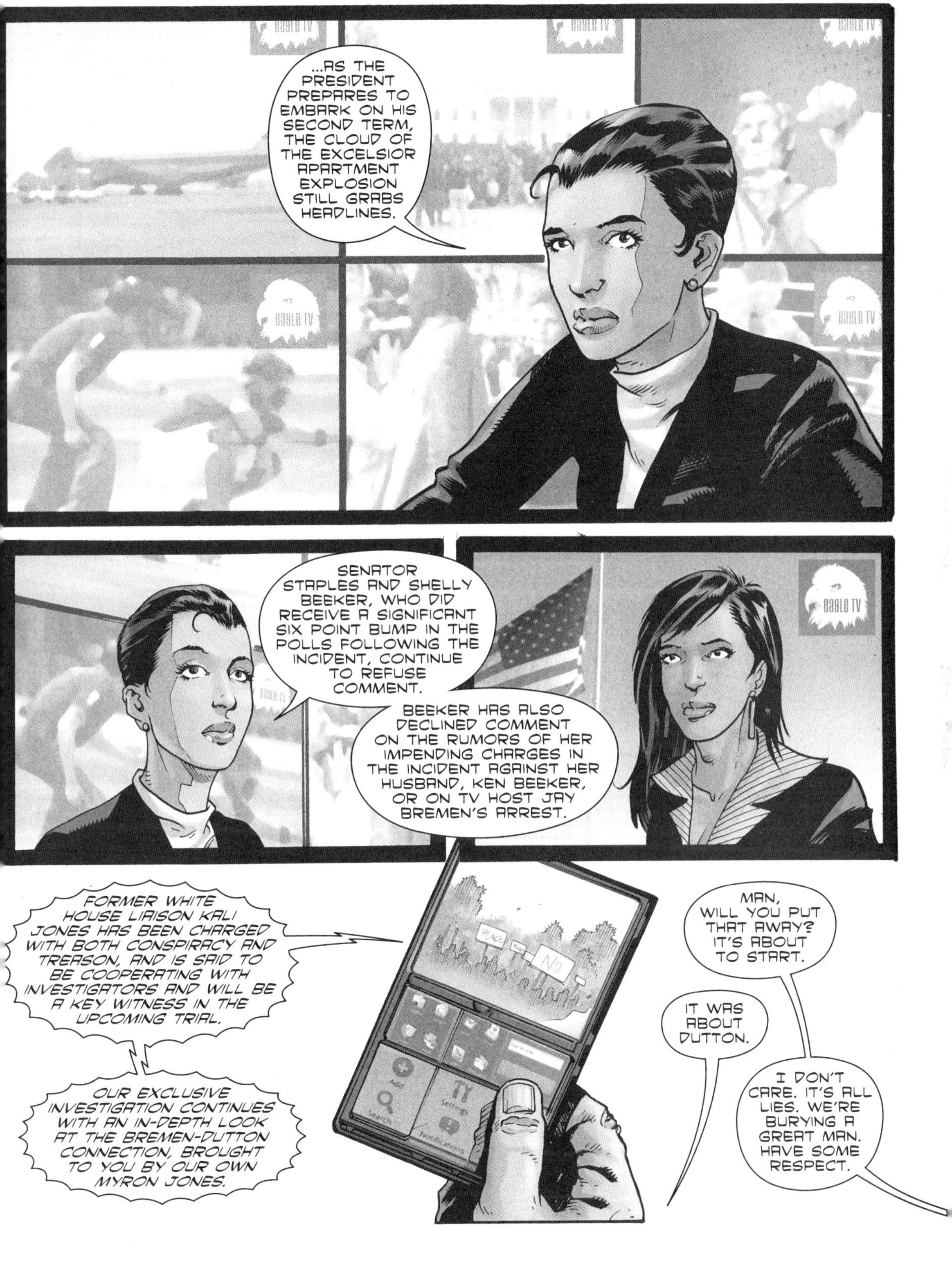

...AS THE PRESIDENT PREPARES TO EMBARK ON HIS SECOND TERM, THE CLOUD OF THE EXCELSIOR APARTMENT EXPLOSION STILL GRABS HEADLINES.
SENATOR STAPLES AND SHELLY BEEKER, WHO DID RECEIVE A SIGNIFICANT SIX POINT BUMP IN THE POLLS FOLLOWING THE INCIDENT, CONTINUE TO REFUSE COMMENT.
BEEKER HAS ALSO DECLINED COMMENT ON THE RUMORS OF HER IMPENDING CHARGES IN THE INCIDENT AGAINST HER HUSBAND, KEN BEEKER, OR ON TV HOST JAY BREMEN'S ARREST.
FORMER WHITE HOUSE LIAISON KALI JONES HAS BEEN CHARGED WITH BOTH CONSPIRACY AND TREASON, AND IS SAID TO BE COOPERATING WITH INVESTIGATORS AND WILL BE A KEY WITNESS IN THE UPCOMING TRIAL.
OUR EXCLUSIVE INVESTIGATION CONTINUES WITH AN IN-DEPTH LOOK AT THE BREMEN-DUTTON CONNECTION, BROUGHT TO YOU BY OUR OWN MYRON JONES.
MAN, WILL YOU PUT THAT AWAY? IT'S ABOUT TO START.
IT WAS ABOUT DUTTON.
I DON'T CARE. IT'S ALL LIES. WE'RE BURYING A GREAT MAN. HAVE SOME RESPECT.

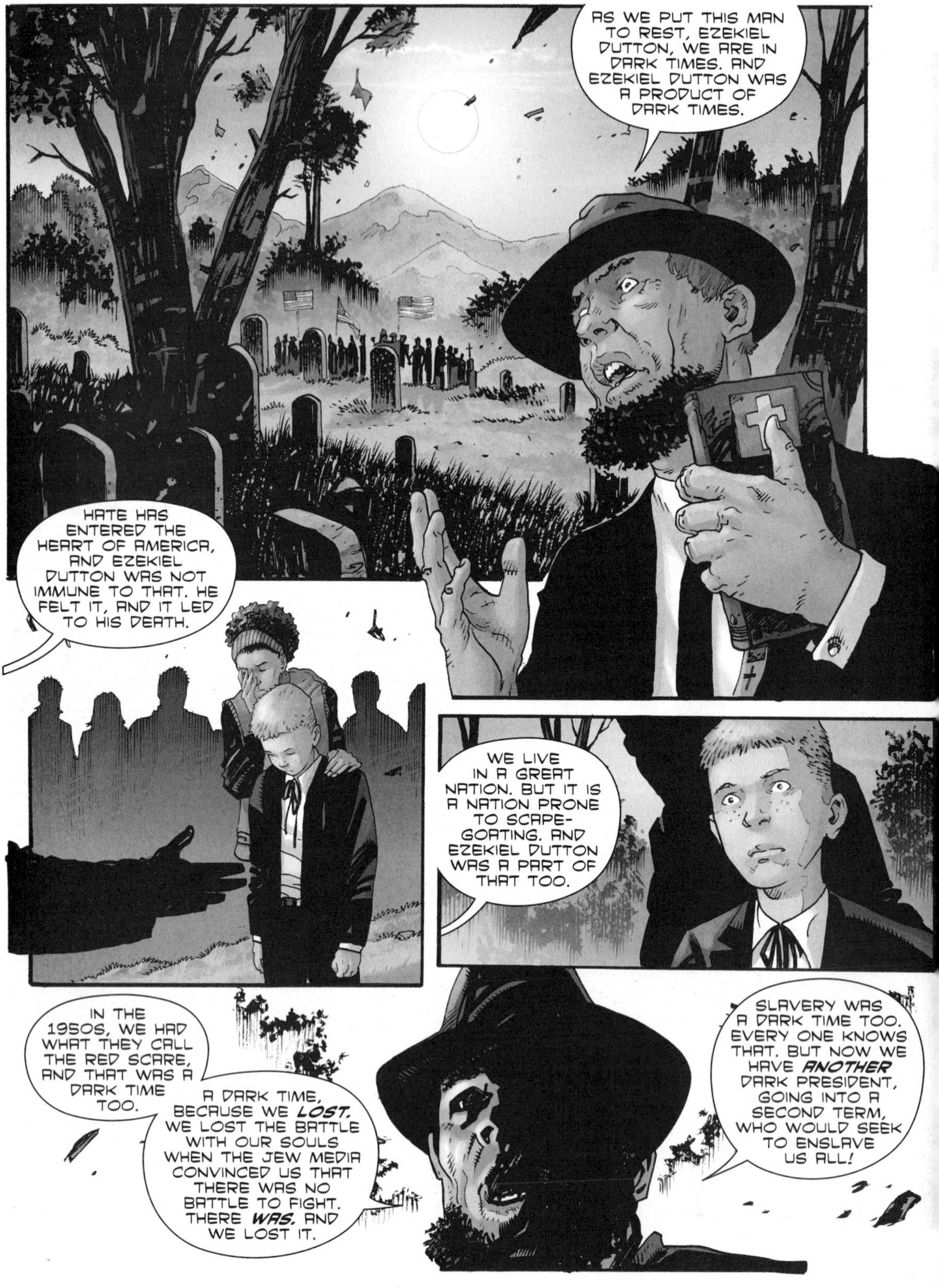
AS WE PUT THIS MAN TO REST, EZEKIEL DUTTON, WE ARE IN DARK TIMES. AND EZEKIEL DUTTON WAS A PRODUCT OF DARK TIMES.
HATE HAS ENTERED THE HEART OF AMERICA, AND EZEKIEL DUTTON WAS NOT IMMUNE TO THAT. HE FELT IT, AND IT LED TO HIS DEATH.
WE LIVE IN A GREAT NATION. BUT IT IS A NATION PRONE TO SCAPE-GOATING. AND EZEKIEL DUTTON WAS A PART OF THAT TOO.
IN THE 1950s, WE HAD WHAT THEY CALL THE RED SCARE, AND THAT WAS A DARK TIME TOO.
A DARK TIME, BECAUSE WE *LOST.* WE LOST THE BATTLE WITH OUR SOULS WHEN THE JEW MEDIA CONVINCED US THAT THERE WAS NO BATTLE TO FIGHT. THERE *WAS.* AND WE LOST IT.
SLAVERY WAS A DARK TIME TOO. EVERY ONE KNOWS THAT. BUT NOW WE HAVE *ANOTHER* DARK PRESIDENT, GOING INTO A SECOND TERM, WHO WOULD SEEK TO ENSLAVE US ALL!

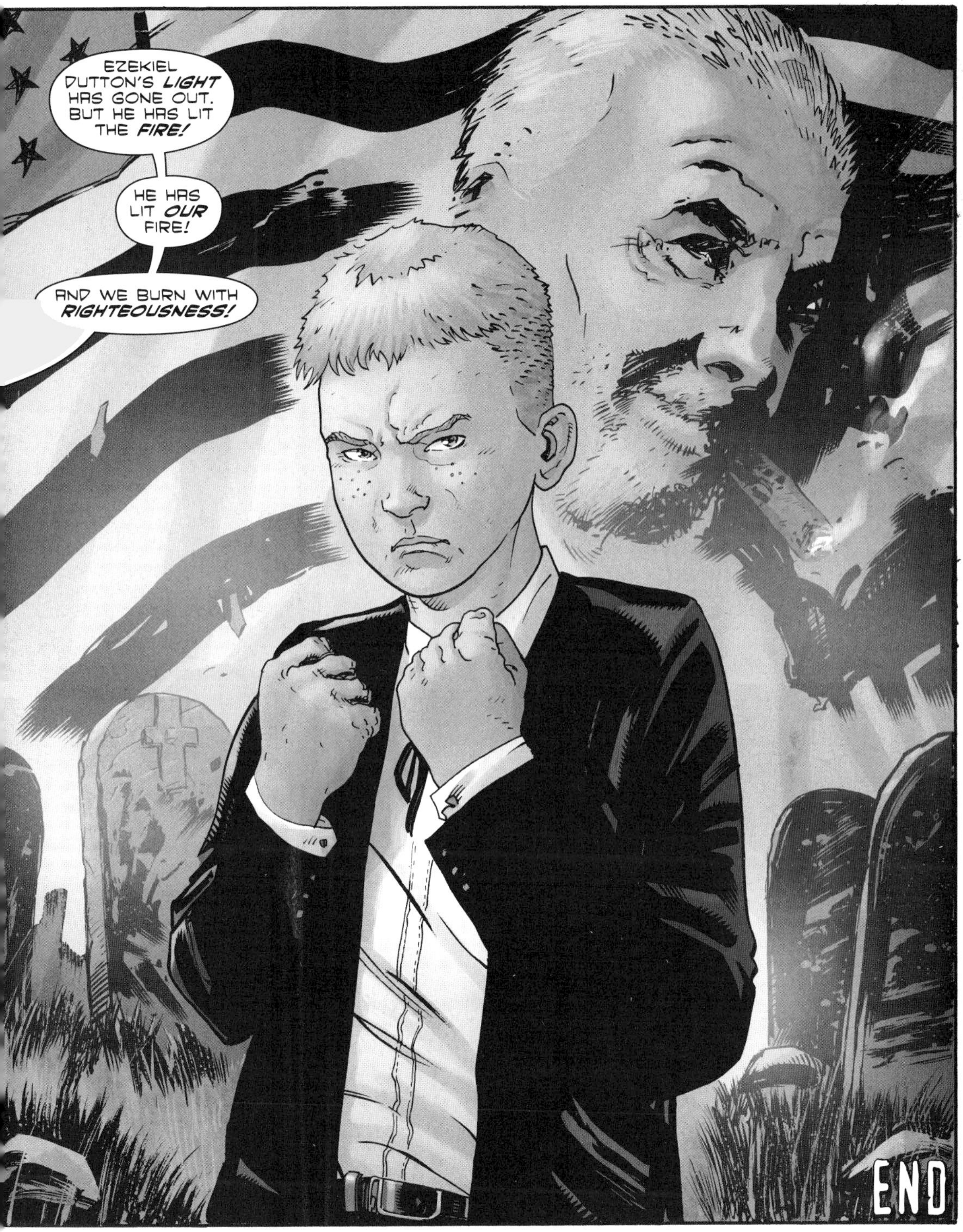
EZEKIEL DUTTON'S *LIGHT* HAS GONE OUT. BUT HE HAS LIT THE *FIRE!*
HE HAS LIT *OUR* FIRE!
AND WE BURN WITH *RIGHTEOUSNESS!*
END

Mat Johnson is the author of the graphic novels INCOGNEGRO and DARK RAIN, and the novel *Pym*. He teaches at the University of Houston Creative Writing Program and the Voices of Our Nation (VONA) program.

Andrea Mutti is the artist of THE EXECUTOR and the upcoming Vertigo adaptation of THE GIRL WITH THE DRAGON TATTOO. He lives in Italy.